Deliver Us from Evil

ALSO BY THE AUTHOR

To Encourage the Others
The Day the Laughter Stopped
Beyond Reasonable Doubt?

Deliver Us from Evil

by David Yallop

Coward, McCann & Geoghegan
New York

Acknowledgments

I would like to express my gratitude to the many who can never be publicly named and to the following:

Josephine Ayres. Alan Bailey. Dennis Barker. Ann Beasland. David Beryland. *Bradford Telegraph & Argus.* Tricia Calvert. Nicholas Chapman. Peter Cobb. *Daily Mirror.* Gypsy da Silva. Celstino Elia. Mike Emery. Cyril Emmerson. Barbara Field. *Halifax Courier.* Jan Hancock. Jack Hickes. *Huddersfield Examiner. Keighley News.* Graham King. The Ladies of the Night of Bradford, Leeds, Manchester, Huddersfield and Preston. *Lancashire Evening Post.* David, Beryl and Graham Leach. Tracy Leung. Jack Windsor Lewis. Irene Macdonald. Keith MacPhail. Clown Marsden. Alfred and Lorna Merrell. Thomas Miller. Lauris Mitchell. Fred Newell. Michael Nicolson. George Oldfield. The staff of the Graham Poulter Advertising Agency. The Press Association. Geoff Robertson. Rob Rohrer. Anna Rugolskyj. John Rundle. Stephen Shaw. Diana Simpson. Harry and Olive Smelt. Frank Smythe. Patricia Soliman. Keith Stoll. Fran Walsh. Barry Wilkinson. Jim Wire. Brian Worsnop. *Yorkshire Evening Post. Yorkshire Post.*

Library of Congress Cataloging in Publication Data

Yallop, David A.
  Deliver us from evil.

  Includes index.
  1. Sutcliffe, Peter. 2. Crime and criminals—England
—Biography. 3. Murder—England—Biography. I. Title.
HV6248.S69Y34   364.1′523′0924 [B]   81-7810
ISBN 0-698-11113-3   AACR2

Printed in the United States of America

To Anna—my best friend

Author's Note

This book is the product of two and a half years' intensive research. It was virtually completed prior to January 1981. The main text of the book stands as it did then. It was written without the benefit of hindsight. I believe that this book raises many important issues and questions, not least the one that I wish to direct to the Chief Constable of West Yorkshire, Ronald Gregory. In June 1980, during my second interview with Assistant Chief Constable George Oldfield I stated: "I believe that the man you are looking for is a lorry driver who lives in Bradford and works in the Baildon/Bingley/Shipley areas of that city." How, Chief Constable, could one man arrive at that correct solution? A solution that eluded your police force for five and a half years?

1

To commit murder is easy. To get away with murder is more difficult.
He smiled at the thought. He could afford to indulge the smug
feeling creeping up from the pit of his stomach. He stopped
pacing, poured another cup of tea, added milk and a carefully
measured two spoonfuls of sugar.

He checked his watch. Nearly five o'clock on the evening of
Friday, January 2, 1981. A new year, full of promise for many, had
just begun. If his expectations for the year were realized, all the
new year held for a number of women was brutal death.

He began to pace again and found himself staring at his
reflection in a mirror. He smiled at himself. *What was it that the
blonde who had survived had said?* "He was good-looking, with come-to-
bed eyes."

He continued to stare at his reflection. That same blonde had
given a very accurate description of him. It hadn't made any
difference. He'd committed murder many times before that
particular attack. He'd committed murder many times since. Even
the police did not know exactly how many. They were still
insisting that he had murdered that woman in Preston in 1975.
What was her name? Harrison. Joan Harrison. Well, they were

wrong about that one. That other man could take the credit for that. That other man who also claimed the victims that were *his* and *his* alone.

It had made murdering that much easier. Had probably helped him enormously on the number of occasions he had been interviewed by the police. They had questioned him quite a number of times. He'd walked away from every interrogation.

He checked his watch again. Plenty of time. He'd told the wife he intended to go out tonight. She was happy watching TV. Just as well. He could hardly take her along with what he had in mind.

He sipped his tea and recalled some of the moments of the past five and a half years. The recollection that he had not always achieved total success, that there had been some women who had survived, brought a frown to his face. But he would never forget other moments. Successes scattered over half a decade. Successes that had made him the best known unknown man alive in the world today.

His wife. His family. His workmates all knew him by his real name. None, not a single person, suspected that this quiet married man living in Bradford was the Yorkshire Ripper.

Images of dead women swirled into his mind. As an automatic reflex his right hand closed, the grip tightened, the knuckles whitened. For once the action was harmless. The hand held no hammer. Still, the hand clenched ever tighter as in his mind's eye their faces came into focus.

Later he kissed his wife goodbye, climbed into his Rover car and headed for Sheffield.

Flossy paused in her writing. Her dissertation on the violence contained in *Wuthering Heights* lay momentarily forgotten on the grass. Plenty of time for O-Level exam cramming. She tickled Monty's ear and stretching out on the lawn listened to Radio 4. She must remember to tell Lauris that they had played "I don't know how to love him." They'd seen the movie three times in one day. Taken sandwiches, bought soda and virtually bedded down in the Ritz cinema.

She smiled at the recollection of the know-it-all who had sat behind them during the third showing of *Jesus Christ Superstar*.

He'd gone on and on about this song, said it was all wrong having it sung by such a pure innocent voice, that it needed the voice of a whore, of a prostitute, the voice of experience. Someone like Edith Piaf. At that point, thank God, the know-it-all's girl friend had silenced him by saying that she thought Edith Piaf had been a bit busy when they had recorded "Jesus Christ Superstar," busy being dead.

Flossy wondered yet again about the future. Should she go on and take A-Level exams and go to a university or should she try some of the local farms for a secretarial position? Typing would help. She just loved being close to animals. She laughed at the particular animal closest to her at that moment, Monty, the family dog. Panting in the early summer heat. "Well, Mont, might be an idea to get some O-Level passes first, eh?" At sixteen and a half years of age there was plenty of time to consider the future. First a little thought for the past. The violence in *Wuthering Heights*.

A few miles from where the Brontës lived is the town of Keighley. The early morning of July 5, 1975, saw the official beginning of a reign of violence no fiction writer would dare conceive.

To a casual observer it would seem that the slim, attractive blonde was involved in a serious argument with the two West Indians who accompanied her. Bibby's Club at Bradford did not, however, feature high on a casual observer's itinerary. The customers went there to drink and dance, not observe. Anna Rogulskyj did indeed have a grievance but it was against the man she lived with rather than these two listeners who were in danger of suffering grievous bodily harm to their eardrums. Vincent tried in vain to mollify her. "Life is too short, baby. Why not live and let live?" Unimpressed with this particular philosophy, Anna continued to list the faults of Jeff Hughes, the man she was planning to marry. She might for the moment still retain the name of her Ukrainian ex-husband, but her temperament was firmly locked in her Irish roots. Eventually Vincent pointed out that it was past midnight and offered to drive Anna to her Keighley home. She declined their offer to come into the house with her. Better to try, without the help of well-meaning friends, to patch up the argument that had sent her out in the first place.

"Jeff. Jeff. Where are you?" She wandered from room to room. The shirts she had ironed for him earlier that day were gone. So was her cat. So was Jeff.

She put on a record. Poured herself a stiff drink. He'd obviously moved back to his own place in the town center. What really enraged her was that he'd taken her little cat. God knows why— just to spite her, she supposed. He didn't even like it—refused to call it by the name she had given it—declaring that "Dum Dums" was no bloody name for a cat. He'd called it "Bluey." It might be two o'clock in the morning. So what?

Her shoes clattered on the pavement as she walked down Highfield Lane. She turned into Mornington Street, deserted as the town slept. Not a soul to be seen, at least not by Anna Rogulskyj. She crossed the wide North Street, passing close to the police station. Down Alice Street, past the Ritz cinema. A few moments more and she was in the cobbled alleyway where Jeff lived. Take her little cat, would he? She banged on the door. Without waiting for a response she banged again and again. If there was anyone inside, he was unimpressed with the pounding and the shouting. She had, however, attracted the attention of someone else.

Anna continued to pound on the door for a while. Eventually the anger and frustration ebbed.

As a parting shot she took off one of her green high-heeled shoes and smashed a ground floor window with it. She partially crouched as she replaced the shoe on her foot. As she did a figure moved rapidly from the shadows but Anna never saw or knew what hit her. He swung the hammer clenched in his right hand. Once. Twice. Three times. The blows smashed into her skull. The attack had been so fast. So sudden. Not a single cry came from Anna. She was deeply unconscious from the first blow. He stood, gasping for breath above her still body. The blood was seeping from the head wounds across the cobblestones.

He lifted her skirt. Pulled down her panties and, putting the hammer into his pocket, produced a knife. He began slashing across her abdomen. The frenzy in him, that had until this moment been under complete control, began to take over.

"Who's out there? Who's making all that noise?"

He froze. A moment of panic as he stared blindly in all

directions. *My God, who was it? Where were they?*

"Come on. What's going on out there?"

Finally he saw. It was a nearby neighbor disturbed by this stupid bitch. Thank God, the fellow had stopped to put his pants on before opening his door. The man stood peering out into the dark, attempting to focus in the dim light. The frenzy in the attacker had died away completely now. Once more he was totally in command. Totally in control. Frightening command. Unnatural control.

When he spoke the voice was calm. He slipped the knife back into his pocket. "There's nothing to worry about. You go back inside. Everything's all right now."

The neighbor was nearly satisfied but he paused a moment longer. "Are you sure?"

Again the attacker was calmness personified. "Yes. Nothing to worry about."

The neighbor nodded and, turning back inside, closed his street door. If he had stayed a few moments longer, if his eyes had grown just slightly more accustomed to the night, he would have seen the body of Anna Rogulskyj lying on the cobblestones, between the legs of the reassuring stranger.

He stared down at the inert figure and smiled. *No time for any more work now. Best away in case that curious neighbor decides to call the police. Must have the luck of the devil to have got away with this.* He bent and rearranged her skirt. A moment later he was gone and Anna Patricia Rogulskyj was alone in the alley.

She was found at 2:20 A.M. lying in a pool of her own blood. Alive but critically injured, she was rushed first to a nearby hospital, then transferred to Leeds General Infirmary. There a priest gave her the last rites of the Catholic church as she was prepared for her long and delicate skull operation. The force of the blows had fractured the skull in several places. She has lived, but the tale she has to tell is not one that the police give credence to. Anna is convinced she knows the identity of her attacker. She is equally convinced that it is not the Ripper and freely names a man living in Keighley. Unimpressed, the police were a great deal more interested in what that neighbor had to say about the man he had spoken to in the alleyway. Investigating officer Detective Superintendent Peter Perry listened as the neighbor strained for details.

"Difficult to be exact about his age. In his twenties or thirties. He was small. I'd say five feet eight inches. He was wearing a checked sports jacket."

The superintendent was puzzled. Nothing had been stolen. No sexual attack. All likely friends and acquaintances of the victim had been accounted for. Anna had no convictions. It was indeed baffling. Things like this did not happen in a nice respectable town like Keighley. Why, the place did not even boast a red-light district. All that kind of nonsense was left to Bradford and Leeds. Why should someone come prowling around Keighley, looking for an attractive woman in her midthirties, apparently a total stranger, to murder? For murder it would have been but for the disturbed neighbor. The attacker certainly had murder in his heart and now only regret that he had not begun with a total success. A regret surprisingly shared by Anna Rogulskyj.

"No, not Anna. It will never be Anna again. I'm Joanna now. Anna died that night and I wish I had died with her. I wish I had died that night. Then I would have known nothing. I wish I had not had that operation. That there had just been the blackness and then no more. If I had known what lay ahead for me I would have refused what they termed 'a life-saving operation.' My life is ruined. So I've had fifteen thousand pounds from the Criminal Compensation Board. So what? No amount of money can give me back my anonymity, can give me back my lost boyfriends. Can remove the stigma of the Ripper."

In the days that followed that first attack he listened eagerly to every newscast and scanned the papers. Something had clearly gone very wrong. If he had killed her, surely it would be front page news? Eventually he found a few lines on the attack. *Damn that interfering neighbor. Still, there must be millions of men in the country who answered such a generalized description. Pity that it was mentioned in the local* Keighley Times; *might now have to venture farther afield for the next one—and there certainly would be a next one.*

2

Beryl watched anxiously as the two girls attempted to emulate the California surfers. With awesome power the wave rose; one moment the girls were standing shrieking with laughter on its crest, the next they had vanished. Beryl died one of those thousand deaths that all mothers die and then smiled as she saw their heads bob above the water and Flossy wave to her. She waved back. David trickled sand through his fingers.

"You can't take every wave for her that she's going to face in life, you know."

She smiled and sat beside him.

"I know. Suppose I'm still trying to cut the umbilical cord." Her smile bubbled to laughter. "Listen to me. Just listen to me. Summer holiday in Cornwall. Nothing to worry about except eating fresh fish, buying sombreros, swimming, surfing, and sunbathing. Our daughter gets nine O-Level exam passes and I'm worrying about a wave."

"She's done very well; they were mostly good grades too."

"Really, David. You sound like one of her teachers. Such grudging praise. Give her due credit."

Flossy and Gillian lay bellies-down on their boards, idly

paddling in the shallow water. Flossy considered the question as she watched a small crab dance a lunchtime quadrille in search of food.

"If you'd invite Roger Daltry, Lou Reed, and Mick Jagger, I'd be grateful."

"Are they all just for you or were you planning to share them with me and Lauris?"

"I'm generous to a fault," Flossy said. "If you can persuade them all to come to a barn dance on your father's farm, I'm prepared to share. Tell them there's a barbecue as well. That should clinch it."

"Bound to. If I can get them to come early they can give us a hand whitewashing the barn. I'd love to see Roger Daltry covered in whitewash."

Flossy's eyes opened wide in mock wonder. "So would I, Gillian. So would I. As it is I suppose we'll have to make do with the Young Farmers Club."

The car moved at a leisurely pace toward Halifax. At the wheel he glanced at his watch. *Quarter to nine—the night was but a pup. Plenty of time to have a look around Halifax. Nice town.* Bits of it were pure Hovis country. The Keighley road began to drop steeply as he neared Halifax. He glanced around curiously as if seeing it all for the first time. In a way he was. He had never hunted in Halifax before. It was five weeks since that night in Keighley. Five weeks in which the nation had enjoyed a magnificent summer, and while most had sunbathed, he had brooded, attempted to put the attack on Anna Rogulskyj from his mind. To forget those moments in the alleyway behind the Ritz cinema. Guilt? Regret? Remorse? No, simple dissatisfaction. His vanity was offended at the lack of total success. Suddenly aware that he had driven into heavy rain, he switched the wipers on and smiled. Perhaps the change in the weather indicated a change in his luck?

Harry Smelt sighed with content: young Stephen tucked up in bed, daughter Julie out with her friends, wife Olive out with hers, a glass of home brew in his hand and a good murder thriller to watch on TV. What more could a man want? Friday nights in the

Smelt home had about them a ritualistic quality; the predictability added to and enhanced the enjoyment for the middle-aged couple. Olive's hen parties were a source of some amusement to her husband. He couldn't for the life of him see the point of going into Halifax pubs and buying ale that was inferior to his own brew and paying a great deal more for the dubious privilege. Still, she enjoyed it. Harry read a preview in his evening paper on the program he was waiting to see, "The Marcus Nelson Murders." Apparently it had been so successful in the States that they had created a series out of the idea and called it "Kojak."

The man came out of the pub, pulled his collar up against the driving rain, and walked quickly back to his car. *Nothing in that one.* He recalled there was another nearby in Horton Street. *Not worth driving; might as well leave the car where it was and walk.* He checked his appearance in the second driving mirror, the one that was permanently facing him. Vain. That second mirror was a mute testimonial to his vanity. While the sleepy-looking eyes checked the appearance, his right hand automatically felt for the hammer that rested in his pocket. Doubly reassured, he opened the car door.

"Come on, Olive. Let's give this one a go. Can't be any worse than the Queens. I've seen graveyards with more life."

The two women hurried into the warmth of the saloon bar of the Royal Oak. Olive scanned the faces, looking for the missing members of the Friday night clan.

"Must be this rain that's keeping 'em in, Jean. Same again?"

Jean nodded as they approached the bar.

"Two lagers, please."

The television program was living up to expectations. An intriguing story of a New York detective who, having put a case together and duly got his man convicted, was now doubting the man's guilt and had begun to reinvestigate. Julie popped her head around the living room door.

"Just letting you know I'm back, Dad. I've brought Sal in for a chat—is that all right?"

Harry, deeply immersed in helping the detective find the correct solution, spoke without moving his eyes from the television.

"If you're going to chat, best stay in kitchen."

"Righto. I'll make you a coffee."

Julie vanished and Harry was back on Fifth and Forty-third.

He turned the car aimlessly toward Saville Park. There must be nearly one hundred thousand people living in Halifax and yet his search was proving fruitless.

Turning into Saville Park Road, he cruised slowly toward the moor. *Perhaps the rain was keeping them all indoors. This was a likely area, though. Never know what you might find out here.* He glanced at his watch. Quarter past ten. If he drew a blank here there was still time to look in at the Royal Oak.

"Right, Olive, what's it to be? One more with this pair of comedians or fish supper at Pearson's?"

Olive considered. It had not been one of their merriest Friday evenings. In fact, it had been a miserable night. She could always get the fish supper for Harry and herself at their local shop. The younger of the two men winked at her.

"Come on, Olive, worried about getting fresh?"

"Fresh indeed. I'm stone sober and for that I'll have a Copper Beech sherry, please. A large one."

The young man laughed. "Just as well we're dropping you home. Get on bus and you'll be attacking conductor, after a large one of those."

The car stopped near the bus stop on Boothtown Road. Olive clambered out from the back.

"Thank you, lads. I'll tell Harry you were asking after him."

The car pulled away as Olive turned toward the fish shop.

It was in darkness. She'd missed supper. *Now I'm for it,* she thought. *Better get home quick and get frying pan on.* Olive turned and moved toward the ginnel, an alleyway that bisected a series of roads. As she did he stepped from the shadows and moving close to her, spoke quietly.

"The weather's letting us down, isn't it?"

With a start of surprise Olive uttered an automatic response.

"What? Oh yes, I suppose it is."

Then he was gone, into the dark. She stared after him for a moment and thought perhaps he must be a little stupid. Then, her mind fully concentrating on what was going to replace their nonexistent fish supper, she began to walk toward her home.

"I'm going to be in trouble," she observed to nobody in particular.

The television program was moving to an exciting climax. Yet again Julie put her head around the door. Harry, transfixed, waved a hand.

"No, love, I don't want another coffee."

"Dad, there are two girls at door asking for you."

It was clearly a conspiracy, a deep-laid plot to prevent his ever knowing whether he would have guessed the solution. With a sigh Harry got up and walked to the back door.

"Is your name Smelt?"

"Ay, what do you want?"

"We've got your wife in a house round t'other side and she's been hurt."

Harry reached for a jacket and spoke to his youngest daughter. "Mum's had an accident, Julie. Probably fallen over. She'll be fresh, you'll see."

Julie and her friend giggled and Harry followed his callers up the street.

As he approached the house his pace instinctively quickened at the sight of the ambulance. In the kitchen Olive was being worked on by the two ambulance attendants. There was blood pouring down her face. Her white blouse was rapidly turning crimson. Neighbors were busying around making tea, offering cigarettes. Despite his initial shock Harry retained his laconic humor.

"Well, this will probably teach you to know when you've had enough."

Olive mumbled a response. An ambulance attendant paused from wiping blood from her face.

"I think it's a bit more serious than that."

The next few hours blurred for both husband and wife. At two-thirty in the morning one of the doctors joined Harry in the waiting room at Halifax Infirmary.

"She's as comfortable as we can make her for the time being."

"Thank you, Doctor. Sorry to put all of you to this trouble. She must have had a bit too much and slipped on her way home."

The doctor looked intently at Harry.

"Why do you say that? Is your wife a heavy drinker?"

Harry smiled. "No, it's just that tonight she went out for drinks with friends."

"Her injuries were not caused by a fall or a stumble, Mr. Smelt. She's been violently assaulted."

Harry was quite literally struck dumb for a moment. The doctor continued.

"It is not a sexual assault, you understand. At least, it doesn't appear to be. But this is certainly no accident. The police will have to be informed. Do you want to do it or shall we?"

It was all moving too fast for Harry.

"Er, I'd prefer it if you informed them. You'll know who to speak to. What details to give them . . ." He tailed off helplessly.

Yet again events became blurred. Strangers coming asking him details. Police officers arriving asking him questions. This wasn't like it had been on TV that evening. It wasn't like that at all. Harry kept shaking his head, a gesture designed to throw off what was clearly a bad dream, but the dream kept on going.

"And would you know where these people live?"

"What?"

"These people who you say were with your wife tonight."

"What about them?"

"We would like their addresses, Mr. Smelt."

"Yes, yes of course."

He realized with a start that the police officers were talking to him in his own home. He had no recall of the journey back from the hospital. At about five o'clock in the morning the house was finally silent. What was he going to tell young Stephen? How do you tell a nine-year-old boy that his mother is in the hospital with head injuries? Injuries not sustained in an accident but wounds deliberately inflicted. Who would do that to your mother, Stephen? Who would actually *want* to hurt like that? These were things that happened on telly. Happened to other people. Things you read about in papers, then forgot about. They were not things that happened to you. To Stephen's mother? To your wife?

Early on Saturday morning Harry visited his eldest daughter, Linda. Married, twenty-five years old, she could be relied on for help; but first there was the task of telling her too that extraordinary things had happened to their ordinary family.

At ten o'clock he was telephoned by the hospital. He had told Stephen that his mum had been taken a bit ill and was in the hospital. The phone call was to tell him just how "ill" Olive was.

There were severe cuts above both eyes. There were lacerations on the head. Olive's skull had suffered a double fracture. Harry listened numbly to the catalogue of injuries. The doctor advised him that they wanted to rush Olive to the intensive care unit at Leeds General and that they would like him to travel with her, "just in case." Harry put the phone back on the hook and stood staring out the window of the small living room. Sightlessly he gazed at the nearby kiln chimney that dominated the immediate area. Slowly, very slowly, it began to sink in that she was possibly dying. He looked around the room at the small ornaments, at his chair, at her couch. With a start he realized that less than twelve hours earlier he'd been sitting in this room, engrossed in a television drama. Then the only problem on his mind had been an impending promotions board before which he was shortly due to appear.

"I'd love a cup of tea."
Olive looked up directly into the nurse's face above her. The nurse, with Olive's head cupped in her hands, smiled down.
"See what we can do when we get to Leeds."
The ambulance swayed as it sped along the highway to Leeds. Harry held tight to one of his wife's hands as if by doing so he could insist that she stay alive.
"Soon be there, love."
He smiled wryly to himself. Funny how one also coped with the

great crises of life with a cliché. He patted his wife's hand.

"Soon be there, love."

LEEDS GENERAL INFIRMARY. INTENSIVE CARE UNIT. NEU-
ROLOGICAL WING. A fast montage of signs, of strange noises and
smells, of people totally preoccupied with their own problems, of
staff who felt that if only there were not so many patients then
they could all get on with their real work; but there were the other
kind too.

"Mr. Smelt?"

Harry stood on hearing his name. He was beginning to respond
like one of Pavlov's dogs. Puzzled, he stared to his left; there was
no one there. The doctor, standing directly in front of him, spoke
gently.

"Thought you might like to see Mrs. Smelt's X-rays."

"Thank you. How is she now?"

"As comfortable as we can make her for the time being."

The doctor moved to a small display unit and, flicking a switch,
revealed two skull X-rays, one frontal, one profile. With a shock
Harry saw the profile of a smashed coconut shell; the photograph
showed vividly how the skull had been broken inward.

"We have two options. We can hope that there has been no
permanent brain damage of a serious nature and that the pressure
on the brain caused by the blows will automatically ease. Alter-
natively, we can risk an operation which may cause further
damage. We are inclined to take the first option."

"I see."

The doctor considered Harry for a moment.

"I think the best thing you can do now is to go home and get
some rest. Spend some time with the rest of the family. We'll let
you know if there's any change in your wife's condition."

Harry became aware that he was walking through the streets of
Leeds. It was Saturday afternoon and the streets were full of
weekend shoppers. He realized that he too was carrying a bag, a
plastic bag. He opened it and saw his wife's blood-stained
clothing. Then he remembered. They'd given it to him before
he'd left the hospital.

It was all becoming more and more unreal: he was in the middle

of Leeds on a sunny Saturday afternoon in August 1975; his wife
was lying critically ill in the hospital and people were milling
about, laughing, smiling, getting on with their lives as if nothing
had happened. It was not fair. It was not right. They really should
be showing some respect. He had physically to check himself from
remonstrating with a laughing group that passed by. He shook his
head. Time to catch the bus to Halifax. Get back to the family.

He turned out of Boothtown Road into Woodside Road.
Puzzled, he saw tremendous activity. Everywhere there were
policemen. They were searching in gardens. Going through
garbage cans. Taking statements from residents. He wondered
what could have happened. Then he remembered.

As he turned into Woodside Mount, neighbors approached him.
He responded automatically to their questions.

"Yes, she's as well as can be expected. Yes, I will. Yes I'll tell
her. Yes, thank you. Yes, thank you."

With relief he reached his own door. Entering he saw that his
family was gathered. Linda, his eldest daughter, rose and poured
him a cup of tea. As she handed it to him, she showed him the
evening newspaper: the attack on Olive was front-page news.
Harry shook his head.

"God, we can do without that, surely?"

"But what happened, Dad?"

"Dunno, but it looks a real set-up. This attack on Mum must
have been planned."

Unprompted and uninvited, several men suddenly appeared in
the kitchen.

"We'd like you to accompany us to the police station, Mr.
Smelt."

"But I've only just got home."

"Yes, we know, we've been waiting for you. Hospital told us
they'd given you your wife's clothes. Would that be them?"

"Yes."

"We'll take them if you don't mind. You'll get them back, of
course. Right—shall we go then?"

The police station was in one respect similar to the hospital.
Everyone seemed to have an allotted task, or at least acted as if he
had. Harry was shown into an interview room. The two who had
kept him company from his home were with him. Behind the desk

was a third. Holding one of the walls up was a fourth. One of them silently pointed to a vacant chair by the desk. As Harry sat, the man behind the desk leaned forward.

"How do you get on with your wife?"

The one holding up the wall asked, "What time did you go out last night?"

The one standing closest to him inquired, "Is she faithful?"

The fourth just stared at him.

Bemused, Harry struggled to respond.

"I get on all right with her, I suppose."

"What does that mean? Is it a happy marriage?"

Harry shrugged.

"It has its ups and downs. Don't they all?"

"What time did you go out last night?"

"You mean, what time did I come in, don't you? I didn't go out once I had come home from work. Not till they sent for me after the accident, that is."

The one preventing the wall from collapsing on them all smiled at that.

"Accident. What bloody accident? You're not talking about what happened to Olive, are you? That were no accident, Harry."

They were very free with their "Olives" and "Harrys." He hadn't been given any names for them. The one seated behind the desk clearly fancied himself a marriage counselor. He adopted that confiding air of bureaucratic concern.

"Now, Harry. Would you *really* call it a happy marriage? I mean, why weren't you out with your wife?"

"Because every Friday she goes out with friends, it's a regular hen party."

The marriage counselor looked pained.

"Now, she wouldn't do that if it was a happy marriage, would she, Harry? Why does she do that? Who does she go out with?"

It had been a long twenty-four hours for Harry. It was going to get longer. He struggled to answer their questions. He realized that of course he would be their first suspect, hence the line of questioning. But still . . .

"Now, your wife was attacked last night at about eleven forty-five."

"I suppose she must have been. I was called out at about ten to twelve."

"According to you, you were at home sitting watching the telly when your wife was attacked?"

"Yes, that's right."

"Can you prove that?"

"Can I what?"

"Prove that you were at home."

"My daughter and her friend were there."

"That's not quite right, is it, Mr. Smelt? They were in another room."

"They were in the room next to me."

"Another room."

"Well, yes."

"Now, while they were chatting in the kitchen, is it possible, Harry—and please listen carefully, we do need your help—is it possible that you went out of the front door, ran along the gardens, around the side of the row of houses, waited in the dark, attacked your wife, then ran back along the gardens and sat back down in front of the telly? Is that possible? After all, how long would all of that take you?"

Harry considered.

"It wouldn't take me long. But my timing would have to be bloody perfect. I would also need telepathic powers to know exactly when Olive was coming down that ginnel so that I would catch her just on that corner where she was found. I would also have to be certain that Julie and Sandy wouldn't walk through from the kitchen and discover I had just popped out to attack my wife. I would also need something to attack her with and somewhere to hide that something. Of course I would have to stop on my way home at this preplanned hiding place. I would also presumably have put on overalls, a mackintosh, gloves and a mask—now, all of this would have slowed me down a bit and if Julie and her friend had walked in while I was putting this lot on, or taking it off, they might have thought I was dressed rather oddly for watching 'The Marcus Nelson Murders.' Other than those points, yes, it's quite possible."

They all stared at him. The one holding up the wall shoved a piece of chewing gum into his mouth.

It was becoming just like on television and Harry did not find this realization made it any more tolerable.

"Now, I've been very patient. I realize that you have a job to do. But you are not going to accomplish that job by asking me silly bloody questions. I've had nothing to eat for nearly twenty-four hours, I've had no rest and I want to have a bath. I'm not answering any more of your questions."

The frustrated marriage counselor looked annoyed.

"Oh yes, you are."

"Oh no, I'm not."

On cue—he had after all been listening carefully—yet another plainclothes officer entered the room. He walked up to Harry, with his hand extended, a broad smile on his face.

"Harry, I'm Detective Sergeant Hands. How do you do? Now look boys, Harry can't be feeling very well. He's not up to answering any questions right now. Look at him. He's all in."

Clearly, Detective Sergeant Hands also watched crime thrillers on TV. Clearly, all of the Halifax C.I.D. did. It was nice-guy time.

By Sunday evening Harry had made a thirty-page statement. He had responded well to the gentle questioning of Hands, who had assured him that every detail of their married lives, every friend met and long forgotten, all should be recorded, any of those insignificant little fragments would perhaps provide the answer, give them the key to the puzzle as to why someone should want viciously to attack Olive Smelt. As he finished signing the last page Harry looked across the desk at the detective sergeant.

"You've got thirty good pages of reasons, right here, why I should want to nobble my wife."

Weeks later Hands was to give his response to that remark.

"If you had wanted to do your wife in, Harry, I think you'd have done it before now. And I think you'd have got away with it."

But that was weeks later. In the meantime the nightmare continued for the entire family.

"I've sent for the chopper man, Olive. I've sent for the bugger.

It'll be the chopper man any minute, love, so for Christ's sake tell me who did it to you."

Olive stared at the huge man. He wore the permanent expression of a man who having just had a rugby ball stolen from him, was prepared to kick the shit out of life until he recovered the ball. His name was Dick Holland. Detective Chief Inspector Dick Holland. He was also head of Halifax C.I.D. Right now as he sat by Olive's bedside in Leeds, he appeared to want his ball back very badly.

"Come on, lass. Stop sodding about. I'm telling you, chopper man is on his way."

Olive looked at him with puzzlement.

"Who's chopper man?"

"The pathologist. Professor Gee. He examines the dead ones."

Olive snorted indignantly.

"Does he indeed. Well, you tell him to bugger off. He'll have to wait a while before he gets a look at me."

Holland smiled at her. They were two of a kind, he and her. He knew where he was with a Halifax woman.

"Olive, this man who chatted to you at the top of the ginnel. Apart from the remark about the weather, did he say anything else? Anything at all?"

"No, just remarked about the weather letting us down. Then he was gone. Do you think he did this to me then?"

"Dunno. Now, what about Harry? I gather you two had some differences over the years. Are you covering up for him? Come on now, Olive."

"I'm not covering for anyone. If it was Harry did this I'd tell you and sod the consequences. Last I remember was that fellow talking about weather then he walked off and I started to walk down ginnel. That were it."

Holland looked worried.

"No, Olive, it weren't it. You were found at the bottom of that alley, not at top. It would have taken you at least two minutes to have walked from where you had this conversation about the weather to where you were found. Now, there's no blood between the two places. We are certain you were attacked where you were found. What happened when you turned to walk down that alleyway? Did you talk to someone else? Did you meet someone else? What happened in those two minutes, Olive?"

Olive strained to recall any fragment that had previously eluded her. If only the pain in her head would ease. If only they'd give her a cup of tea.

"You're covering up for someone, aren't you."

It was delivered as a direct accusation rather than a question. It came not from Holland but the large plainclothes policewoman seated on the other side of her bed.

"You're covering up for your husband."

This time her comment came as a statement of fact. Olive looked at her.

"Don't be bloody daft."

The policewoman, who would not have disgraced a rugby team, herself almost shouted.

"If you don't want him locked up, we do. Next time it might be a five-year-old child. Might be someone worthwhile."

Holland observed his colleague for a moment.

"Officer."

"Yes, Mr. Holland."

"Keep your mouth shut. Further, it is to remain in that position until you are off duty."

He paced the room. Pausing at the window he gazed out and considered the situation. She had survived. First account in the *Evening Post* was fun. According to that he was five foot ten and spoke with a foreign accent. Four days later the Yorkshire *Post* had said the police were looking for a yellow car, believed to be a Ford Escort, with a black racing stripe. Well, he hoped they found it. After an early report that said she was very poorly, the latest news was that she was improving. If only those car lights had not gone on. She would have been worse than poorly. Pouring another cup of tea, he sat and brooded.

At precisely that moment the man hunting him was sitting with a cup of tea in a hospital annex, also brooding.

So we are looking for a man about five foot, eight inches tall. Quite good-looking or, as Olive said, "He wouldn't frighten anybody." Well, he'd frightened you, lass, near out of this life into next. Slightly wavy hair. Dark. Long sideburns. Spoke with a Yorkshire accent. Must be half a million like that in the county, though they didn't all go around with an iron bar or a hammer smashing women over the head, thank God.

"Mr. Holland."

The slight figure of pathologist David Gee approached him. Prematurely balding, his domelike head served to enhance his professional status. The tall policeman rose.

"Got something?"

"Well, I had a little trouble initially. Mrs. Smelt was disinclined to allow me to examine her. Apparently you'd told her I only look at corpses. After we'd overcome that problem, yes, I did find something interesting. She has two slashes in the small of her back; each is about six to eight inches long. They have clearly been caused by a sharp instrument. The clothing had first been lifted before the marks were made, then the clothing was rearranged. That was precisely the same procedure involved with a woman I examined last month, except in her case the marks were made on the stomach. Her name was Anna Rogulskyj."

Holland never forgot a face or a piece of evidence on a crime. It was as if Gee had pressed a very specific button.

"Anna Patricia Rogulskyj. Aged thirty-seven years. Divorced. Living in Keighley. Found at about two-twenty hours on the morning of Saturday, fifth June, this year. Three lacerations to her scalp consistent with being hit on the head with a hammer. Slash marks on stomach caused by a sharp instrument. But I thought you said Olive Smelt was attacked with an iron bar?"

"An iron bar or a hammer. Difficult to be precise."

"So I'm looking for a man who randomly attacks women?"

"It would seem so."

"And he's now done one in Keighley and one in Halifax?"

"They do appear to be linked."

"I'd like another word with Olive. Have you finished examining her?"

"Yes, but if you could be gentle . . ."

"Of course, Professor Gee."

Holland strode into the ward. The curtains were still drawn around Olive's bed. He coughed and called out.

"Are you decent?"

He entered the inner sanctum. A movement of his eyes dismissed the policewoman. Sitting near to Olive, he took one of her hands.

"You should be honored. That was Professor Gee that's been looking at you. He only looks at dead ones."

"Then what's he looking at us for?"

"Because I've got influence."

"Is that why he came to measure us up, then?"

"Ay, that's right."

"When he saw these marks on my back?"

"Yes."

"He seemed surprised. He said 'Oh my God. Come and look at this.' And when the others were looking, he said, 'I've seen this before.' What did he mean by that?"

"Olive, you are very lucky to be alive. I sent for the chopper man because I didn't think you were going to live. Today's not the first time he's examined you. As for the marks on your back, I think they remind the professor of another case, that's all. Don't let that worry you. Where do your panties come up to, Olive?"

"How do you mean?"

"Over your bum. How far up your back?"

"You're married, aren't you?"

"My, but you're a hard case, Olive."

"Well, what kind of question is that to ask me? If you want to know about panties, ask that bloody dragon with you, though I should think hers are welded on."

Holland could not resist smiling at her.

"Judging from your husband's statement, Olive, you have had a better social life than I've ever had. When I've caught this bugger, you and I will have a night out."

It was clear to Holland that Olive could not tell him any more. Equally clear that, if her husband was responsible, then she did not know it. What was indisputable was that she was a very lucky woman. Had a young man nearby not chanced to say goodnight to his girl friend at that moment and turned on his car lights, the man bending over the unconscious body of Olive Smelt would have finished what he had clearly set out to do. Yes, Olive was a very

lucky woman. And Harry a very lucky man. Of course in the days
that followed he had to grow used to hearing that he'd been
arrested and charged. He grew used to a silence descending like a
fall of snow whenever he entered a local shop.

Their children too were fortunate that they still had both
parents. They learned to cope with the jibes that implied their
father had attacked their mother. Later they learned to cope with
other rumors, too, when the word was that Olive had been
attacked because she was a prostitute. Young Stephen was
sometimes found crying in the street; Julie grew accustomed to
hearing her mother discussed in the same breath as the weather,
and Linda had a nervous breakdown. Olive and Harry themselves
also made adjustments. Harry worked in a rehabilitation center
and was now married to a woman who was a prime candidate for
such a place. Harry adjusted to the fact that his wife had become
withdrawn, morose, acutely depressed and very dangerous; on one
occasion he found himself half conscious on the living room floor
after Olive had lunged at him. Olive adjusted too. To the pains.
To the confusions. To the fears. To the hatreds. To the
uncertainties. The pains came in the head; sometimes they were
sharp, sometimes dull and constant. The uncertainties came when
she considered why it should have happened to her. It was as if
that moment in the alleyway had robbed her of far more than two
minutes. Her very personality had gone. She simply did not feel
Olive any more. That feeling gave birth to fear and that to hatred.
Hatred for all men, and if Harry happened to be the nearest, so be
it. Sometimes she felt like sticking a knife between his shoulder
blades.

Stephen might well lock the door to protect his mother but
thoughts and imaginings come straying through the cracks in the
doors. Some come unaided, like the doubts about each other and
the doubts about friends. Over the years other problems have
come through the letter box, with the daily newspapers. Other
problems have come on the telephone. Like Yorkshire *Post*
reporter Claudia Cook, who was interested in the fact that because
of chronic headaches Olive sometimes got up at night. That
became an item to the effect that the attack on Olive had affected
their sex life. Or David Bruce, reporter for the *Evening Post*, who
inquired of Harry, "Have you ever stopped to consider that your

wife might be a prostitute?" That delicate question and response achieved immortality under the headline "What the Ripper Has Done to my Wife."

But long before that, the mystique was growing around the man who had attacked Anna and Olive. It was said he came and went in the night like an invisible man. That he knew exactly where the police were and where they were not. He was credited with extraordinary powers, astonishing gifts. The folklore about him began very early. If Olive had been attacked in the area where the stranger had casually remarked to her about the weather, then why was there not a trail of blood to the spot where she was found, two minutes' walk away? Had she been carried? Had she been placed in a car and driven there to be dumped? It puzzled the police. Dog hairs on Olive's clothes that remain unidentified puzzled them some more. The fact that her panty hose did not even have runs in them. That her white high-heeled shoes were unmarked; if he had dragged her all that distance the shoes would have been badly scratched. If he had carried her, not only would he but the walls of the ginnel would be covered in blood. The answer is simple. It usually is. Nothing to do with her attacker's magic powers. She was attacked at the bottom of the alleyway. Not the top. She was attacked exactly where she was found. Olive's mind has wiped the previous two minutes from her memory bank. The tragedy is that she cannot do the same with some of the succeeding years.

3

"Darling?"

"Yes, love. In here."

His attractive wife put her head around the sitting room door.

"Just going for breath of fresh air with Mum and Dad. You want to come?"

He rose from the armchair where he had been brooding and smiled as he approached her.

"Bit tired, darling. I'll stay here and put my feet up."

He held her head in his hands and kissed her. The kiss grew longer. She pulled away with a giggle.

"Thought you were tired. You get some rest and we'll see what happens when I get back home."

"Promise?"

"Promise."

A moment later he heard his wife and her parents close the front door and walk down the path. He returned to the armchair. He'd hidden it well but inside he was boiling. Two attempts and they were both still alive. Next time he had to get it right. Next time he had to finish the job.

Hands in pockets, he began to pace the small room cluttered

with furniture. He stared unseeingly at a memento from his father-in-law's native Ukrainia. Clearly he had been choosing the wrong areas. What was needed was a big city. A place where he could fade in, then out. Somewhere with plenty of women. Then he could get his own back. *All those bitches out there, any one of them could knock out a dozen children. Here it was October 1975. Married fourteen months and still no child. Twice she's become pregnant. Twice she's lost the baby through a miscarriage. It wasn't right. It wasn't fair.* The anger in him began to well up. He was determined to get his own back, to kill a few of those cows who could pop out kids like peas from a pod. If he had his way he intended to put a stop to a few of them. When he got hold of the next one he was going to . . . He switched off the anger and the images that came to his mind as calmly as someone switching off a light.

Where next? Someplace where that bloody Black Panther wasn't likely to be. Almost drove into a police checkpoint after Halifax. The sooner they caught the Black Panther the better. Robbery, kidnapping, and killing post office officials was child's play to what he was planning.

He considered the places he had already tried. Keighley, a fair-sized town, over fifty thousand people, lot of light engineering, plenty of money knocking about, but clearly a shortage of women walking alone. Seemed to be the same in Halifax, even bigger, with ninety thousand people. It might well have the headquarters of the world's biggest building society, plenty of candy from Mackintoshes and raincoats made nearby from Gannex but it was short on unescorted women. He'd been lucky to find that one on her way home. Then she'd bloody well survived. Suddenly it came to him. So obvious that he was puzzled why the solution had taken so long to work out.

Whores. Prostitutes. No need to stalk them waiting for the right moment. Why, just pay your money and they came with you willingly. Into the dark. Into fields, alleyways, deserted areas. He'd seen enough of them while driving the truck. In Leeds. Here in Bradford. All over the place. He'd used them. Now he would use them for a different purpose.

He got out his highway maps of Northern England. Staring at the map, he began to assess the various possibilities. He needed a city with a good inner road system that linked with the highways. They would be essential for getting out fast if he had to. His eye fell on Leeds. Only ten miles from his doorstep. Again it seemed so obvious he could not understand why he'd ever bothered with the other places. And he knew just the place in Leeds. Excited, he decided to check it out. His wife would think he'd just gone out for a drive. Which is exactly what he intended to do. He carefully combed his hair and winked at his reflection. A few minutes later he was driving through Bradford. Anyone who had observed him would have seen a good-looking man of thirty. Good head of dark hair. Under six foot tall. If they had spoken to him they would have discovered a quiet, pleasant, unassuming, gentle man. Absolutely ordinary in every way. Except one. He was planning murder. As he walked quietly around Chapeltown the excitement inside him grew. He'd read somewhere that the government was anxious to create a mobile and flexible work force with no real cultural or national roots. They'd certainly succeeded here. Manchester, London, Birmingham, Nottingham, Glasgow, the West Indies: They were all represented among the prostitutes who inquired if he was "Looking for business?" He strolled down Reginald Terrace. Fine Edwardian houses, built for the carriage trade. Even earlier, men such as the Lords Allerton and Airedale and Sir John Barran had chosen to build their homes in this area. Earlier still, the gentlemen of Leeds had defeated the gentlemen of Wakefield at cricket. The Countess of Mexborough had presided over archery contests. Now a polyglot of women from fourteen to sixty sold their bodies for five pounds a time while black pimps presided over them, checking the takings that were dutifully handed over twice nightly, for fear of mugging, and doling out beatings if the girls were considered to be standing up on the job.

He saw all of this as he walked the area. He listened while sipping a beer in the Hayfield. He brushed aside the propositions that he was offered in Spencer Place. He wasn't ready, not yet.

He stood quietly in the Gaiety watching a middle-aged stripper playing with her nipples and stroking the hair that rose from between her legs. A topless waitress, swinging a tray and chewing gum, approached his table and mechanically replaced the half-full ashtray with a clean one.

"This drink finished with, love?"

"No, but I'd like another. Pint of bitter."

"Right."

He watched as she bounced to the bar. He saw the men leer and nudge each other as she approached. Most were watching the stripper moving in jerks to the disco beat. Like a massive overweight puppet being pulled from on high. *Pull her and it would wipe that stupid permanent grin from her face.* He saw that most of the men, far from demonstrating any excitement or enjoyment, were watching the stripper with something akin to hatred. It was certainly contempt that showed clearly on so many faces. *They must feel the same about this as me.* It's all bloody filthy. The whole lot of it. They use sex to sell cars, to sell vacuum cleaners, curtains, shampoo, everything, everything. And here in this pub in Leeds they were using sex to sell sex. All you had to do was walk a few yards out of the Gaiety and there would be a whore waiting for you. He wondered if the prostitutes gave the strippers a cut. He'd like to give that bitch cavorting on stage a cut. Like to give her quite a few. That would slow her down. He found that his grip on the glass was tightening, his teeth were clenched. With an enormous effort he made himself relax. Carefully he looked around to check if he had been observed. They were all too busy looking at the show. The girl with the bouncing breasts walked to the table. Her breasts were virtually level with his mouth. For a moment he had an overriding desire to bite her above one of her breasts. Not in love. In hatred.

"That'll be forty-seven pence."

He placed a fifty-pence coin on the tray and indicated that he did not require change.

"God, the last of the big spenders has hit town."

He stared at the retreating naked back and visualized two slash marks across it. Sipping his drink, he continued to watch the audience.

Down Vicar Lane he walked and smiled ironically at the incongruity of the name. No self-respecting vicar would be seen down here.

In the Robin Hood. The Star and Garter. The Duncan. The Regent. The Scotsman. The White Swan. They were every-where, simply everywhere. As the days and the weeks melted by, he began to observe patterns of behavior. Certain whores used certain pubs. Most had favorite beats and most had favorite places to take their clients. By discreetly following in his car he began to build up a detailed knowledge of the vice life in Leeds. He had always prided himself as a planner. *Reconnaissance. You couldn't beat it. It had been the same at woodwork lessons as a boy; what was it the teacher was so fond of saying—"Measure twice and cut once." Good maxim for life, that. Keep the risks to a minimum.*

He managed to get into a shebeen in Sheepscar. An illegal drinking club full of multicolored dregs. He watched the whores drunkenly leaning on men who were total strangers to them. The women were being groped and pawed; in one instance a man, scarcely able to stand up, lifted a whore's skirt and inserted his penis from behind. The whore just went on talking, to the intense delight of her listeners.

He got up and walked out.

He walked again through Chapeltown and saw the once fine houses, now long decayed and made into many cramped apartments. He walked past the Warsaw & Riga Stores, past a Polish social club, Zermansky's the Solicitor. He crossed the road by the Sikh temple that rose from the remnants of an English parish church. Two men passing a bottle of meths to each other sat on the corner of Reginald Terrace. He paused as a car, slowly cruising, the driver peering out into the dark, went by.

The area lacked a health center, a library, playing fields, a launderette, even litter baskets. What it had, and it had them in abundance, was whores and their attendant essentials, pimps and johns.

He walked down Reginald Terrace again. Once fine gardens were now overgrown and full of refuse. A rat scuttled across the dimly lit road. Yet another prostitute approached him. She was young and attractive. He stood very still as she walked toward him.

"Are you looking for business, love?"

"How much would it cost me?"

"Five pounds. Only five pounds. I can give you a good time for that. Would you like me to suck you off instead? Still only cost you a fiver."

He stood and considered the variety of propositions. After all that he had seen and heard he was tempted. Strongly tempted. Instinctively he felt his right hand pocket for his hammer. It was empty.

"'Fraid it will have to be another night. Haven't brought the necessary with me tonight."

"Never mind, love. Come back and see me when you're fixed up."

Oh, she could rely on it. If not her, then one like her. He would get fixed up all right and he would come back. Tomorrow.

She wandered down the road, oblivious that death had just brushed by her. Her dated miniskirt just covering her backside, black leather boots, blond hair piled high. Dressed to kill and be killed.

He began to walk slowly across Chapeltown Road; he had parked the car near Potternewton Park. He had recently read of protests by local inhabitants. They were angry at the rat-infested places that many of them lived in, angry at the damp, the bugs, the decay, the squalor; they were particularly angry about the prostitutes and their clients. In the late 1940s there had been a campaign to rid the area of whores. The press had cooperated by giving those found guilty of "street walking" prominent publicity. It had worked, or had seemed to. There was a campaign now in 1975 for similar action. He agreed that there certainly should be action. What he had in mind was very specific action. He paused and gazed across the park. He saw a line of men, each a few yards apart from the next. His eye followed the line. Standing with her back to a large tree was a prostitute. Even from this distance he could clearly make out the white thighs. Between her outstretched legs the figure of a man was moving urgently. After a moment or two he stopped, broke free from the woman and quickly moved away. The line shuffled forward.

"Who's next?"

"I'd like the large cotton wool and this bottle of shampoo, please."

Flossy began to wrap the items as Lauris sidled up to her.

"Tea break after that one."

Flossy nodded. "One pound twenty-five, madam. Thank you."

The two girls sat in the booths thoughtfully provided by the drugstore management.

"I'm going to get that new Max Factor lipstick and two pairs of panty hose and if there's enough left over, David Essex singing 'Hold me Close.' Oooh, I wish he would."

"It isn't number one any more, you know. Art Garfunkel's 'I Only Have Eyes For You' has taken over."

"Well, when I buy a copy that'll put it back at the top, won't it?"

"Flossy, you've got all your wages spent before they're half earned."

"Well, we get staff discount. Seems silly not to take advantage of it. I know the idea of taking these Saturday jobs was to save up, but we've plenty of time to do that. Just think, we'll be able to buy all our Christmas presents here at Boots. We'll save a fortune. Rugby Club tonight?"

"We're supposed to be working towards our A-Level exams. I've got stacks of homework to catch up on."

"Lauris, I'm beginning to think you've been brainwashed. It's Saturday. Look, we're working. Being good little girls. Instead of being out horseback riding . . ."

"We're buying up half the place," Lauris interrupted. "Do you think Ray and his friend will be there?"

"At the Saturday night disco? Now, where else would they be? Not doing homework, that's for sure. Perhaps I can persuade Mum to drive us over to the stables tomorrow."

"That'll be great." Lauris checked her enthusiasm. Flossy noticed the change of expression.

"What's the matter?"

"Well, if we skip homework tonight, we simply can't again tomorrow. I'm having enough trouble with English Lit as it is."

Flossy uttered an exaggerated sigh.

"All right, Lauris. Tonight the disco. Tomorrow the homework. Sounds like Adolf Hitler."

They exploded into fits of laughter. Lauris recalled a tidbit of gossip.

"Linda Stevens came into the shop just now. She'd just heard that we've been asked to design the poster for the grammar school boys."

Flossy beamed.

"Was she just a tiny bit jealous?"

"Oh, I would say just a tiny bit. Couldn't talk of anything else, then walked out without her change. Wait until she hears that we're going to be *in* their revue as well."

"I think that might well reduce her to total silence, at least for an hour."

They burst into giggles again. Saturday afternoon, with the world stretching to infinity, or at least as far as the Rugby Club disco.

"I only have eyes for you," Wilma McCann half sang to herself and half to her children, who watched as she prepared to go out. Sonje at seven years of age, the eldest of the four asked, "Will you be late, Mummy?"

Wilma wriggled into the tight-fitting white, flared trousers as she joined in a litany that was familiar in the McCann household.

"Not too late, Sonje."

"How late's that?"

"Never you mind, miss."

"Can we watch telly?"

"For a bit. Be sure to get them all to bed."

"Yes, Mum."

Wilma smiled as the children scurried into the living room. Separated from her husband for the past eighteen months, the twenty-eight-year old woman relied heavily on Sonje to organize the home. The seven-year-old had responded well, freeing her petite, strawberry-blond mother for what she considered was "the good time"—a multitude of boyfriends and a nightly tour of certain Leeds public houses. Someday she would get around to divorcing Gerry, not that the fact that they were still technically man and wife had inhibited either of them. He lived with his girl friend Pauline in another part of Leeds and Wilma had her freedom and her children at Scott Hall Avenue. As she buttoned up her pink blouse and put on a short blue bolero jacket, her image of chic contrasted markedly with the home she was leaving. Unwashed clothes, an unmade bed, dirty china, mute testimony to an indifferent housewife. The thin Scots face stared back at her from the mirror as she carefully put on lipstick.

"Royal Oak to start with," she announced to her reflection.

In the living room the children stood in line for a goodbye kiss.

Three-year-old Angela, the youngest, asked, "Going to tuck me in and kiss me goodnight, Mummy?"

"Sonje will do that, won't you?"

"Yes, Mum."

"Goodnight kids. Be good. I'm going to town."

A moment later she was gone. Not out of the front door, past curious interfering neighbors who might well report her again to the child welfare authorities. Better by the back exit. Down by the side of the playing field. What they didn't know couldn't hurt them. How she looked after her kids was her affair.

The following morning at about four o'clock Sonje crept into her mother's bedroom. The bed was empty. The young girl was puzzled. Her mother had come home late before, many times. But never as late as this. An hour later Mum still had not come back. Sonje looked at the clock. She knew the buses would be running again soon. Waking the others, she helped them to dress. The four children walked down Scott Hall Road to the bus stop. It was bitterly cold and foggy but the first bus was bound to have Mum on it. They waited two hours but Mum never came. Unknown to them, the children had walked within one hundred yards of their mother. She was stretched out on the grass of the nearby playing field. Dead.

The police teleprinter stirred into life.

From Det. Chief Supt. Hoban, C.I.D. No 2 Area, Leeds.

To all divisions, surrounding forces and police reports. Ref previous teleprinter message 79/30-10-75, re murder of Wilma McCann, 26 years, at Leeds.

Post mortem examination reveals that the deceased had multiple stab wounds to the abdomen, chest and throat, probably inflicted by a knife with a blade of approximately 4" in length, ¾" wide, with one edge sharper than the other, possibly a pocket knife. McCann also suffered severe lacerations to the skull and fractures in the region of the crown, these apparently having been inflicted by a heavy instrument similar to an axe. It is known that there is missing from the deceased's handbag a white purse with clasp on top with the word "Mummy" on the front. It is believed the purse contained approximately £6 cash.

At 1 A.M. on 30-10-75 the deceased was seen to leave a local club (Room at the Top, Sheepscar, Leeds).

At 1:10 A.M. it is known she was stopping motorists at the junction of Sheepscar Street South and Roundhay Road, Leeds, attempting to obtain a lift and it is known from an eyewitness that a semitrailer with a dark colored cab and possibly a tarpaulin sheeted load stopped at the junction of Roundhay Road and Sheepscar Street South alongside Wilma McCann and it is believed she had a conversation with the driver. The location in question is the main route from the A.1. (North) Wetherby Traffic Circle to the Leeds Inner Ring Road which services heavy goods vehicles traveling to the M.62 (East) to Hull and the M.62 (West) to Manchester and Liverpool. Although an extensive search has been carried out in the vicinity of the crime the murder weapons have not yet been found and it is requested that any bloodstained instruments which could possibly have been used to commit this crime and should be found should be retained for forensic examination.

No mention of the head injuries or of the weapon believed to have been used to inflict them should be disclosed to the press. Any information concerning this murder should be passed to the West Yorkshire Metropolitan Police Murder Room, Tel 35353, Ext 2034, 2025 2031.

Message Ends.

Wilma's mutilated and partially clad body had been seen by a milkman at 7:41 on Thursday, October 30. Within a few minutes the Prince Philip playing fields were alive with the men and machinery of a murder investigation. Before the Leeds town hall clock had struck eight the head of Leeds C.I.D., Dennis Hoban, was gazing down at Wilma McCann. The chief superintendent was no stranger to violent death. He had met murder on the way more than fifty times and more than fifty times had found the answer to the puzzle. Scores of commendations to his credit. He had an ability to use the news media to advantage that was second to none, and every reporter in the north of England had Hoban's home phone number. Brave, only months before he had defused a time bomb in a Leeds store rather than risk the delay before the army could get there. Hoban was indeed a man of many talents. He began to bring some of them to bear within hours.

The first press conference on the murder took place less than three hours after the milkman's discovery. Hoban wanted publicity on a number of fronts and for a number of reasons. He was acutely aware that many of the reporters would consider this just a "fish and chips murder," today's news, tomorrow's dinner wrappings. He was also aware that with the Black Panther still at large any crime stories that did not feature that particular individual would get low priority with editors; but Hoban had a couple of aces. Four, to be precise. Sonje, aged seven, Richard, aged five, Donna, aged four, and three-year-old Angela.

Within two hours of the discovery of their mother's body, the four children had been placed in temporary care. They had also been photographed for the press.

Subsequently "Uncle" Dennis called on the children with bags of candy. He told them what had happened to their mother and questioned them closely about the many other "uncles" they had acquired over the years.

The fact that Wilma had over thirty boyfriends would undoubtedly sell newspapers. The fact that four young children had been orphaned might help Hoban catch the man who murdered her. The Chief Superindendent declined to give the press precise details but instead referred to "multiple stab wounds" and stated "we are looking for a vicious and sadistic killer." He told reporters he was anxious to trace her movements for the previous day and evening, that reports were coming in of sightings in various pubs, that anyone who had seen her in the previous twenty-four hours should contact the police, as of course should boyfriends "for elimination purposes." By early afternoon the story and the children's photograph had been given prominent coverage in the Leeds and Bradford evening newspapers.

Slowly the 150 police officers working on the investigation began to put some of the pieces of the puzzle together.

It was established that Wilma had left home at half past seven that evening. She was seen in a variety of pubs. At twenty to ten she was in the Royal Oak. At ten o'clock she was drinking in The Regent. At ten-thirty she was in the White Swan. During the course of the evening she consumed at least fourteen whiskies. At one o'clock in the morning, after spending the previous two hours in the Room at the Top Club, she emerged and began to weave her way roughly in the direction of home. She decided to hitch a ride and while walking past the Pointers Arms in Sheepscar jumped out into the path of an oncoming car. This eccentric and highly dangerous technique was apparently a favorite with Wilma. The startled motorist, having managed to avoid hitting her, wound down his window to find himself confronted by a swaying Scot who, clutching a carton of curry and chips, demanded a lift to the Scott Hall Road. The motorist declined the offer of her company and pointed out he was going in the opposite direction.

Undaunted, Wilma flagged down a truck and clambered into the cabin. Four hundred yards farther on she clambered out again; the truck driver was bound for Lancashire and did not feel like making a detour.

Doggedly, Wilma set out once again toward her home. Having stopped another motorist who was also traveling in the opposite direction, Wilma offered her services as a prostitute. The driver declined.

On the corner of Meanwood Road and Barrack Street she was picked up by a "West Indian" about thirty-five years of age, wearing a dark jacket and a gray trilby hat. He was driving a "K" registered red Avenger. He had a full face, a thin black mustache, rounded to the corners of his mouth. The time of this pickup was 1:20 A.M. Wilma climbed into the passenger seat and the car moved down Barrack Street in the direction of Chapeltown. This man, the last person but one to see Wilma McCann alive on this earth, has never come forward. Never been "eliminated" from the police investigation. That fact nagged at Hoban. As did Tommy.

Tommy was one of the many men in Wilma's life. About thirty years of age, five feet eleven inches tall, slim-built with black hair worn to the collar with an exaggerated wave at the front, he was a Scotsman with an accent as broad as Wilma's. On the twelfth of October, eighteen days before her death, Tommy was known to have had a furious argument with Wilma in her home. He threatened to knife her, a threat he had made more than once during previous arguments. There was evidence that indicated Tommy was a long-distance truck driver. Whatever his occupation, like the black man in the red Avenger, Tommy has taken to the hills and stayed there.

Hoban eliminated twenty-nine men friends of Wilma's during his investigation. Initially he thought that jealousy or revenge might have been the motive, but the condition that Wilma McCann had been found in argued against that theory. Lovers often kill, but the sheer savagery of the attack on Wilma brought to mind something far more unusual: the random homicidal killer.

Yet for all that violence, not a sound had been heard by the caretaker or his wife who lived in a bungalow on the edge of the playing fields. True, their dog, a South African ridgeback, had barked at about ten-thirty that evening but when Margaret Bould peered out into the mists there was no sign of anyone. The following morning when her husband pulled back the bedroom curtains he was confronted by a uniformed policeman with the body of Wilma. How on earth had she been murdered without the Boulds' hearing a sound? Perhaps the body had been dumped there?

Wilma's handbag strap was looped around her left wrist as if one of her last thoughts had been to hang onto her meager possessions. Six buttons lay on the grass near her body. Five were from her blouse, one from her blue bolero jacket. Her brassiere was pushed up, exposing her breasts. Her slacks were pulled down around her knees. Her panties were in their normal position. There was a positive semen reaction on the back of her slacks and her panties.

Her head had suffered two lacerations, one of which had penetrated the full thickness of the skull. There was a stab wound in her neck. There were a further fourteen stab wounds in her chest and abdomen.

Death had been caused by a combination of the injuries: none of the wounds alone would have proved fatal. They were caused by a blade that was not less than three inches long and three-quarters of an inch broad. One edge of the instrument appeared to be sharp and the other rounded. None of the stab wounds had penetrated Wilma's clothing. As with the earlier attacks, he had lifted the clothes to stab and mutilate.

The end, when it came for Wilma, had been mercifully fast.

She had been standing on the bank. Slipping not an axe, as the police have incorrectly stated, but his ball peen hammer from his pocket, the murderer struck her rapidly twice on the head. As she lay on the grass, deeply unconscious, he plunged the knife into her. Again and again. He concentrated particularly on the area where women carry the growing child. The life-force area.

In such a manner died a mother of four young children. The man that took her life took a memento of the occasion: the small white plastic purse that Sonje had given her mother. On it the little girl had written carefully with a ball-point, "Mummy." Inside was a photograph of Tommy. The purse is still missing.

This time the "chopper man," Professor Gee, had only a corpse from which to elicit information that would subsequently contribute to an inquest jury's verdict of "Murder by person or persons unknown." By the time that verdict had been reached, detectives had interviewed seven thousand householders and six thousand truck drivers.

Statements by the hundreds had been taken. Friends, boyfriends, clients, and acquaintances had been traced, sometimes after many painstaking hours and days of investigation. All had been questioned. Her four previous convictions for drunkenness, theft, and disorderly conduct were considered to see if they could yield a clue. Other good-time girls, known to be friends of Wilma's, were pulled into Millgarth police station, Leeds, and asked to give the story of their lives.

The term "good-time girl" is not a polite euphemism for "whore" or "prostitute"; it is one of the many grades used by the vice squads. Sometimes a good-time girl will ask for money, other times she will not. The name of her particular game is a good time.

From Wilma's friend's who fell into this category, the police obtained precisely the amount of help that they had anticipated: none at all. Rule one on the street is, Never help the enemy.

Slowly a picture, not merely of the last hours but of most of Wilma's life, had been built up, but her murderer remained a figure in the October mists.

Detective Chief Superintendent Dennis Hoban did not like it, he did not like it at all. He liked to get his man and this bugger had got away. The same hour that Wilma had been found on the grass, a man had also been found, less than a mile away, in a telephone booth; he too was dead. He had been strangled. A woman was arrested within hours. That was the kind of conclusion to a murder investigation that Hoban preferred. As the weeks went by and the investigation was inevitably wound down, Hoban worried from time to time. That inexplicable something in him that made him a good detective told him that whoever had killed Wilma McCann would not stop there. He felt sure he would strike again. He was right.

4

He could feel that inner coil beginning to tighten again. The compulsion was returning. *He wondered if it was safe so soon. It was less than a week since that night when he'd picked her up in Leeds. It had been so easy. God, so easy. It had helped of course that she was well under the influence. Good point to remember. Try to pick ones who've been drinking. It slowed their reactions. Made them far more vulnerable.* Fortunately there was no guilt within him. Not a shred. If there had been he would have given himself away when the police stopped him. It turned out to be a routine check for the bloody Black Panther. He had nothing in the car that would arouse suspicion. It was licensed and he had a driving license and registration papers to show the police officer. That wasn't so much luck as good planning, though.

His greatest piece of luck so far was unknown to him. For a long time he assumed that the police realized that the attacks at Keighley and Halifax had been committed by the same man who had murdered Wilma McCann. In fact, it was years before the police worked that one out. Or admitted the connection.

He laughed as he walked down Leopold Street, Chapeltown. Virtually outside the synagogue a young girl was soliciting. Around the corner by the church there were two more, and he had just walked past a couple of whores looking for business outside the Sikh temple.

In the 1950s J. B. Priestley had observed that Chapeltown "still retained traces of that restless glitter which is the gift of the Jew." If he had taken a look around now he would note that the only glitter was on the diamond rings worn by the pimps.

Of course the wealthy Jews had moved out of Chapeltown years ago. Now they were in Moortoom and Alwoodley.

The synagogue was now a nightclub, but he saw that the Star of David still hung on the wall. Rod Stewart's recording of "Sailing" came blasting out of the club into the street. Nobody cared.

The carriage trade had saddled their horses and moved out long before even the exodus of the Jews. There might well be over twenty nationalities still living in Chapeltown but the overriding impression he gained as he walked the streets on November 5, 1975, was that he was in Yorkshire's Harlem. Those fascinating Poles, Punjabis, Latvians, Russians, and Puerto Ricans clearly did not consider tonight—Guy Fawkes night—a cause for celebration. Perhaps they were all Catholics. A gray Rolls Royce went slowly past him; he did not get the impression that the driver was looking for a guy.

There was a lot of activity in the area this evening. The ruined derelict buildings had proved irresistible hunting grounds for young gangs seeking bonfire material. All Chapeltown was dotted with fires. He would have to wait for a while. Wait until there was less activity on the streets. Wouldn't do to be seen by too many people who might remember him. He smiled to himself. The excitement within him was growing by the minute, but it was an excitement that was under very exact, very precise control. He was totally in command. He knew that a few streets away his Ford Capri was parked. He knew that in the car were his hammer, his knives, his screwdrivers, all that he needed. In a couple of hours he'd pick up one of these whores, take her to a real quiet spot and murder her. Now, to kill time—he smiled as the phrase came to his mind—to kill time he would stroll around and decide who the lucky girl was going to be.

He walked up Spencer Place. God, there were more out tonight than he'd ever seen. He'd wondered if murdering Wilma McCann might have frightened some of them away but here they were, lit by the flickering bonfires, miniskirted, high-heeled and every color of the rainbow. Blondes, brunettes, black afros, redheads—you could probably get a green-haired one if you asked at the right address.

A red car drove past him quickly; he recognized the number. It was a vice squad car. They were as well known in the district as the ice cream vans.

A moment later there was a tremendous noise of smashing glass. He stood rooted to the spot. A gang of teenagers, virtually all black, had turned and stoned the car. A large brick had hurtled through the windshield and the car had crashed into a tree. Instinctively he moved toward the scene of the crash, then his control factor took over. He couldn't go to help. Bloody silly to think he could.

Suddenly the area was alive with police cars. Sirens wailed from every direction, all converging on Rossington Grove. A large bonfire served to illuminate the scene. The red vice car had been turned upside down. God alone knows what had happened to the two policemen inside. A helmetless uniformed policeman hurtled past him in pursuit of a young West Indian. German shepherd dogs had been let loose. Violence all around him. It was time for him to leave. To creep quietly away unnoticed. This was no place for him. He would have to come back another night.

The two plainclothes police officers had not, as the black kids believed, been about to put their bonfire out, neither had they been about to arrest any of the teenagers who were throwing fireworks. As members of the vice squad it had been vice that they were pursuing when their car was wrecked. Constable Alan Mann and Sergeant James Carter both suffered fractured jaws, facial cuts, and bodily injuries. A year later when the Guy Fawkes bonfires were again lit in Chapeltown, neither man had been able to return to duty.

The seeds of that violence had been planted long before by many people. The flowering has yet to come. November 5, 1975, was merely the first blossom.

He shook his head as he read the accounts of the bonfire night violence. If the youth of today had no respect for law and order, what was the future going to be like? Tossing the paper to one side, he turned back to his map of the north of England. His finger traced over the highway links between the cities for the hundredth time.

She tilted the bottle of cider to her mouth and felt the sweetness of its contents run down her throat.

"Come on, Joan, save some for me."

Laughing, she passed the empty bottle very carefully to the man at the next sink.

"Thanks."

He tipped the bottle to his mouth.

"Yer bitch. It's empty."

Joan roared with laughter and raised a suds-covered hand to her forehead and rubbed an itch with her arm.

"Don't worry, luv. I'll buy you a pint at lunchtime."

"Well, all right then. But remember, the first round's on you."

Joan Harrison smiled, the slow, almost glued-on smile of the alcoholic. It was not yet noon but already her mind was softened with drink, already she was under that very pleasant, gentle haze. It might slow the brain but it deadened the pain. It blurred the memory. Some would find that a disadvantage. Joan Harrison considered it a definite bonus.

Twenty-six years of age. Married twice. Separated for two years from her second husband, Paul. She did not mourn the dead marriages, either of them; what she yearned for was the two children, her daughters. One now lived with her mother in Chorley, the other had been taken into care in Preston. Into care, bloody care. In court they'd said she was "a complete wreck of a human being." What did they know about bringing up a young lass? It was *her* lass. Tears began to well in her eyes. A combination of the cider and the memories. What she needed was more of the former and less of the latter.

She had wandered from man to man. From situation to situation, both work and personal. Now in November 1975 her friends were mainly prostitutes, drug addicts, and alcoholics. She shared a common interest with each element.

Proud Preston, that was what they used to call this place. Not much to be proud about now, not from Joan Harrison's point of view. What was she doing washing bloody plates in a hostel for the homeless? Must be something to do with that saying about "give me a child for seven years and I'll give you a Catholic for life." After all, this hostel was called St. Mary's. Old habits do indeed die hard. The man at the next sink grinned with what was left of his teeth.

"It's lunchtime."

She smiled back at him.

"That's very good. You win first prize."

"And what's that?"

"Any drink of your choice, as long as it's cider."

The interchange was greeted with roars of laughter from various parts of the kitchen, demonstrating not only their deep love of ritual but also an awareness that they were all in the shit together.

Joan dried her hands and turned to the others, who were busily engaged divesting themselves of aprons, overalls, and other chains of office.

"Where shall we go, then?"

"Where do we always go for lunch?"

Joan smiled; she enjoyed their community jokes.

"We go to the nearest church. The one with a public bar and a saloon. And what's the boozer called?"

The answer came roaring across the kitchen.

"St. Mary's."

Curious name for a pub. Still, the cider tasted good.

At half past three that afternoon, Joan, her young face even more bloated than usual, staggered back into St. Mary's hostel for the homeless. The fragments of her awareness told her she had beds to make. She fell on the floor, giggling. An assistant warden attempted the impossible.

"Now come along, Joan. This will never do."

"I am sailing. I am sailing. On the sea. On the sea."

Joan's sense of pitch was on a par with her grasp of the lyrics.

The assistant warden gamely battled on.

"Joan, I think you ought to go home."

"Want to go to bed. I want to go to bed."

There had not been many times in her life when Joan Harrison had been granted her wish without argument, cajoling, or the playing of one of the many other emotional cards of life. On this occasion she did not have to even reach for the pack.

"All right, Joan, I'll find you a bed."

Joan beamed. At last a little bit of justice. A short while later she was still smiling as she snuggled between the clean sheets.

She continued to smile in a drunken haze as she heard the door open, then close. She knew exactly who had come into the small cubicle. Always, always, in life there is a price to pay. At least that had been her experience. Nothing is for nothing. She turned and gave her best come-on smile to the assistant warden. At least she considered it was her best come-on smile. In reality it was a glazed, stupid, vacuous, drunken grin. The assistant warden, with his trousers rapidly falling, was too preoccupied to consider the smiles. Stripping, he climbed into bed. As if in reflex Joan turned onto her back and, opening her legs, guided his penis into her.

The assistant warden of St. Mary's hostel for the homeless briefly forgot that he lived and worked in a sordid dying northern city of England. Soon, all too soon, he had an orgasm. God damn it, why was it always so fast? So soon? Why did Preston always come roaring back into the thinking mind so quickly?

He didn't know it then, that assistant warden, but the fact that he had taken and used the living body of Joan Harrison was going to cause him an enormous amount of aggravation and trouble with the police. Perhaps there is some higher form of justice after all?

Joan slept on after the warden had returned to his official duties. The drink induced an unfitful sleep but at nine o'clock that evening she awoke. She licked her lips, dehydrated; her first thought was the same as every alcoholic's: she needed a drink. Beer, cider, that medicine with the morphine in it, anything.

Staggering out of bed, she splashed water on her face. It was a pointless exercise. She shook her head, again and again, in an attempt to clear the muzzy clouded sensation. It was useless; there was only one cure and that was a drink. She stared long and hard at her wristwatch. Concentrating on the dial was very difficult, very confusing. Finally she arrived at the conclusion that the combination of the hands on the watch and the darkness outside indicated that although it was night, the pubs were still open.

She opened her black, shiny handbag and took out her purse.

Christ, it was empty. She'd been too bloody generous at lunch-time. She considered the possibilities. One, go to Blackburn, see her friend Pauline and borrow some money from her. No, that was too far. Two, try and get an advance on next week's wages from St. Mary's. No, the assistant warden would be off duty by now. Three, go and see David. Yes, that was the one. David Keighley would give her a bob or two. He didn't approve of her drinking, but still he did want to marry her. She'd rented a room from him in June of that year; three weeks later she was living with him. He'd even bought her a ring. She smiled as she looked at it. He was nice, was David.

By quarter to ten she was home at David's. By twenty past ten she was out again. Without a loan. He'd refused to give her money for drink. Pleaded with her to stay at home. Have some food. Well, stuff that. She didn't need something to eat, just something to drink.

She wandered out of David's home in East View. At the bottom of the road she paused for a moment. Directly opposite was Preston prison. No bloody good going there for a drink or to put the touch on somebody.

She turned and walked down Church Street. Plenty of pubs down here. Plenty of discos too. If there was nobody she knew in the pubs she could always try somewhere like Scamps. If the discos proved useless, she still knew one or two places in Church Street. Not exactly pubs or discos, more derelict buildings or open spaces where the winos gathered. She liked being with them. No crap about them. You just screwed and got pissed. No bollocks about this or that. Just got on with what it was about. Really about.

A car stopped beside Joan. She gazed at the man behind the wheel. He looked all right. Well, perhaps she could do a bit of business first, then have a drink afterwards. Always somewhere to get a drink in Preston, if you had the money. She moved over to the car.

"Are you looking for business?"

"Yes. How much?"

Normally, like any northern prostitute, she would pitch the price according to the appearance of the client. Get a guy talking in a handmade suit and it's going to cost him thirty. Rough-looking clothing reduced the price to what the handmade suit could have had it for, five pounds.

Joan was too anxious for a drink to auction her body tonight.

"Five pounds."

"O.K. Get in."

She walked around to the passenger seat, he unlocked the door from the inside. As she entered the car he was surprised to see that in fact she was not as old as the street lighting had indicated. He leaned past her and locked the passenger door.

He put the car into gear and moved away.

"Do you know a place?"

Oh yes, she knew every place in Preston that it was safe to use for business.

"Yes, you'll come up to a church in a moment. Take the second on the left past that. You don't sound like a Preston man."

"I'm not. Just passing through town."

"Well, we'll have to see if we can't show you a good time before you pass through."

"This one here?"

"That's it. Now turn right at the bottom then take the first left. We can either use your car or there's some rental garages I know. They're not in use."

"The garages sound fine. How far are we from them now?"

"Oh, not far."

"Right. I'll stop here, then, and we'll walk the rest of the way. Don't want to disturb the neighbors, do we?"

"What a thoughtful man."

"Oh, I try to think of others, you know."

He stopped the car and they got out. As he did, he slipped the lock on the passenger door from the inside. Locking his own door, he walked to her. She tucked her arm inside his as they strolled along Frenchwood Street. On the other side of the road three men were giving every impression of having just survived an earthquake. He frowned as Joan giggled at them.

"Friends of yours?" There was an edge to his voice that she did not hear.

"Yes. Happen they are. Grand lads."

"Look like winos or tramps."

"Yes, they are." She laughed. "That's why they're trying to hold the pavement still by laying on it. They're all right."

He looked at the figures in disgust. Filth, absolute filth. They had stopped by a small building.

"Here we are, love."

He glanced around. The three winos, having somehow clambered to their feet, were staggering off in the direction of Church Street. Slowly his head turned nearly full circle. Multistory carpark in darkness. Convent, mosque, bus depot, all in darkness. A train pulling out of nearby Preston Station was the only sound. Joan misunderstood the precautions.

"Come on, luv, no need to be nervous. I'll give you a really good time."

If she could have seen the expression on his face perhaps some warning bell would have penetrated her drink-softened faculties, but the darkness masked the malevolence. They stepped inside.

"Now, my motto is business before pleasure."

Without a word he handed her a five-pound note.

"Thank you, luv." She unclipped her shiny black plastic handbag. Taking out her purse, she folded the five-pound note inside it. She placed her handbag on the floor of the garage. Bending down, she removed one of her boots, then lowering her slacks she stepped out of the leg. She repeated the process with her panties. She braced herself against the garage wall. She was ready.

A moment later he had entered her. Lifting her brassiere to play with her breasts he discovered to his surprise a second brassiere. She offered no explanation. For some irrational reason the second brassiere irritated him, vexed him. Quickly he lifted it up. He admired the well formed breasts, fondled them and then suddenly began to kiss and suck the left breast. The comfort and satisfaction he sought eluded him. The anger in him began to rise. Moving his mouth a few inches above the breast, he bit. He bit deeply. He heard her gasp with pain. The gasp aroused him to the point of orgasm.

By now the sexual activity was having an effect on Joan, she too was aroused. The pain, the noises, grunts from his exertions, the realization that he had climaxed, all served to arouse her. She uttered a small groan of disappointment as he pulled away from her. He was still hard. The idea that had been dancing just short of his consciousness from the moment they had entered this garage now came to the forefront. He smiled with excitement at the possibility.

Quickly turning her around, he attempted to bugger her. His actions were those of a boy who expected at any moment to have his name called by the teacher for misbehavior. To his surprise she reacted with a laugh and, pushing her rump toward him, quickly guided his penis inside.

He shook with excitement, the realization of the act causing him to tremble. We all have dark little secrets. Many of us take our secrets to the grave, untold. Here in a grubby little deserted garage in Preston this man had chosen to share one of his dark secrets with this woman, a total stranger. He didn't even know her name. Clearly Joan was enjoying the act. This drove him to even greater heights; yet again he had an orgasm and within moments, just like that naughty schoolboy, his delirium of pleasure turned to revulsion. For a moment he felt self-disgust but rapidly he corrected this error. He was still inside her, her body half leaning away from him. He smashed her on the back of her head. She groaned as she fell to the floor.

He stood over her, gasping, not with the effort of the blow but with the recently finished sexual act. As he zipped up his trousers his disgust welled up within him. Shame and hatred intermingled. He began to kick her. He kicked her on the face. On the head. On the breasts. On the body. On the legs. He kicked her and went on kicking her long after he had kicked the last spark of life from her body.

Eventually he felt cleansed. He stood over her breathing deeply, in total control again.

He dragged her body a few yards farther away from the door, just in case the garage should have any other visitors that night. His sense of neatness was offended at the sight. He had too much self-respect to leave her like that. Putting the panties and tights back on the bare leg might prove difficult, so leaving them lying free he worked her legs back into the slacks and pulled them up. Leaving the inner brassiere above the breasts he pulled down the outer one to mask them. The boot that Joan had removed, he stuffed tightly between her thighs. Eventually after a struggle he managed to remove her overcoat; this he placed over her body, taking particular care to mask the face.

He began to move out of the garage but saw the black handbag still standing neatly on the floor where Joan had placed it.

He picked it up and, opening it, rummaged among the contents. Eventually he took them all out and pocketed them. Having parked Joan Harrison in eternity, he left the garage.

He began to retrace his steps towards his car. As he walked he checked and rechecked. Testing for error. Ensuring that all aspects had been considered. He stopped. Here he was walking through Preston in the small hours of the morning clutching Joan Harrison's handbag. True, there was no one around. But suppose her body was found before he was clear of the town? Suppose they put up a road block? Equally he might drive into another police checkpoint for that bloody Black Panther. Best get rid of the bag here in Preston.

He hid the handbag in a refuse dump some 400 yards from the garage. The purse he tucked under a bush in Avenham Park a little farther away. No point in making it easy for the police by leaving the purse in the bag. He smiled as he looked at the rings and lighter and the odds and ends that until a few moments ago had been just about the only possessions of Joan Harrison. The three rings looked good. He yawned. It had been a long night. Slowly the car turned back into Church Street.

Joan Harrison may have counted the regulars of Skid Row as friends, but she clearly lacked the kind of friend that comes looking for you. It had been Thursday evening on November 20, 1975, when she popped out for a quick drink from her "home" with David Keighley. On Sunday the police called to tell him she had just been discovered in the garage.

Distressed, David Keighley told first Wilf Brooks of Lancashire C.I.D., then the press, of his love for the murdered woman, of their plans to marry the following year and of how he had given her a ring.

Another friend who received the news with shock and disbelief was Pauline Storey, the friend Joan had considered traveling to Blackburn to see on the night of her death.

When Pauline learned of her friend's murder she promptly offered to help the police. This annoyed the man she was living with. James Plunkett was no lover of policemen. When Pauline, who was eight months pregnant with his child, told him of her plans to place an "In Memoriam" in the local newspaper for Joan Harrison, his annoyance became rage. It seemed to him to be adding insult to injury to waste money on a drunken whore. He and Pauline began to fight. The fight ended with his death; he was knifed by Pauline.

In February 1976 Pauline was acquitted by a jury of the murder of James Plunkett, but the damage had been done. The ripples of evil spread far and touched many.

The bite mark above Joan's left breast was considered by a variety of forensic experts, among them a Liverpool dentist, the late James Furness, who was a specialist in forensic odontology. This science has recently been used by the C.I.D. in London when in a deliberately set nightclub fire thirty-two people perished. In some cases all that remained to assist identification was the teeth.

James Furness was fond of observing, "People can lie through their teeth, but their teeth cannot lie." The odds against two people with a complete set of thirty-two teeth producing identical bite marks are the same as the odds against identical fingerprints—two point five billion to one.

It was clear to Furness that the marks on the breast of Joan Harrison had been put there very shortly before death. What intrigued him was the clear gap in the front upper teeth that the marks indicated.

Equally foolish was the decision to have sex with Joan before murdering her. Surely her killer knew that his blood type was rare?

The Lancashire police began to organize saliva tests. Anyone who secretes in semen will also secrete in saliva. They tested over six thousand men. Not just friends and acquaintances. Not just the bemused inhabitants of Church Street and its environs. The crews of twelve ships that chanced to be in the port of Preston at the time found themselves spitting into small glass reusable jars.

If any thought was given by the Lancashire C.I.D. of linking this murder with that of Wilma McCann's, it was quickly forgotten. The police in Preston were sure that their fugitive was a local man. When the purse was found two months later and then the handbag in June 1976, they regarded this as confirmation that the murderer was a local familiar with the area. The contents of the purse and handbag, like the man that took them, are still undiscovered. The drunks still stagger through Church Street. If they lived in Baton Rouge they might well have become immortalized by now in a song. But who cares a damn if you're busted flat in Preston?

5

They were riding John Wayne style with the addition of screams and shrieking laughter as Flossy and Lauris hurtled across the fields. Horses and riders exuding clouds of steaming breath into the crisp November air. The frosted grass crackled beneath the hoofs.

With Flossy's mother bringing up the rear they approached a large hedge. Lauris sailed over, as did Flossy's horse, without its rider.

"You are supposed to stay on when you take a jump, Flossy."

"Oh, anyone can do it that way. Thought I'd be different."

Her mother drew close.

"Are you all right, dear?"

"Yes, of course I am. I want to try that jump again."

"Are you sure that's wise?"

"No."

Lauris and Flossy's mother kept well out of the way as, having remounted, Flossy urged the tall horse at the hedge. A moment later she spoke to the watchers.

"Now you must admit, that was a considerable improvement. I must have been half over before I fell off that time. Is this what they mean by saying it's great exercise, Mum?"

"Darling, I don't think you should try again."

"Mum, if I don't do it now I never will. Like falling off a bike."
She rubbed her backside.

"Except it's just a little bit higher. Don't worry, third time lucky, they say."

"Oooh, isn't he gorgeous. Just look at that mouth."

The mouth in question belonged to Freddie Mercury, lead singer of a pop group, Queen. Flossy and Lauris lounged on the floor watching the group perform "Bohemian Rhapsody," lost in a private fantasy that they were simultaneously sharing with several million other teenagers. At the end of Top of the Pops they resumed their conversation at precisely the point they had stopped it thirty minutes earlier.

Lauris clapped her hands.

"Now, there are a number of extremely important, in fact crucial, decisions that have to be made."

"What are we going to wear to the grammar school play next week?"

"That is item one. Item two is, who are we going to chat up after we have watched all those boys make fools of themselves?"

"Right, I suggest we move item two until the last on the grounds that it is the most interesting subject. All those in favor?"

"Carried. Then the next item is the grammar school revue, which two certain girls, having already designed the poster for the boys, are now actually going to appear in."

"You do realize that Linda Stevens will probably have a fit in the playground when she sees you actually kissing a boy onstage?"

Flossy adopted a regal stance, and with a regal wave observed, "As long as she doesn't faint while I'm actually kissing the boy."

"Then we have to discuss the lunchtime disco we're going to run for our third-formers."

"And then we must discuss the grammar school dance. And we haven't even got to Christmas yet."

It was at the grammar school dance that it happened. Flossy had gone with the expectation of a fun evening. She got a great deal more than she had ever anticipated. She fell in love.

"Who is he? Who is he? Quick, I have to know."

"Hey, steady on, Flossy. You're spilling my drink. Who is who? No, that's not right. Should it be who is whom? Or should it be . . ."

"Lauris."

"It's a cousin of mine, actually. His name's Benjamin. We call him Ben."

"Ben." Flossy repeated the name. There was a faraway look in her eyes. The hall was full of the sound of Queen. Lauris bounced up and down with excitement.

"Listen, Flossy. It's Queen. 'Bohemian Rhapsody.'"

"Who?"

"No, not The Who, Queen."

Flossy continued to gaze into the middle distance. Lauris affected slight hurt.

"Well, I thought it was funny."

"What's funny? I think it's a very nice name."

Lauris looked closely at her friend.

"Flossy, are you all right? That was cider we had to drink, wasn't it?"

"Yes, of course it was. Now, Lauris, I think we should go and sit down."

"I don't want to sit down. If I stand just here, that rather sexy-looking Mike Goldsmith may well ask me to dance with him."

"Lauris, you can dance with him anytime. I want to talk."

"Flossy. Have you gone mad? We can talk anytime. I want to dance. What do you want to talk about, anyway?"

"About Ben."

"Cousin Ben! Have you gone bananas? I don't come to a dance to talk about my family."

"But he's different."

"All right, he's different. Now, can we get on with dancing?"

Flossy smiled at her friend.

"Yes, of course we can. Then, afterwards."

"Afterwards?"

"You can tell me all about Ben."

So they had finally arrested the stupid bastard. Once again he read the new item that told him that a man called Donald Nielson had been remanded for a further three weeks. He'd already been charged with the murder of Lesley Whittle; presumably they would bring him to trial on that first and then do him for the murder of the three post office people later. He chuckled at the thought that the Black Panther had finally been caged. That would mean an end to police roadblocks. Other than those that might happen after his own activities, but then he planned for them anyway. It would mean an end to coppers all over the place. He clapped his hands and rubbed them in satisfaction. What a lovely Christmas present. Before he was finished they would have forgotten all about the Black Panther—it would be him they were talking about. It was just five days to Christmas, not really time to plan another one and carry it out this week, particularly as he'd promised to spend Christmas with the family. Perhaps a little walk about? Why not a stroll around Chapeltown to see if things were back to normal after the Guy Fawkes bonfire-night violence and of course Wilma McCann's death?

He drove slowly, yet again familiarizing himself with the familiar. Every street. Every turning. Which were cul-de-sacs. Which were one way. Like a London taxi driver on the "knowledge," he was preparing himself for his work. He turned into Blackman Lane and stopped at a small shop.

Leaving his car, he surveyed the street. The tramp was wearing three overcoats. His hair was a Jacob's coat of colors, black, white, red, the streaks extended to a long beard. The eyes had the look of a man staring at hell. The shirt could have been black or gray or simply filthy. In one hand he clutched a bundle, in the other an open bottle of wine; at least it was a wine bottle, whatever its contents might be. He stopped very close, swaying.

"Money. Need money." He extended his hand and lifted his face in expectation. He was met by a gaze that literally made him blink in fear. Pure reflex cut through his addled responses and propelled him back a step. Then, turning, he shuffled quickly up the street. He had indeed stared at hell. The face that had frightened him reverted from normality to a mask and with a final glance at the vanishing tramp looked around. Houses were mostly derelict. Dogs were foraging in abandoned garbage cans. Everywhere was decay and neglect. He was seeing more and more of this since he had begun. He turned back to the small shop and entered. A middle-aged man, his right hand below the level of the counter, eyed him warily.

"Bar of that chocolate, please."

The shop owner relaxed and reached for the chocolate.

"Oh, and an *Evening Post*, please." He placed a pound on the counter and, picking up a copy of the paper, noted that there was another item on Donald Neilson. He'd enjoy reading that later. He turned back to the shopkeeper.

"Have they got demolition going on around here or something? I just had a wino trying to beg in the street."

The shopkeeper shook his head as he handed over the change.

"This is a clearance area. They say rats leave a sinking ship. They might well at sea. On land they move in. Those boards on front windows. I have to keep them there, otherwise the scum just smash windows and climb in. Been raided five times in the past eighteen months by the scum."

"You're joking."

"I wish I were."

"What about police?"

"Now thee's joking. Bloody useless. Old people around here do not go out after dark."

"But this is the middle of Leeds."

"No, lad. It *seems* to be. This is the jungle. I've been here twenty-one year. Can't wait to get out now. There's no moral fiber in country any more. Worst mistake they ever made was getting rid of the rope and doing away with the birch. Bring those back and give these buggers a taste of it. Then we'd see some improvement."

It was by the shopkeeper's standard a very long speech. Exhausted, he slumped on his stool and stared glumly at the enormous pair of breasts that confronted him on the cover of a magazine. Following the shopkeeper's gaze, his customer was reminded of why he had come to Chapeltown.

"Good night, then. And take care."

"Don't worry, lad. I keep hammer under counter now. Next time the buggers try anything they'll get it." He smiled at his customer, who returned the smile with an even broader one. He was still grinning as he climbed behind the wheel of the Ford Capri and moved deeper into Chapeltown. The shopkeeper was

right, of course, absolutely right. Well, he was doing all he could
to bring back the old standards. Restore the old virtues, at least in
one area. Pity he had promised to spend Christmas with the
family. He felt the urge to get back on the job right away, but it
would need careful planning. Everything had been perfect so far.
It must stay that way.

    Emily Jackson sat in her kitchen and considered the morning
mail laid out on the wooden table. It might well be the season of
peace on earth and goodwill to all men, but apart from a number of
cards that extended the season's greetings there were another
three bills, two of which were offering to extend something
warmer than greetings if they remained unpaid. Emily stood up
and having poured herself another cup of tea, walked to the
window and considered a few of the realities of her life.
    She was forty-two years of age and had been married to Sydney
for nearly twenty-three of them. Like every other marriage, theirs
had highs and lows, though as she considered the situation that
Christmas week of 1975 it was difficult to remember the highs; it
often is when you are at the other extreme. Four children; Neil at
eighteen years more than pulling his weight in the family roofing
business; ten-year-old Christopher and eight-year-old Angela.
Then there was Derek, he would be going on twenty, if he had
still been alive. Five years earlier he had tumbled out of a
bedroom window and fallen to his death. She had never really
taken to their home in the village of Churwell, just outside Leeds.
Since her eldest son had died, Emily and Sydney contrived to
spend as little time as possible in the place. They had determined
to live for the day and enjoy life to the full, but Churwell or nearby
Morley were hardly able to satisfy such a philosophy. The night
life of Leeds had a great deal more to offer: lively pubs, plenty of
bingo, and people who might help them find what they were
looking for. All Churwell had to offer was three pubs and pork
pies. There had to be more to life than that. Sydney entered the
kitchen. Pouring himself a cup of tea, he observed the scene: his
wife standing at the window and the bills fanned out on the table.
He sat and stirred his tea.
    The only sound apart from the clink of the spoon on china was

the chattering of Chris and Angela making the most of their Christmas vacation by pillow-fighting.

"We've another three bills, Syd."

"So I see."

"Two of them are threatening court action."

"I can read."

"We've got to do something about them."

"Ay, put them with the other buggers."

"Syd, we've got bills for nearly three hundred pounds."

"Emily, I can do no more than work my balls off. I work every bloody day. I don't know where the money goes. You tell me. You do the books. Where does it bloody go?"

She turned from the window and stared at the hunched, defeated form of her husband.

"It goes, love. It just goes. There's never enough of the bloody stuff. We've got to do something about it, Syd."

He looked at her.

"What do you suggest I do, rob a bank?"

"No, I've got a better idea."

She had his undivided attention now.

"I'll go on the game."

"You what?"

She elaborated as if to a child.

"On the game, Syd. Become a pro. I've been chatting to a few of the girls in Leeds."

"Have you, now?"

She smiled with the knowledge that there was not going to be any real argument. She always knew when her point of view was going to prevail. Confident with that inner knowledge, she elaborated. She told him of the easy money to be earned as a prostitute, of the figures that she had heard prostitutes boast of making, even if one deducted fifty percent for exaggeration, there was still a bob or two to be made.

Sydney was a man who worked with his hands; as such he was practical, and tested any idea for its practicality.

"Where did you have in mind to work, then?"

"Oh, somewhere in the Chapeltown area."

"What, among all those pimps around Reginald Terrace or

Leopold Street? They wouldn't stand for it unless you worked for them."

"If you think I'm working for a black pimp, you're bloody well mistaken," she retorted indignantly. "I'm working for us. For you and me and our kids, to keep bloody wolf from door, before the bugger comes to this table and sups with us."

"Where are you going to work, then?"

"What we'll do is this. We'll put mattress in the back of our van. Each night we'll drive into town and park in the Gaiety parking lot. You can sit in the pub and have a drink. If the johns I pick up have a car, all well and good, I'll use that. If they don't, I'll take them in back of van. I'll work until closing time each night, then come home with you in the van. I'll just work a few of the streets near the pub. A couple of the girls said I can work with them if I like."

Sydney smiled. "I'm surprised they don't resent the competition."

It was his wife's turn to grin.

"Sydney. I'm forty-two years of age. I've had four children and I'm hardly a sex kitten."

"Well, I can't keep up with you. Never have been able to. We both know that."

He smiled, this time not at her, more to himself. "The amount of men you've slept with since we've been married. If you had charged each of them, every time, why, I'd have biggest roofing business in West Yorkshire by now."

The observation caused no offense, mainly because of its inherent truth.

"Well, Syd, from now on I'm charging them all. Except you."

Emily went on the game, the same night, December 21, 1975. She had never lacked sexual confidence and rapidly adjusted to her new profession. By day she was the dutiful mother and wife. Caring for her children at their Churwell home. Driving her husband in the van to his work; Sydney had never driven. Answering the telephone, sending off bills, exchanging pleasantries with her neighbors in the village or acquaintances in nearby Morley. At night she entered her other world. A world of johns, prowlers, men of all shapes, sizes, and colors with a variety of demands and needs. If she had combined both worlds for long enough they might well have collided. Perhaps she might have had a request for "business" from one of the pillars of Morley society. Some women stay on the game for years. Emily managed barely one month.

On Tuesday, January 20, 1976, Emily and Sydney drove into Leeds at 6:00 P.M. She parked the large Commer van in the parking lot of the Gaiety public house.

The van presented an incongruous sight as a mobile brothel, the double ladder being left on top for the following day's tiling work.

Emily lit a cigarette as she climbed out of the van. Syd continued to sit in the passenger seat for a moment.

"Fancy a drink before you start, Emily?"

"No thanks. I'll have one later. See you soon."

She waved her hand and strolled off toward Gathorne Terrace. Climbing out and leaving the van unlocked for Emily and her clientele, Sydney entered the pub.

It looked as if it would be a good evening. Emily had earned her first five pounds before seven o'clock. Returning to the area of the Gaiety, she sat on a small wall and chatted with a girl friend who chanced to be passing. Within a few minutes the friend, Maria Sellars, pointed to a jeep parked nearby.

"What's he looking at?"

Emily turned and stared at the driver. She continued to talk to Maria for a few minutes, but all the time she was quietly watching the driver of the Land Rover. Satisfied that he was a potential client, she tapped Maria on the shoulder.

"I'll see you later."

She strolled to the vehicle.

"Are you looking for business?"

"Yes. How much?"

"Five pounds."

"Right, jump in. We'll go and find somewhere quiet."

Maria watched as the Land Rover drove off.

At 10:30 that evening Sydney came out of the pub. Closing time and Emily was not back. He lit a cigarette and waited. Fifteen minutes later he was still waiting. Locking the van up, he phoned for a cab and returned home.

*　　*　　*

Emily Jackson's last customer on the evening of January 20 quietly opened his front door and slipped into the hall. He stood for a moment breathing heavily.

"Hello. Somebody there?"

It was his mother-in-law, peering down from the landing. He stood totally still in the darkened hall.

"Just me, Mum. Didn't mean to disturb you."

She began to come down the stairs. He looked at his hands and jacket. They were covered in blood.

"No, Mum. You go back to bed."

She continued to come down the stairs.

"I'll just make you a pot of tea."

"No, really. You go back to bed. I'll make it and bring you a cup."

She paused on the stairs. The panic within him was total yet his voice remained gentle, calm, caring.

"Go on, Mum. You fuss me far too much. Back to bed now, and I'll bring you some tea and biscuits."

For a moment it seemed that she would continue to walk down the stairs, then smiled and turned back.

"Such a good boy. So kind."

He called up to the departing figure.

"Be up in a minute."

Quickly he moved into the kitchen. Turning the tap on with an elbow, he held his hands under the water until it ran clear. He stripped off the jacket and turning it inside out folded it. There was blood on his trousers too. He'd have to get rid of the clothes. That could be done tomorrow. He removed his heavy boots and carefully washed them in the sink. They'd come in handy again. Remembering his conversation with his mother-in-law, he put the kettle on. Checking his face in a mirror, he saw a few spatters of blood. Moments later they too had been removed. As he moved around the room making tea, placing cups on a tray, he mentally checklisted. The weapons he had used were safely locked away in the car. The bloodstained clothing would have to be put with the tools before he went to bed.

A short while later the hands that had killed Emily Jackson were pouring tea and passing biscuits.

* * *

The following morning, just before eight o'clock, a young man having parked his car near the busy Sheepscar–North Street junction chanced to glance over at a bundle on the ground by a cul-de-sac. At first he thought it was a dummy. He strolled over to have a closer look.

The teleprinter in Millgarth Police Station clicked on automatically as its message went out.

From the ACC Number 2 area, West Yorks Metro Police.

To all divs West Yorks, all surrounding forces, police gazette and police reports.

The body of Emily Monica Jackson, 42 years, home address 18 Back Green, Churwell, was found in a derelict building in Manor Street, Leeds 7, at 8:05 A.M. today, 21st January, 1976. It is known that the woman has recently been an active prostitute in the Chapeltown area of Leeds. When found she was wearing blue, green and red checked overcoat, blue and white horizontal striped dress, white sling back shoes, fawn handbag, black panties, brown tights.

It is known that between the times 6:10 P.M. and 10:30 P.M. Tuesday, 20th inst, she was in possession of a blue Commer van with ladders on the roof, reg no B N K 953 K.

This vehicle has been found in a parking lot belonging to the Gaiety Hotel, Roundhay Road, Leeds, approx half a mile from the scene of the crime, and any sightings of the woman or the vehicle should be notified to this office.

The deceased suffered severe injuries to the skull, believed caused by a hammer, and multiple stab wounds to the chest, abdomen and throat, possibly caused by an instrument similar to a Phillips screwdriver (cross pattern type).

Assailant may be heavily bloodstained and is believed to have been wearing heavy ribbed rubber boots or heavy Wellington boots.

Though there has been no sexual interference to the vagina, the bra was moved to a position above the dress and there are several indications that the person responsi-

ble for this crime may also have been responsible for the
death of the prostitute Wilma McCann at Leeds on 29/30th
October, 1975.

Motive appears to be hatred of prostitutes.

Particular attention should be paid to persons coming
into custody for the footwear described, who may have a
vehicle containing tools of the type described and which
will perhaps be a workmans van.

A search of records for persons convicted of serious
attacks upon prostitutes would be appreciated with details
to this office. Telephone number Leeds 35353 Ex 312 to
315.

Authorizing officer DCI Bullock.

Message ends.

The previous October, Detective Chief Superintendent Dennis
Hoban had been called to the Prince Philip playing fields to lead
the investigation into the murder of Wilma McCann. Now, in the
following January, he was called to a site less than two miles from
where Wilma had been discovered, to investigate what was at the
time thought to be the second murder by the same person.

It was clear to Hoban that Wilma and Emily had died by the
same hand. The pathologist's report (again the post mortem had
been performed by Professor David Gee) left Hoban in no doubt.
While over one hundred detectives began to piece together the
last hours of Emily Jackson's life, conducted a pattern search of
the partially derelict industrial park where her body had been
found, appealed for witnesses, checked alibis, and performed the
tasks that were routine in such an investigation, the man in charge
was looking at a post mortem report that was far from routine.

There were the extensive injuries to the head caused by a
hammer, injuries consisting of lacerations, and a number of skull
fractures.

There were the stab wounds to the lower neck, upper chest,
lower abdomen and the back, apparently caused by an instrument
similar to a Phillips X-shaped screwdriver. Emily had been
stabbed fifty-two times.

As in Wilma McCann's case, her brassiere has been pulled
above the breasts. On one of her thighs the impression of a heavy-

ribbed rubber boot or a Wellington boot was found.

From Hoban's first press conference a number of descriptions of the man he was seeking were given to the press. Dennis Hoban observed, "I believe the man we are looking for is the type who could kill again. He is a sadistic killer and may well be a sexual pervert."

He revealed to reporters that Emily Jackson had been stabbed with a ferocity "that bordered on the maniacal."

On Friday, January 23, 1976, the national press of Great Britain first coined the phrase that would eventually sweep around the entire world. They referred to a "Jack the Ripper Killer." The man's mystique was growing hugely. It grew even larger when the press wrongly reported that Emily's murderer had driven off in the blue van, a "fact" now enshrined in two books. The van did not move from the lot after Emily had parked it on the last evening of her life. It was discovered at the same spot by the police. Sydney Jackson confirmed that he had locked it the previous evening. Yet because the bar owner chanced not to see it at closing time the theory goes that having murdered Emily, her killer had audaciously brought the van back to the pub. In such a manner has the folklore that surrounds this man taken root and flourished.

As the investigation continued, officers yet again experienced a wall of silence from the Chapeltown prostitutes. One of them, a twenty-two-year-old named Joan, did respond when the police appealed for help. She told them, "The week before Christmas I had my nose broken by a man in the street. He just walked up to me and said 'How's business?' and before I could answer he punched me. I've been dead scared ever since."

Loudspeaker pleas for help interrupted the weekend football and rugby matches. Police vans toured the city displaying large photos of Emily. Cinemas and bingo halls interrupted proceedings to broadcast police appeals for help. A week later Hoban got what he considered to be his biggest break. Maria Sellars came to tell Hoban of her conversation outside the Gaiety with Emily on the evening she was murdered. Maria not only had an excellent memory but unusually good powers of observation. She recalled the Land Rover that had lingered while she talked to Emily; she also remembered the driver. Of the Land Rover, she told Hoban, "It was green in color. It had a hard top which was darker than the rest of the body. The passenger door appeared to have been patched up with a gray or a silver paint. The windows on the passenger door and the driver door were normal. There was a small aerial on the front nearside wing near the windscreen. The vehicle had bench seats."

The above is an extraordinary tribute to the investigating abilities of Dennis Hoban. Very few people, certainly not a frightened nineteen-year-old woman, would normally have come up with such an exact description. It was the result of many hours of patient, careful questioning. If the description of the vehicle is extraordinary, the details that Hoban managed to elicit from Maria about the driver are astonishing.

"He was a man aged about fifty years. He was of fat build. His hair was mousy-colored and was of ear length. He had a full beard that was unshaped. He had ginger or blond-colored sideburns, they were the same color as the beard; eyebrows, sideburns and beard were very bushy. He had a round nose, it seemed to be squashed. His eyes were almost closed, giving the impression that he was going to sleep. His face may have been scarred. His left hand was certainly deformed, it had a very distinctive scar, as if it had been burned. The scar extended from the knuckles on the back of the hand to the wrist. It was normal skin color but stretched and wrinkled.

"I believe he was wearing a plain gold square-topped ring on the third finger of his left hand and also a plain gold ring on the second finger of his left hand.

"He was wearing a dark blue working jacket. I think it was a parka type. He had dark blue overall-type trousers. His footwear was black, possibly boots or Wellingtons with a thick sole pattern. His clothing was dusty. He looked like he had just come from working on a building site."

The details appear to cover virtually everything except the man's name and address. As detectives redoubled the efforts to obtain information from prostitutes in the area, they became quietly optimistic. The man that Maria had described was also known to some of the women who walked the streets. Details of other clothes the man had been known to wear were obtained.

Estimates of his height were given by women who had certainly been in a position to know. They said he was only about five feet two inches. The women told the listening officers that they believed the man was Irish; some seemed to think he was known as Sean. Others recalled him as wearing a dark gray overcoat, a white shirt, a colored tie, a dirty blue cardigan with two square pockets, dark gray trousers, a brown leather belt, brown slip-on shoes.

In less than two weeks from the discovery of Emily's body the police issued a composite photo of this man. The *Daily Mirror* ran a small story: "Ripper Hunt for Mister Hairy Hands." Other papers talked of "Yorks Murders; Hunt for This Man."

Police are in fact still hunting for him, five years later. The black man in the Avenger car and boyfriend Tommy, both still missing and needed for elimination purposes in the case of Wilma McCann, now had a third to keep them company, the small Irishman in the Land Rover. Perhaps the reason this man, who was no more than one of Emily Jackson's last customers, has not come forward can be found in the heading the Yorkshire *Post* put over his police composite: "The face of a killer."

This particular killer was to acquire over the years a "face" for every day of the week.

The day that Emily's body was discovered, Hoban had no concept of a hairy-handed Irishman to put in the frame. He began where Dick Holland before him had begun when investigating the attack on Olive Smelt: with the husband.

Sydney was pulled from his Churwell home shortly after nine o'clock in the morning. He was hit, emotionally speaking, hard, fast and often that day.

They told him his wife was dead. Minutes after he had made hasty arrangements for the children to be cared for he was rushed to the Leeds mortuary to identify what was left of Emily Monica Jackson. The next stop was the police station. Thirteen hours later Hoban was aware that he needed to look farther afield. He knew as much about Sydney Jackson as Sydney himself did. He had used much of it against the man in an effort to break him. He had succeeded in breaking Sydney. Indeed, the man was reduced to tears as he kept on insisting to Hoban, "I didn't do it." Hoban reasoned with him. Told him that many a man who discovered his wife was unfaithful had extracted revenge. Surely if it was ever justified it would be if you discovered your wife was on the game? Sydney was obliged to admit that he knew his wife was a prostitute. That he had done nothing to dissuade her from this activity. That he had accompanied her on her forays into the Chapeltown area, looking for clients. The contempt with which this information was received was yet something else for him to bear.

His ordeal was only just beginning; when the police had had their fill, when his wife's murder had become merely another statistic, when her personality was reduced to a still photograph and no more, Sydney Jackson continued to suffer, to adjust, to cope with a life without his wife, with his three surviving children, and perhaps most horrendous of all the problems to cope with, the unspoken ones. The look from a neighbor. The glance that he would get in one of Churwell's pubs. The odd way that conversation would freeze when he entered a room, or there would be a fit of coughing, or someone would hail him heartily, too heartily.

What preoccupied them in the village of Churwell and nearby Morley was not that Emily Jackson had met a uniquely horrible end. Not the way her body had been mutilated. Not even the fact that she had been killed by a man who was destined to become the country's most infamous murderer. All of that was interesting, of course. It gave a number of them that dubious quality of fame by slight association. The "I know him well—he fixes my roof for me" school.

What really boggled the locals was the fact that Emily Jackson had become a prostitute. That really excited their imaginations. People who should have been occupied with sex were instead preoccupied with sex. Tongues wagged long and hard as they talked of Emily and her van, and her mattress, and of how the Jacksons tried to solve their financial difficulties.

6

He read the news story again and again. As he did the smile on his face developed into a laugh. Eventually he was filling the room with laughter. It was such a bonus. She had lived on the outskirts of Morley. That fact made her death all the sweeter. Morley was where that bloody Donald Neilson had come from. Well, he'd paid the Black Panther back with interest for all the roadblocks he'd had to avoid. For all the extra precautions he'd been forced to take.

That thought would keep him going for a while. He knew that after nearly being discovered by his mother-in-law he would have to wait some time before the next one. Wait until he had his own home. Just him and the wife. There would be plenty of space then. Would only have to keep check on one person, rather than three, in his own place. Have to buckle down, work hard, and save for that house deposit. He would volunteer for as much overtime as he could get. Work all the long hauls. If he got any foreign work then he might get opportunity to kill again; otherwise it would be safer to wait until he and the wife were comfortably settled in a home of their own. One large enough for children.

More than anything he wanted children of his own. Sons and

daughters to love and enjoy as he watched them grow, taught them his values.

The weeks slipped by into months as he concentrated on building up his savings. The thought that the sooner he acquired a home of his own the sooner he would have a safe base to venture out to murder from, spurred him on. His continued inability to create children was a constant source of anger. Although he had planned to wait, by early May 1976 the desire to kill again was predominant.

Carefully he combed his dark hair. Staring at his reflection in the second driving mirror he adjusted his tie. For once he was well dressed to kill. He loosened the jacket of his smart black suit. The hammer and knife in his pockets were distorting the jacket. Much easier to carry in a donkey jacket but his wife had insisted that he change from his working clothes before going out for "a late drink."

Driving slowly along the Chapeltown Road he saw a young black girl clearly the worse for drink and clearly looking for business. He stopped the car close to her. Moments later Marcella Claxton was sitting beside him. The twenty-year-old West Indian suggested the Soldiers' Field in nearby Roundhay. He smiled, it was curious how these women picked such perfect places to die in; playing fields, alleyways and now a darkened park.

He drove the car onto the grass, away from the passing traffic, away from the late night buses, into the black night. As they clambered out of the car the hammer fell from his pocket. Marcella saw him desperately searching in the grass for the fallen object.

"I hope that wasn't a knife."

"It was my wallet. Just strip."

The look of hatred on his face caused her to back away instinctively. No time to find the damn hammer now. He came at her with the knife. As he stabbed her again and again in the face and the head she screamed and staggered a few yards from him. Panic surged through him. He ran back to the car and trod on the hammer. He picked it up. For a moment he considered attacking her again but those screams might have already alerted people in the nearby houses. Moments later he was speeding towards Bradford. Again and again he cursed his bad luck.

Stopping the car on the outskirts of Bradford he checked his appearance. There was no blood on his face, hands or suit. *Going to need a new car.* Now he would definitely have to wait for a while. He had left her alive, he was sure of that. She might be able to give a description. He would just have to work harder at his lorry driving and at his planning. Next time there would be no suit. Dropping that hammer had given him a nasty fright.

Behind him he had left a twenty-year-old woman with serious head injuries that required over fifty stitches. Marcella was indeed able to give the police an accurate description of her attacker and his car but it served little purpose. *The police failed to link the attempted murder to him.*

He relaxed as the days went by without a visit from the police to the engineering works or his in-laws home.

Given time, they would probably think he had stopped for good, that the—what was it they were calling him, "the Yorkshire Ripper"—had gone away. But he'd be back. With his hammer, screwdrivers, and knives. He picked up the newspaper again. There was a small piece about this man they were comparing him with. This Victorian Jack the Ripper.

Between August 31 and November 9, 1888, five women died at the hand of Jack the Ripper. No one was ever arrested and charged for these murders. From those two facts a thousand myths have sprung. A folklore has been woven around the identity of the Ripper. So powerful have the myths and fancies become that often, far too often, they are quoted as "facts." In much the same way "facts" are asserted about the "Yorkshire Ripper." His predecessor, that Victorian Jack, has been credited not only with a variety of identities but also a variety of deeds. One newspaper will assert he murdered ten. Another that he killed eight.

The Victorian Jack murdered five times. No more, no less.

1. On the 31st of August 1888. Mary Ann Nichols, at Bucks Row, who was found with her throat cut and with slight stomach mutilation.

2. On the 8th of September 1888. Annie Chapman, at Hanbury Street: throat cut, stomach and private parts badly mutilated and some of the entrails placed around the neck.

3. On the 30th September 1888. Elizabeth Stride at Berner Street: throat cut, but nothing in shape of mutilation attempted. *And on the same date:*

4. On the 30th September 1888. Catherine Eddowes, at

Mitre Square: throat cut and very bad mutilation, both of face and stomach.

5. On the 9th of November, 1888. Mary Jane Kelly at Miller's Court: throat cut, and the whole of the body mutilated in the most ghastly manner.

The above details are a verbatim quote from confidential notes made by Sir Melville MacNaghten, who joined Scotland Yard as an Assistant Chief Constable with the Criminal Investigation Department in 1889, the year after the murders. The notes are dated February 23, 1894. No one who has seriously researched the Victorian murders disputes that the number of victims is five, yet still one reads that Jack killed twenty.

The identity of the person responsible for the deaths of those five prostitutes in Whitechapel has generated much speculation. Here are just a few of those who have been "put in the frame" for the carnage that occurred in just ten weeks of 1888.

There is "The Lodger," usually portrayed as a man prone to quote large chunks of the Bible from memory. He clearly indicates his profound hatred of whores, prostitutes, or as they were rather quaintly known during the reign of Queen Victoria, "unfortunates." "The Lodger" has been given many names and many professions: medical student, lawyer, vicar, something in the city. Whatever the profession, the philosophy is always the same. He is a religious maniac who has been placed on earth for just one purpose, to exterminate all whores. "The Lodger" theory gained enormous credence after a fictional story by Mrs. Belloc Lowndes was published in a magazine in 1911. Her story subsequently sold half a million copies in the next ten years.

Possibly the strongest candidate in this section of the "Hunt the Ripper Stakes" is Montague Druitt. The main evidence against the wretched man appears to be the fact that he committed suicide by drowning sometime during December 1888. The logic appears to be that as the series of murders had ceased the month before, then Druitt fits the bill.

George Bernard Shaw, writing at the time of the murders, considered that the man responsible was a social reformer of perhaps a somewhat extreme persuasion. He observed: "While we conventional Social Democrats were wasting our time on education, agitation and organisation, some independent genius has taken the matter in hand. . . ." Conan Doyle considered that Jack the Ripper was a man disguised as a woman. Another suggestion is that the murderer was a woman disguised as a man, a Jill the Ripper, possibly a demented midwife or a bungling abortionist covering her tracks. This latter theory has among its advocates ex-Detective Chief Superintendent Arthur Butler of New Scotland Yard. His crazed abortionist has an accomplice called "Fingers Freddy."

In his *The Mystery of Jack the Ripper*, published in 1929, author Leonard Matters told the world of a deathbed confession made by a Dr. Stanley in Buenos Aires. The confession had been made about 1909 to a fellow doctor, who recounted it some thirty years later to Matters. Doctor Stanley had apparently taken to the streets of Whitechapel in 1888 in search of the woman who had brought about the ruination of his son. The woman in question was Mary Kelly, the Ripper's fifth and final victim. It transpired that Dr. Stanley had chopped up the first four while seeking Mary. Whether this is a case of mistaken identity four times over is not made clear. Perhaps the Whitechapel fog was even thicker than usual on those occasions? Apparently Dr. Stanley's son had spent a naughty week in Paris with Mary Kelly and had returned with a memento other than a model of the Eiffel Tower. Mary had given him "the disease." Two years later Stanley Junior died of "the disease" and Stanley Senior exacted his terrible revenge. Two of the many flaws in this particular solution to the mystery of Jack the Ripper are that to contract any form of venereal disease and die of it within two years is a medical impossibility, and Mary Kelly was found at the time of her death to be suffering only from alcoholism.

In the ninety-two years since the awful events in the East End of London occurred, many have had the finger of accusation pointed at them. All of the following, it has been asserted, are the real Jack the Ripper: The Duke of Clarence, eldest son of Edward VII. A Russian anarchist or Tsarist double agent whose name might have been Kosmanski or Klosowski or Ostrig or Pedachenko or Konovalov. A Jewish slaughter-man, or *shochet*, usually identified as John Pizer, known as Leather Apron (in fact Pizer was a cobbler). Sir William Gull, Queen Victoria's doctor. Barrister John Kenneth Stephen, son of a judge, cousin of Virginia Woolf, and tutor to the Duke of Clarence. Various intimate friends of Oscar Wilde. The entire Masonic movement. Finally, a committee that included Queen Victoria, Prime Minister Salisbury, the Freemasons, Sir William Gull, Sickert the painter, Sir Charles Warren, the chief commissioner of Scotland Yard, Sir Robert Anderson, Inspector Aberline, and various other members. It was evidently a very large committee.

All these and a great many others have been put "in the frame" while Ripperologists play the game of "hunt the Ripper." Of course, some ninety years after the horrific events it can be reduced to a game. There was no such element of sport in the minds of the British public in 1888.

In the sordid gaslit streets of Whitechapel, none laughed as the Ripper killed again and again. This occurred in an area where official estimates of "the poor" were nearly one hundred thousand; where police estimated that there were over a thousand prostitutes, just in Whitechapel alone, an area under a square mile; where sex of any description with man, woman, or child could be purchased for twopence; where the overcrowding ensured that forty to fifty people living in a house designed for three or four was a common occurrence; where immigrants formed the vast bulk of the population. Where people paid that same twopence just to lean on a rope stretched across a room, as a cheap substitute for a nonexistent bed; where a prostitute often carried all her worldly possessions on her back; where pubs were open throughout the night and if one drunken prostitute were to vanish from the face of the earth or be found murdered it caused no bother. Into this area where the mists and fogs lay heavy even in summer came Jack the Ripper. There were no fast-car escapes for him. No highways to transport him to another city within the hour. A hansom cab clopping its way through the cobblestones was the best that the Victorian Ripper could hope for. All of his victims were heavy drinkers. All were prostitutes. All were murdered within shouting distance of safety, yet none were heard to shout.

The police investigators were never able to build up a satisfactory description of the Ripper. It all begins to have an eerie familiarity. The police of 1888 labored without the aid of much that their modern counterparts take for granted. Fingerprinting as a science lay many years in the future. Blood typing was unknown. Telecommunication consisted of getting a senior officer to the scene of the crime by a hand-delivered telegram. Mary Kelly's eyes were photographed because of the widely held view that the last image a dying person sees is retained on the retina. While nonsense like this ran about, so too did Jack the Ripper, a five-times murderer, who got away.

Now, in the latter part of the twentieth century, nearly one hundred years later, another man was getting away with murder. Despite the massive advances in forensic science, despite all the technology that aids the police.

She shifted her stance and by slightly opening her legs she made the tight black skirt rise provocatively higher on her thighs. Her long dark hair fell freely to her shoulders. Despite the fact that it was winter she wore no overcoat, or even a jacket. Her white blouse was unbuttoned to below her breasts, revealing, as she turned slightly, that she was wearing no brassiere. She took the cigarette from her mouth as he slowly approached.

"Looking for business, love?"

He responded with a silent shake of the head and continued at the same measured pace along Leopold Street.

What he saw angered him. Just over a year before there had been panic in these streets after Emily Jackson's body had been discovered.

The numbers of street girls had initially dropped dramatically. He had read with satisfaction that many had retired from the game. Now, in early February 1977, there seemed to be a greater number than ever in Chapeltown. If they had forgotten him, then it was time they were given something to remember, and the sooner the better.

Reaching the end of Leopold Street, he crossed Chapeltown. He had left the Ford Corsair parked securely by the Hayfield. Outside the Hayfield pub as he approached he saw a blond prostitute arguing with a black man. Indifferent or oblivious of his approach, they continued as he drew within earshot.

"I'm telling you, Jimmy, that's all I've earned tonight. Twenty-five pounds isn't bad."

"It isn't good, baby. Better move that tail of yours faster. This is

Saturday night. Supposed to be the best night of the week. It's
nearly ten o'clock and all you can hustle is twenty-five. Bad scene.
Very bad scene.''

The blonde launched into a defense as he passed by. The
conversation had left a bad taste in his mouth; he needed
something to wash it away.

"I'm telling you, it's a fact. One million dollars a minute, for
every single minute of the day and night, is spent on military
activities.''

He sipped his drink unobtrusively in a corner of the room.
Nearby an aged seer was holding forth to a mixed gathering of
West Indians, Pakistanis, and a few prostitutes. It was the
prostitutes who attracted his attention rather than the seer. He had
all he needed in his car. He hadn't planned on getting back to
work tonight, but if the opportunity presented itself he intended
to take it.

"A few miles away from this pub it were. Home of a family
called the Kithinghams. They lived at Allerton Hall and they
always buried their dead at night.''

For a moment the seer had his undivided attention too.

"Apparently it were a very ancient custom. Interring dead
members of your family at dead of night by candlelight. The
Kithinghams would walk through streets all holding burning
torches and bury their loved ones.''

"Go on, you're pulling our legs.''

"I'm not. This is Gospel.''

He moved away to another part of the bar but his eyes never left
the prostitutes. *Don't know about burying them at night but with luck
one of them is going to die tonight.*

He moved slowly, almost gently, through the crush at the bar. It
was the normal last-orders rush. He waited patiently and eventually was served with a beer. He moved away from the crowd
again, back to a corner of the room.

"Don't cry for me, Argentina. You know I never . . .''

"You stupid cunt.''

The drunken singing had been terminated with a spilled pint
down the front of the singer's skirt. The accident was greeted with
roars of laughter. His eyes narrowed as, sipping his beer, he
surveyed the clientele in determined pursuit of an enjoyable
Saturday night.

In the parking lot of the Hayfield he paused for a moment to check the direction she was taking. She crossed the road and, walking down the road a short distance, turned into Cowper Street. Good.

He moved quickly to his car and unlocked the door. Already he could feel the excitement mounting, spreading slowly through his body. The sensation was similar to downing a very large brandy and feeling its effect move through the body. But this sensation was a hundred times better. There was a tightening as the heart began to beat just a little faster. A clearance of thought, a clarity of mind. Reflexes, reactions, became incredibly faster. He possessed an alertness similar to one of the beasts of the jungle when it was engrossed in hunting defenseless prey.

He turned the car right into Chapeltown Road. Driving slowly, he turned left into Cowper Street. He drove slowly, very slowly. For a moment he thought he saw what he was seeking but it was just a girl with her boyfriend. He continued driving along the street seeking the prostitute he had selected in the pub.

Past the school and then he was confronted with Spencer Place running left and right in front of him. *Which way? Which way had she gone?* As he paused for a moment he saw a young woman emerge from a block of flats and begin to walk slowly along the street. He studied her. Attractive, yellow two-piece cotton suit, dark coat, calf-length boots. The boots particularly caught his eye. She drew level with the car. He leaned over and wound down the window.

The teleprinters in police stations in Leeds, Halifax, Keighley, Pontefract, Castleford, and many other points in the West Yorkshire area came to life with a jolt.

From Detective Chief Supt Hobson.
To all divisions and surrounding areas.
At 7:50 A.M. today Sunday 6.2.77, the body of a woman was found at the rear of sports locker rooms on Soldiers Field (a sports area), Roundhay near to West Avenue, Leeds.
The body was found to have severe head injuries, a cut throat and stab wounds to the abdomen.

Description. 20-30 years, 5' 7", long dark hair, medium build, wearing a blue and white checked blouse, brown cardigan, zip-up front, with yellow trim on edges, yellow two-piece cotton suit, fawn three-quarter-length suede coat with fur down front, brown calf-length boots.

An incident room has been set up at Millgarth Street Police Station, tel no 35353 ext 314/315.

Message ends.

Chartered accountant John Bolton got a great deal more than exercise on that particular Sunday morning jog. Yet again it was shortly before eight o'clock in the morning that the gruesome discovery was made. At first Bolton thought it was someone who had been taken ill. He called out.

"Hello. What's the matter?"

He approached the still form. Her face was turned toward the grass and covered by her long hair. He brushed the hair to one side. Saw the blood on her neck. The eyes glazed, staring and lifeless.

This time the police officer summoned to the scene to take charge of the investigation was Detective Chief Superintendent Jim Hobson. Seven months earlier when Dennis Hoban had been promoted to deputy assistant chief constable for crime, Hobson had taken over as head of Leeds C.I.D.

As he gazed at the still form of the unknown woman he began to consider the similarities between this murder and the still un-solved murders of Wilma McCann and Emily Jackson.

Again Professor David Gee was brought to the murder scene so that the initial medical examination could take place before the body was moved.

Yet again the disciplined routine that was automatic when a suspected murder was being investigated moved into action.

Hobson strolled across the grass on this sunny winter's morning, discussing the pathologist's initial findings. What Gee had to say served to confirm his own view. After a break of just over a year, the murderer of Wilma McCann and Emily Jackson had returned with a vengeance. The sheer savagery of the attack transcended what had gone before.

Gee's subsequent full post mortem confirmed that the person

responsible for the death of this still unknown woman had gone beserk.

She had been struck three times on the head with a hammer and this time there was no doubt of exactly what kind of instrument. It was a ball peen hammer. It has been designed for a number of uses, beating out sheet metal, hammering rivets into boilers; it is used sometimes on leather work, or on other occasions by plumbers. There is a man living in Yorkshire who has found another use for it. He fractured this particular woman's skull with blows of such severity that a circular piece of skull actually penetrated her brain.

As she lay on the grass, deeply unconscious and dying, he had stabbed her in the neck. He had then stabbed her in the throat. He had then stabbed her three times in the abdomen. These blows were of such severity that her intestines had spilled out.

She had been wearing panty hose and two pairs of panties. One pair had been removed. Her right leg was out of her panty hose and the panties that had been taken off had been stuffed down into them. The three-quarter-length suede coat was draped over her buttocks and thighs. Her brown calf-length boots were draped neatly over her thighs. Her handbag was nearby and there was no indication that anything had been stolen from it. Unlike the situation with previous victims, her brassiere had not been moved.

Tests indicated that she had sexual intercourse at some time in the twenty-four hours before her death. Her time of death was thought to be at about midnight.

During the course of that long Sunday, February 6, 1977, the one hundred investigating detectives began to feed information back into the Incident Room at Millgarth, Leeds.

Door-to-door inquiries at the fashionable houses and blocks of flats that overlooked this pleasant, pretty park brought little relevant information. Residents told the police that the area was a favorite for courting couples and sometimes prostitutes. This hardly came as a startling revelation to the Leeds officers, who knew every single site used by the Leeds prostitutes.

The woman had been found just behind the locker rooms of a sports pavilion, and when football teams arrived a few hours after the investigation had swung into action they found their matches canceled. Curious passersby on tops of buses whose routes ran right through the park and very close to the screened area where the body had been found had a bird's-eye view of a great deal of activity that would have meant precisely nothing to them. But it would be something to tell the family over Sunday tea. Eventually the quiet, patient investigation bore fruit. Yet again the police teleprinters throughout the county stirred to life. It had been exactly twelve hours since the breakfast jogger had found the body.

HQ Admin Rom Det Ch Supt Hobson, Incident Room, Millgarth St, Leeds.
To all divisions and surrounding areas.
Rev previous TPM 144 6.2.77.
At 7:50 Sunday 6.2.77. the body of Mrs Irene Richardson, born 23.3.48. 1 Cowper Street, Leeds 7, was found at the rear of sports locker rooms on Soldiers Field (a sports area), Roundhay near 90 West Avenue, Leeds 8. The body was found to have extensive head injuries, a cut throat and stab wounds to abdomen.
This woman has been living in Leeds area since October 1976, when she came to Leeds from London, having worked in hotels in the metropolis. She was reported missing from home by her husband from Blackpool in March 1975.
Inquiries are requested of all persons coming into police custody for bloodstains on their clothing and also inquiries at dry cleaners for any clothes with blood on them. Any replies to Incident Room, Millgarth St Police Station, Leeds. Tel No 0532 35353 Ext 314/315.
Message ends.

So the woman in the grass had a name, an identity. She also had two children. They were living with foster parents at the time of her murder. This brought the total of children made motherless by this man to nine. There would be others, many others, to add to that number.
No sooner had one piece of the puzzle been put into place with the identity of the victim than further information set the teleprinters in action once more.
Yet again the source was Hobson in Millgarth.

Wanted for elimination purposes in connection with the murder of Irene Richardson in Leeds on 6.2.77.

Steven Joseph Bray, born 13.7.38, CRO 3319357 WRC 1771360.

Bray is also an absconder from Lancaster Prison since 1.3.76, having failed to return from home leave. Police Gazette 2376 Item 8 refers.

Description. Born Greenwich, London 13.7.38. 6 ft tall. Heavy build, fresh complexion, black hair, brown eyes. Extensively tattooed.

Message ends.

Steven Bray was entirely oblivious of the fact on that Sunday evening, but he had suddenly become the most wanted man in the entire country.

Bray was already being sought by the police prior to the death of Irene Richardson. In March 1976, while serving a prison sentence at Lancaster, he had failed to return after being granted home leave. Now, nearly one year later, the man on the run was hunted by every police officer in the country. As the lover of Irene he was sought by police working on a premise supported by many years of hard evidence. Most murders are "within the family," or "domestic," to use the Home Office description. Approximately seventy-five percent of murders fall within this category. Husbands and wives either legal or *de facto* murder each other far more frequently than passing strangers.

As the police probed the backgrounds of Bray and the murdered woman a curious state of affairs was revealed.

On Saturday, January 22, Irene Richardson and Steven Bray were due to be married at Leeds Register Office. They had lived together since Bray had absconded from Lancaster prison, first in London and subsequently in Leeds. Bray, former seaman, chef, nightclub doorman, clearly did not feel like adding bigamy to his list of achievements. With a wife still living in Hull, he was conspicuous by his absence from the Register Office. So was Irene Richardson. She had a husband and two children living in Blackpool. News of her death was the first of many shocks for the family. Her husband, George Richardson, refused to accept that his wife had become a prostitute. He told the police, "She was sick, she just could not settle down."

Further investigation established that in the last two weeks of her life Irene Richardson had descended into a living hell. Deserted by Bray, unable to obtain work, even in the menial occupation of chambermaid, practically penniless, she wandered the streets of Chapeltown, sleeping in a public toilet room, reliant on the charity of a few acquaintances for a bath or somewhere to change. She had set out from Cowper Street for Tiffany's Club, hoping to see Bray, who had previously worked there as a doorman. The prospect of earning a few pounds had put her beside the man in the white Ford. Within one hour she was dead, stretched out on the grass of Soldiers Field. He had carefully placed her coat over her body to hide the mutilations. Doing so made it seem to his mind that the event had never taken place. The reality underneath that coat was that Irene Richardson had left her living hell forever.

For a few weeks it seemed to Hobson and his men that the murders of Wilma McCann, Emily Jackson, and Irene Richardson would be solved with the arrest of Steven Bray. It was not to be. On March 15, Bray was caught in London. After intensive questioning he was eliminated from the murder investigation and returned to Lancaster prison.

There were appeals to the public in general and prostitutes in particular; posters with a photograph of the dead woman plastered all over the city in public houses, bingo halls, cinemas and the streets; items on television, radio, and in the press with the ever-increasing use of the description "Jack the Ripper type murders." One hundred police officers were now working exclusively on this particular murder. Fifty-one thousand people were interviewed, over one thousand five hundred statements taken; all this activity eventually became, at the Coroners Inquest, distilled into a verdict that was becoming chillingly familiar:

"Unlawfully killed by person or persons unknown."

But the man responsible had in fact made yet another of his many mistakes. He had presented the police with a complete set of his tire marks. Ever careful, he had driven the white Corsair onto the grass of Soldiers Field, away from the street lighting, into the darkness that is an essential part of the man. What puzzled the police was that the marks indicated he drove either a medium-sized sedan or a van and not a Land Rover. Wrongly convinced that Emily Jackson's client in the Land Rover was the man they were looking for, they now had clear evidence of a totally different vehicle fitted with two India Autoway, one Esso 110, and one Pneumat tire, all of a cross-ply type. Among the vehicles with identical track widths are the B.M.C. Marina, the Ford Corsair 2000E sedan (1966/1970), Hillman Minx Mark VI (1965/1967), and the Singer Gazelle Mark VI. Another car with identical track widths is the Morris Oxford series V four-door sedan.

Detective Chief Superintendent Jim Hobson, known to both fellow police officers and villains as "Lucky Jim," found himself confronted by an adversary with even greater luck. The tires on the front of his car when he murdered sad Irene Richardson were half worn; his luck showed not the slightest trace of wear. Allied to his luck is a shrewd native intelligence and profound cunning. The intelligence told him it was time to try another town. The cunning drew him much nearer to his home, to the streets of Bradford. To Manningham. As he walked down Lumb Lane and saw soliciting prostitutes on corner after corner, he knew that the next one would be even easier.

7

She snuggled closer to his warm body as they swayed to the David Bowie LP.

As the song finished, Flossy and Ben, oblivious, continued to move slowly and suggestively. He looked at her, then gently kissed her cheek. They were no longer just two eighteen-year-olds. Both knew with a certainty that what they felt for each other had never been experienced by anyone. That when they made love it was unique.

Flossy had flowered fast. She was still given to fluctuating moods. To an intensity that caused her all too often to take life too seriously, but now something superb had been added. To all the doubts and insecurities was added a love affair.

"Well, I say sod the Jubilee. All the money that's being spent on it would build quite a few houses or nurseries."

Flossy and Ben, arms linked, joined the heated debate. Bill was holding forth, monopolizing the earnest youthful debate that was going to set the country to rights.

"What does she want for sitting on the throne for twenty-five years? A round of applause?"

"Hey, just a minute. I think the monarchy gives us stability," Ben said, unlocking his arm from Flossy and waving a finger to emphasize his patriotism.

Flossy gave Lauris a "here we go again look" as by silent mutual agreement they both moved to the kitchen. With her parents away on vacation Flossy was for once queen in her own home. No Dad to nag her about his car that she frequently borrowed. No Mum to fret about her progress or lack of it with the A-Level exams. Not even brother Graham—whom she called Crow—Graham, who could always be relied on to provoke an argument. She pottered in the kitchen, opening another bottle of cider. Lauris, busying herself making sandwiches, eyed them lasciviously and groaned.

"Bang goes my diet."

"I don't know why you're bothering, Lauris, there's not an ounce of fat on you. I'm the one who's exploded. You know, I think it's the Pill that's doing it. We ought to have a word with our friendly neighborhood gynecologist. I've put on ten pounds in the last year."

Lauris smiled. "In that case blame Ben."

"I do sometimes. He pointed out that for the past few months both you and I have been gorging ourselves silly at a stack of eighteenth-birthday parties. Typical man. They leave the responsibility of being careful to the woman, then adopt a superior position."

"Really? Which one?"

They giggled helplessly. From the living room The Who could be heard telling all and sundry that they would not be fooled again. The two girls, declining shouted invitations to dance, settled down to their cider and sandwiches.

"Have you decided on which university yet, Flossy?"

"No, I've had interviews at three now. 'Course it all depends on A-Level results. What about you?"

"Probably Nottingham. If I pass. I still wish we were planning to go to the same one, though."

Flossy squeezed her friend's hand.

"So do I. But remember, we agreed. We'd never have any time for anyone else if we went to the same school. Got to make the most of it. That's what Crow's always saying, anyway. You know sometimes I wonder why we're bothering. I'm only majoring in sociology because I'm not sure what to do. Think I'd be far better off working with animals than studying humans. Remember that monkey?"

Lauris laughed as she recalled the occasion.

"Never forget it. Petticoat Lane last winter. It pissed on your raincoat. Flossy?"

"Hm?"

"That pile of sandwiches we've just made for the others."

"What about them?"

"We've eaten them."

"Sssh."

Ben and a few of the others appeared as if on cue at the kitchen door.

"Thought you'd come out to make some sandwiches."

The two girls erupted into laughter. Ben stared at them in puzzlement.

"What's so funny? I only asked about the sandwiches."

That provoked even louder laughter. He scratched his head and turned to Bill.

"Reckon they've been at the cider, if you ask me. Either that or smoking naughty substances."

Flossy turned on him. The venom in her reaction left him open-mouthed.

"We have not been smoking shit and if you think we have, you can bugger off."

Ben moved back slightly as if he had been hit.

"Flossy. It was only a joke."

"Well, we are not amused. At least I'm not."

There was still about her that manner, almost a coldness. It was a side of her that few saw or heard. A previous boyfriend certainly had. The night she had met Ben. At the time of the grammar school dance she already had a boyfriend. Flossy had dispensed with that problem the following day.

"Hello, can I speak to Tony please?"

The lamb had been brought to the phone.

"Tony, this is Flossy. No, I don't want to talk about arrangements for the Christmas party. I don't want to see you any more. I am saying get lost."

The lamb had been slaughtered. Now the same ruthlessness was being directed at Ben, the lamb's replacement.

"I'm sorry, Flossy."

"Sorry. What do you mean 'sorry'?"

"Well, I am."

"You know my views on dope. Christ, you heard me sort Crow

and his crazy friend out. What do you think? That I say one thing and do another?"

Lauris decided it was more than time for the Seventh Cavalry.

"Flossy, you are getting heavy. It was only a joke. Come on, now, it's Easter week. One crucifixion is more than enough."

It had the desired effect. While they were all laughing Lauris built on the foundation.

"I've got a great idea. Let's forget about The Stones and all those other old-fashioned ravers and have a real rave-up."

Bill quickly came to her aid.

"And what does my lady have in mind, the Parrot Sketch?"

"No, you fool. Monopoly."

It was a stroke of youthful genius and took the heat out of the moment. They saw the night out desperately trying to buy Mayfair and mortgage Fenchurch Street Station.

In the morning Flossy and Lauris surveyed the remains of dinner. The sandwiches that had followed were just a fond memory.

"Got stacks of greens and potatoes left over, Flossy."

"Lauris, I am now going to show you what a frugal wife I will be one day."

"I beg your pardon?"

"Bubble and Squeak."

"By the look of those potatoes I think you mean Bubble and Squelch."

"Lauris."

"Yes."

"Thanks for coming to the rescue last night. I'm sorry I got heavy."

"'Got heavy,' the girl says, and with her about to eat five pounds of fried potatoes and greens!"

He parked the car in a side street off of Lumb Lane. It was midevening. The twenty-third of April, 1977. Easter weekend.

Almost directly across from where he had parked was a pub known locally as The Percy and to the passing trade as The Perseverance. It would do for a start. Previous trips had laid the groundwork. He already knew the area well. He was ready but still he remembered the advice given long ago at school by his woodwork teacher.

"Measure twice and cut once."

It had served him well. It would serve him better. He stopped in Lumb Lane and gazed at the scene. One member of the tabloid press had labeled it "the most violent street in Europe." Clearly that writer had not visited certain streets in France, Germany, and Holland. Nevertheless there was plenty of action in Lumb Lane. The government had been talking about "enterprise zones," a concept designed to bring relief to depressed areas. As he gazed about him he concluded that there was already more than enough enterprise in this particular depressed area. He felt something inside tighten. His muscles began to contract. Images and memories of the past began to whirl through his mind. Yet again he recalled his wife's last miscarriage.

"Are you looking for business?"

Just for a moment he was momentarily off guard.

"I'm sorry, what do you mean?"

"Would you like a nice woman to give you a lovely time?"

He was still trying to clear the images from his mind. The tall young Irishman who had approached him took the hesitation for an indication of interest.

"It's my girl friend I'm offering. I can recommend her."

"No, I'm fine, thanks. Just taking a breath of air."

The Irishman eyed him keenly. In his line of business you had to be a good judge of character and a fast one.

"What about a twelve-year-old girl? I guarantee she hasn't started her periods yet."

"No thanks. I'm just going into The Percy for a drink."

The Irishman was not a man to give up lightly. Suddenly he adopted a grotesque pose. One hand on hip, the other pushing his long hair up into a bun. He twisted the top half of his body and lisped.

"Well, what about me, then? Only five pounds?"

To anyone else but the man he spoke to he would have presented a hysterically funny sight. A Dubliner built like a door. Six foot three with a face like an unmade bed. His listener saw none of that. He did not like what he saw. His face reflected that distaste. Like the wino before him in Leeds, the Irishman saw hell staring at him. He had never ever in his life backed down from the threat of violence, but now he took a couple of steps away then turned back to his girlfriend waiting in a nearby doorway. She eagerly looked at the Irishman, who merely slowly shook his head.

Saturday night, the pub was busy. Taking his drink, he edged away from the bar and moved to a corner of the room. The memory of the encounter outside was gone, wiped from the cassette. Now he was back on the job.

The pub door swung open and a group of men wearing Leeds United rosettes stormed through the door. They were greeted with cheers, mainly derisory.

"What happened, then? Beaten by bloody Manchester."

"Their second goal was a yard offside."

This produced loud laughter as the stalwart supporters made their way to the bar.

"We'll have to cheer for Liverpool or Everton in the finals now."

His eyes went past the speaker, a fresh-faced youth, to a group of women sitting with their drinks. Whores, every single one. It was odd how he could spot the whores. Some sixth sense told him which were straight and which were prostitutes. A dark-haired woman in her early thirties caught his gaze and held it. Still staring, she drank her double gin in one and mouthed an open-mouthed kiss at him. He half smiled back but his eyes told her that he was declining the invitation. *Plenty of time. Plenty of time. Be silly to pick one of them up in here, someone might remember. Too much light. Need the darkness, the comforting black night.* He finished his drink and walked out into the night. Checking that the car was still there, he strolled up Lumb Lane to check out the Carlisle Pub.

The dark-haired woman had already forgotten the moment and was getting into her next double gin. Her once attractive features bore mute testimony to the years of dependence on alcohol. Patricia Tina Atkinson, alias Mitra, alias McGhee, had been through as many forms of life as she had names. As the wife of Roy Mitra she had for a while been contented with a life of domesticity. Their three daughters had kept her fully occupied but for the extrovert Tina there were other needs to be fulfilled. She began to indulge in Bradford night life. At the divorce hearing her husband was given custody of the three girls.

As a stripper and go-go dancer what Tina lacked in technique she made up for with a wild abandon. Invariably drunk on stage, she forgot the cardinal rule of stripping. Always control your audience, never let them control you. Her act often finished with the naked Tina opening her legs and straddling a customer's face. Though highly popular with the all-male audiences, she had difficulty obtaining work at respectable pubs.

She became a prostitute and by 1975 was a familiar sight in the Lumb Lane area. She also had a fairly detailed knowledge of the local Manningham police station and the courts of Bradford, where she was convicted for soliciting in 1975.

The evening was beginning to warm up. Tina finished her drink and looked at her watch. Not nine yet. Plenty of time for business later.

"Right girls. It's my round. Same again?"

The clientele in the Carlisle were interchangeable with the lot he had just left. Elderly white people, West Indians, and Asians. Here and there a younger white man. In the toilet his eye caught some unpredictable graffiti. He stared at them for a moment totally bemused. He had been immortalized on the toilet wall of the Carlisle Pub, Lumb Lane. Not with one slogan, but two.

"The Ripper. I'll be back."

The second statement declared, "Fuck them before the Ripper kills them."

Curious they should have him threatening to return to a city where he had not been on the job before. *Soon rectify that. After tonight that threat of returning will carry some meaning.* Ignoring the drink he had left on the counter, he walked straight out of the entrance and turned into Church Street. As he did so Tina Atkinson and her friends entered the Carlisle.

He walked by the parish Church of St. Paul and St. Jude and paused. It was odd how amid all the decay and rotting the pubs and the churches still thrived. He watched as a prostitute clambered into a car containing three men.

The local children were by now all in bed or watching TV. The cleared areas of land that abounded were deserted. He glanced at his watch. Eleven-fifteen. Time to get on the job. Turning, he walked back along Church Street toward Lumb Lane. From the direction of the Carlisle a woman appeared. Half turned away from him, she was shouting a drunken goodnight to her friends. As she turned back she saw a smiling face that seemed somehow vaguely familiar. Tina spoke to him.

"Hello, love. Looking for business?"

"Yes. How much?"

She breathed deeply as she considered. The twelve double gins that she had drunk that evening had blurred her senses.

"Let's see. You got a car?"

He was disinclined to get involved in long conversation. At the moment the street was deserted. No need to press his luck by discussing the bloody weather and standing there until someone came along.

"I've got a car and I've got a fiver to spend."

"Right, then, what are we waiting for?"

He started the car up. He had already surveyed a likely spot but the beauty of it all was that these women knew the places that were really out of the way. Really nice and quiet. It was a case of the whore selecting her own graveyard. She turned to look at him.

"Got a real treat in store for you, love."

"Oh yes?"

"Yes, no back of the car or waste ground. Got my own flat."

He hadn't expected that. This was the first street girl he had encountered who offered that facility. *It was fraught. Best sound it out. Measure twice. Cut once.*

"Oh, I don't know about that. Get me back there and your big black boyfriend comes out of the wardrobe and mugs me."

Her laughter was deep, throaty.

"Don't be bloody silly. I live on my own. I also work on my own. No bloody pimp owns me."

"Are we likely to be disturbed?"

"No, it's a nice, quiet, respectable block of flats. Down Oak Avenue."

"What number?"

"God, you are cautious. Are you a virgin?"

"Now you're being bloody silly. I'm just being careful, we don't want to get arrested, do we?"

"That's why I use my flat. I've already got a record and I've no desire for the Queen to put me up again. I live in a flat at number nine. Do you know where I mean?"

He relaxed. He knew exactly where she meant. He had been right over the whole area. *Measure twice, cut once.*

"Yes, I know, love. That'll do fine."

He put the car into gear and headed for Manningham Lane.

"I've seen you before somewhere, haven't I?"

"Earlier this evening, in the Percy. You were with your friends."

"Was I?"

Too many drinks in too many pubs, he thought. It was curious how they gravitated during the course of an evening. Up and down Lumb Lane. The Carlisle. The Percy. The Queens. The Flying Dutchman. It was a ritual gavotte that he was determined to change to a *danse macabre*.

The car turned off Manningham Lane down Queens Road. They drove past the police station on the left. Outside the station poster blow-ups of the faces of Emily Jackson and Irene Richardson gazed at them as they went slowly by and turned left. A few moments later they were in Oak Avenue. It was a mixture of well maintained Victorian dwellings and modern flats. As he slowed he scanned the road, then relaxed.

"You can park around the back. Won't attract attention then. You know, if you're worried."

He smiled at her. They really were most thoughtful. Quietly they left the car and walked to the front entrance. He tensed again.

"I'm on the ground floor. Flat three."

He merely nodded and held the main entrance door open for her. At the door to number three she stopped and, fumbling in her handbag, searched for the key.

"Now, where did I put it? S'here somewhere." He could hear from an upstairs flat noises that indicated that someone was watching the late night movie.

"Ah, there's the little bugger." She unlocked the door and stepped into the flat. He quickly followed. She had gone three paces when he swung the ball peen hammer and hit her on the back of the head. Instantly unconscious, she began to slump to the floor. He moved with such frightening speed that Tina Atkinson received four blows to the head before she hit the floor. Blood poured from the wounds. He stood quiet, still breathing heavily. In the tidal wave of anger that had surged through him, he had not stopped to consider that despite her assurances there might be a boyfriend lurking in the flat. Stepping over her still body, he went from room to room. They were alone. Bending down, he placed the hammer beside her then removed her overcoat. The dark hair was now thickly matted with blood. Her green eyes stared sightlessly at him. Effortlessly he picked her up and carried her to the bedroom. The rage was still building, fighting to gain control of his every thought and action. One moment he was in command, the next the inner force was master. He ripped open her black leather jacket and pulling open her blue shirt, lifted her brassiere above her breasts. He undid her jeans and pulled them down to her ankles. Then he pulled her panties down. Taking a chisel from his jacket pocket he began to stab at the dead body. Again and again. Turning the body over, he began stabbing the back. Images swam again into his mind. Images that disgusted him: of this woman groaning with pleasure, of the many strange men on top of her, panting with exertion. In his mind the woman was reaching the point of orgasm and the groans were becoming ever louder. He had to stop that groaning, stop that hideous image. He swung the body over onto its back again and began to stab at the abdomen. Always it was that area of woman that he hated most. The malignant life force that had to be eliminated. The images in his mind subsided. The rage had gone. For a moment he stood over her and, panting, spoke loudly to the body that had been Patricia Tina Atkinson.

"Dirty prostitute bitch. Dirty bloody prostitute bitch. No more whoring for you. No more children. No more walking the streets. One less piece of filth. Whore. Bitch. Prostitute."

Then he partially pulled up her jeans, but still the sight of her disturbed him. He turned over the body so that it was lying face down. The brassiere he again left above the breasts. He quickly covered the body with blankets. As he stood beside the bed it looked as if she had merely gone to sleep. That was better. It was as if it had never happened. He knew it had and was glad, almost overjoyed, certainly cleansed.

Moving quietly now, he double-checked that he had forgotten nothing. *Measure twice. Cut once.*

Back in the hall he picked up the ball peen hammer and slipped it into a pocket. By the door he listened carefully. There was no sound other than the late night movie upstairs. Quietly and quickly he made his way out of the block of flats. A moment later he turned his car into the Manningham Road and drove to his nearby home. Despite the paper-thin walls of the flats no one had heard a thing. Despite the fact that the area was still alive with people, no one had seen him or his Ford Corsair. He smiled as he drove home. "God," he said to the reflection in the second driving mirror, "I'm clever. Very clever." Minutes later, with his car parked in the garage, he washed and changed before joining his sleeping wife.

He was unaware that behind him in the flat, he had left a clear footprint on the bed sheet. He was unaware that on one of Tina Atkinson's thighs he had left a bloody hand print.

On Sunday, April 24, 1977, a close friend of Tina's, Bob Henderson, came knocking on the door of flat 3. It was shortly before 6:30 P.M. Getting no reply from his repeated knocking, he found his puzzlement turning to concern. He knew she must be in; apart from the fact that they had arranged to go out for a Sunday drink, he knew she would not have gone out. She never ventured out on a Sunday until the evening. Breaking the door down, he saw first the blood on the hall floor. Running into the bedroom, he saw the apparently sleeping body. He pulled the blankets away. What he saw caused him to scream. He continued to scream and ran in search of the caretaker. Ten days earlier, Tina Atkinson had been delighted when she had moved into flat 3.

"I don't think I'll be looking for somewhere else for quite a time," she had remarked to a friend.

Yet again police throughout Yorkshire were advised that *he* had returned.

The teleprinters were busy.

To Force Control
Attention ACC Western Area and ACC Eastern Area and police reports. Divisions West Yorks and adjoining forces.
From: Det. Chief Supt Domaille.
At 6:30 P.M. 24.4.77 the body of Patricia Tina Atkinson, alias Mitra, alias McGhee, 33 years, was found in her flat at 9 Oak Avenue, Manningham, Bradford. This woman was a convicted prostitute, WRC No. 21684/75. Professor Gee has carried out a post mortem examination which revealed that death was due to 4 blows to the head with an instrument which has not been recovered. There were stab

wounds to the abdomen and possibly to the back which would not have proved fatal.

Inquiries show that Atkinson left the Carlisle Public House, Carlisle Road, Bradford at 10:15 P.M. on Saturday 23.4.77, at which time she was apparently under the influence of alcohol.

The wounds to the head were such that it is most likely that the assailant's clothing will be bloodstained and it is requested that the clothing of any person coming into police custody be thoroughly examined and that enquiries also be made at dry cleaners and launderies.

An Incident Room has become operational at Western Area HQ., West Yorkshire Metro Police, Bradford, Telephone 23422 Extensions 686 and 219.

Investigating Officers Det. Chief Supt Domaille and Det. Chief Inspector Wiseman.

Message ends.

A heavily censored version of the above was promptly transmitted for general release.

In a murder investigation that has from the beginning been bedeviled with suppression of vital evidence from the public the two messages, when compared, graphically illustrate one of the reasons why the police spent five years hunting the world's most famous unknown man.

To: Community Affairs HQ. Press Release.
From: Det. Chief Supt Domaille.
At 6:30 P.M. on Sunday 24.4.77, the body of Patricia Tina Atkinson otherwise known at Mitra or McGhee, aged 33 years, a lady well known in the Manningham area of Bradford, was found in her flat at Oak Avenue, Manningham, Bradford.

She had severe head injuries and a post mortem examination has been carried out by Professor David Gee of Leeds University, who will be making a report to the coroner.

Inquiries reveal that Atkinson left the Carlisle Public House, Carlisle Road, Bradford about 10:15 P.M., Saturday 23.4.77. It is requested that anyone who saw the deceased on Saturday evening or since that time contact the police at Bradford. Telephone Bradford 23433 or any police officer.

Message ends. Sender Quinn Ref XB19 × 25.4.77. Time now 06:47 hours.

Investigations established that she had been to bed with one of her boyfriends.

When Joan Harrison had been murdered in Preston, Lancashire, C.I.D. had compared notes with their colleagues on the other side of the Pennines investigating the killing of Wilma McCann. They had noted the similarities, the repositioning of brassieres, items stolen. Both women had led promiscuous lives. They also noted the differences. Wilma had been stabbed and smashed on the head with either an axe or a hammer. It was considered that Joan had been hit on the head with the heel of a shoe; she had not been stabbed.

When Emily Jackson was murdered, police evidence was again compared. No direct links between the deaths of Emily and Joan were ascertained.

It had been the murder of Irene Richardson that had drawn the investigations on both sides of the Pennines much closer. Irene, like Joan, had had sexual intercourse at some time on the day of the murder but what the police found particularly significant was the placement of Irene's shoes upon her body. One of Joan's boots had been stuffed between her thighs. The Lancashire police still kept an open mind. It could just be bizarre coincidence.

When Tina Atkinson's post mortem established that she too had had sexual intercourse at some point prior to death, certain members of Bradford's police force decided to ascertain if there was a link with the Preston murder. The police were aware that the post mortem on Joan Harrison had given them, in that particular instance, a very specific blood-typing from the semen. Blood type B. The boyfriend of Tina Atkinson was taken to a police station.

The five men were impassive. Some stared at him. Others averted their eyes.

The boyfriend huddled in the corner. Eyes screwed tight. Attempting to block all of this out of his mind. One hand clutched a small bowl. The other pulled desperately at his exposed limp penis.

"I can't."

"Yes, you can. Go on. Get on with it. We haven't got all night."

"But why? Why must I do this?"

"We've already told you."

"I've admitted I went to bed with the girl. Made love to her."

"Made love! Is that what you call it? To a scrubber? To a whore?"

"You shouldn't talk about her like that."

"Just get on with it. Leave the sermons to those in the pulpits."

He was sweating. The droplets were running down his face. Never in his worst nightmares had he conceived a scene like this.

"There must be some other way."

"Shy, are you? Weren't shy when you fucked her, were you?"

"Look, we're doing you a favor. We've got enough on you to arrest you and charge you. Now, if you're as innocent as you say you are, you'll oblige us by coming into that bowl. We only want to check your blood type. As long as it's not a certain type you've got nothing to worry about, have you?"

"I can't do this with all of you standing looking at me."

"All right, we promise not to look. Now get on with it."

Eventually, agonizingly eventually, he obliged them. It was established that he did not have blood type B. Of course there are a number of other ways of ascertaining a man's blood type. Of course afterwards they were very contrite. In truth several of them felt acute self-disgust. They were charming to him. Friendly to him. They even took him out for drinks. They even took him out and organized a girlfriend for him. A new girlfriend.

To help him forget the death of the old one. To help him forget that day in a room in a police station.

Over one hundred policemen flooded into the Manningham district of Bradford. They stopped cars. They knocked on doors. They questioned passersby. They called at the Carlisle and the many other pubs frequented by Tina Atkinson. They questioned the owners of nightclubs, particularly the owners of The International in Lumb Lane, Bradford. When Tina had left the Carlisle she had drunkenly announced that she was going to the International. She had never made that last drink.

The police procedures followed the classic pattern used by the

West Yorkshire Police and by many forces throughout the world. The anatomy of a murder investigation.

At the head of the investigation was Detective Chief Superintendent John Domaille, directly involved in the hunt for the first time. After nearly two years as head of the community affairs department at Bradford H.Q., he had requested a return to the C.I.D. Now he was investigating crime with a vengeance.

A murder incident room was established at the Bradford H.Q. within hours of the discovery of Tina Atkinson's body. Spanning out from that like the arms of a family tree were the crucial subsections. A divisional officer whose duties included arranging for transportation of the body for post mortem and plebeian but essential aspects such as meals and parking facilities for the investigating officers. Not much point in sending police to the scene of a murder if they cannot park their cars.

The community affairs division handled all liaison with the press. It is little realized how crucial a role the media of England play in police investigation. It is a tit-for-tat situation. The police get what evidence they care to let the general public know, across to the nation. The media get stories, fill pages, fill air time. One of the other aspects covered by "community affairs" is arranging a reconstruction of the crime if it is considered by the senior investigating officer to be a useful exercise. Someone has to ensure not only that the media are tipped off to the reconstruction but also that it happens without hitch. Another senior officer handles communications and traffic. Phones, teleprinters, links to mobile police stations, ensuring that when Domaille calls for a car there is one there for him.

An administration section handles other vital nuts and bolts of the investigation: logging the hours worked by police personnel; circulating information to officers; preparing plans of the murder site; cross-checking reports; indexing; following up inquiries already made.

A scenes of crime officer is appointed, ensuring initially that the murder area is cordoned off and that only a very few, privileged people are allowed within that cordon. They are: a photographer, a pathologist, the scenes of crime officer, a forensic scientist, the senior investigating officer, the coroner. That is the definitive list. Subsequently the scenes of crime officer is in charge of the body, ensuring that care is taken in its removal to the mortuary, that the correct procedure is followed at the mortuary, that the body is identified correctly. This officer will also supervise the search of the murder area and be in charge of any exhibits.

Then there is the massive investigation itself. Checking on the family of the deceased, their movements and associates. There are the house-to-house inquiries. The checking out of convicted persons who might be likely candidates to put into the frame. Checking out persons unlawfully at large, such as abscondees from prison or mental institutions. There is the interviewing and elimination of suspects. The interviewing of potential witnesses.

This is the anatomy of a murder investigation. All of the above has been done every time this man has struck. Without success.

Domaille tried every gambit he knew. He told the press that he was in possession of Tina Atkinson's diary. That there were fifty names and addresses in the diary. That Tina "had kept a very good diary, we shall make every effort to trace everyone mentioned in it. It would save a lot of time if those people who think their names may be in it would come forward. Anyone worried about the confidentiality of their relationship with this lady should police stations, ensuring that when Domaille calls for a car there is anyone, personally, about this matter."

Of course if he had acquired the names and telephone numbers of fifty of Tina's "friends" there would have been no need for a public appeal.

The press was advised that Tina had died as a result of "a frenzied sexual attack." It made a good headline but was rather short on factual details.

Further investigation had established that although Tina had left the Carlisle public house at 10:15, an hour later she had been seen nearby. The man with the luck of the devil had avoided being seen by just a few seconds.

A spiritualist held a seance in Tina's flat. It did not take Domaille an inch further forward.

A reconstruction was set up on a Saturday evening with a policewoman posing as Tina walking from the Carlisle to the International Club and then to her flat in Oak Avenue. The exercise brought forward a few people who thought they had seen Tina Atkinson on the night of Saturday, April 23, but it was of little help.

Domaille studied the earlier murders; as a result he got the incident room teleprinter busy again.

From Chief Superintendent Domaille (Incident Room), Bradford.

To all divisions, surrounding forces and police reports.

Re Murder of Patricia Atkinson.

West YKS Ref XB/17/25/4/77

It is desired to trace the following described man who was involved in an incident with a prostitute at Bolton Woods, Bradford, in March 1975 and a similar described man who was seen to pick up Emily Jackson, a prostitute who was murdered at Leeds in January 1976. White male, 30/40 years, five feet eight inches. Stocky build. Ginger-colored hair which was untidy and a gingerish colored beard which was bushy round the cheeks but trimmed under the chin.

Pointed nose and ruddy complexion.

This man was wearing a well worn jacket and blue bib and brace type overalls with a pair of trousers underneath.

It is thought that he had two rings on fingers of left and possibly one on finger of his right hand. The back of his left hand is scarred.

This is described as similar to a burn scar and stretches from the knuckles to the wrist. The back of his right hand is tattooed. This man has the appearance of a workman and probably spends his time in areas where prostitutes are known to loiter.

He has the use of a vehicle and it is thought that he had the use of a Land Rover or similar type vehicle from March 1975 to January 1976.

It should be borne in mind that the Land Rover could have been in the possession of this man because of his employment and that he might not now have access to the vehicle, also it could well be that the beard has been shaved off.

Suggestions as to the identity of this man to be passed to Incident Room, Bradford.

Message ends.

Domaille, like Hoban before him, was anxious for a word with
this man. Apart from picking Emily Jackson up, there was
evidence that in March 1975 the same man had attacked a woman
in Bradford who survived. This attack has never been publicly
linked with the series of murders and attacks under investigation.

In any event, Domaille had no more success than Hoban in
tracing this man.

The day after that Telex was transmitted Domaille tried yet
another tack. He began to trace the previous occupants of flat 3.
They knew nothing of their successor in the Oak Avenue
residence.

While the press talked increasingly of "Jack the Ripper Murders" the story was picked up by foreign press, while other papers
headlined "Ripper Triangle" and yet others reported that warnings had gone out to prostitutes never to accept a lift in a car
without telling a friend the driver's identity or the car's license
number, the daily grind of other police work unconnected with
these murders and attacks continued. The West Yorkshire police
force was being pushed to the very limits.

There were other murders that needed solving, other attacks
that remained on the books. Among them was the Manningham
Rapist, a creature responsible for raping over twenty women.

There was the murderer of Debra Schlesinger, an eighteen-
year-old woman found stabbed to death a few yards from her
Leeds home.

The Manningham Rapist and Debra's killer are both still at
large.

At the coroner's inquest into the death of Tina Atkinson the
verdict was one that was becoming very familiar. A verdict of
"murder by person or persons unknown."

Coroner James Turnbull concluded the investigation with these
words: "We must hope that the police enquiries will bear fruit
sooner or later. And we must hope sooner."

Three more children had been deprived of their mother.

8

In late June 1977 the newspapers were full of reports on the violence outside the gates of the Grunwick factory in London. The fleet was preparing for the Silver Jubilee review at Spithead and British hopes at Wimbledon were making their predictable exits. On Sunday, June 26, the West Yorkshire police were having an open house at Wakefield—a public-relations exercise designed to present the best possible police image. That image was about to get yet again a national scrutiny.

From A.C.C. West Yorkshire Metro Police.

To Chief Constables No 1, 2 and 3 Police Districts, Regional Criminal Record Office, police reports and press office.

About 9:45 A.M. on Sunday 26th June, 1977, the body of Jayne Michelle MacDonald, sixteen years of age, shop assistant, 77 Scott Hall Avenue, Leeds 7, was found in the Adventure Playground Compound, between Reginald Terrace and Reginald Street, Chapeltown, Leeds. The deceased was last seen alive at 10:30 P.M. Saturday 25th June 1977 in the Hofbrauhaus, Merrion Center, Leeds. She is described as follows.

Five feet three inches, proportionate build, shoulder-length brown hair and wearing a blue and white check x gingham skirt, a blue/gray waist-length gabardine jacket, dark brown tights and high-heeled clog-fronted shoes in brown and cream with brass studs around sides.

A post mortem is being carried out by the home office pathologist, Professor David Gee. So far as can be ascertained, the deceased had been subjected to violent blows about the head with a blunt instrument and had not been sexually assaulted. It would appear that the person responsible may also be responsible for the deaths of Wilma McCann at Leeds on the 29/30th October, 1975 (see police reports 703 para 1 dated 31.10.75):

Emily Jackson at Leeds between 20/21st January 1976 (see police reports 758 para 1 dated 22.1.76);

Irene Richardson at Leeds between 5/6th February, 1977 (see police reports 1020 para 1 dated 8.2.77); and

Patricia Atkinson at Bradford between 23/24th April 1977 (see police reports 1071 para 1 dated 25.4.77).

Details of the injuries to the deceased Jayne Michelle MacDonald and the possible links with the deaths of McCann, Jackson, Richardson, and Atkinson should not be disclosed to the press. There is no evidence that Jayne Michelle MacDonald was an active prostitute. The body of MacDonald had been dragged a distance of some 15/20 yards from where the initial assault took place. Her assailant's clothing will be heavily bloodstained, particularly the front of any jacket, shirt, or trousers worn by him.

Examination is requested of the clothing of all persons coming into custody since 10:30 P.M. Saturday 25th June, 1977.

Any information to the Incident Room, Millgarth Police Station, Leeds. Telephone Leeds 35353 Ext. 312 to 315 inclusive or Leeds 454173, Leeds 454197.

Originating officer ACC Crime, West Yorkshire.

Message ends.

The MacDonalds were a close knit family, Wilf was a railway-man, his wife Irene a waitress. Their five children were fortunate enough to have a home environment that apart from instilling in them some excellent values also gave them essential warmth and love. Money was never abundant, but a closely knit family offers more than ample compensation. Jayne, the third born, had a beauty that ensured constant attention. At half past seven on Saturday, June 25, 1977, she kissed her father goodbye with the words, "Won't be late tonight, Dad. I'm going out with a girl friend."

Later that evening as he dozed in front of the television set he felt sure that his daughter had returned about 11:30 P.M. and kissed him goodnight. When his wife came home from work at about midnight they locked up and went to bed.

The following morning while his wife was out collecting the Sunday newspapers he heard a knock at the door. Previously he had taken Jayne a cup of tea and discovered her absence. Answering the door, he was confronted by a uniformed police officer. The following exchange took place.

"Are you Jayne MacDonald's father?"

"Yes, and I'll kill her when she comes in for staying out all night and not letting us know."

"You probably won't have to, because someone's already done that."

A little boy ran into a nearby house where Irene was chatting with his mother.

"Auntie Renee, there's something terribly wrong because Uncle Wilf's crying."

He was not the first child in the area to have been shocked that morning. Two others had gone to the adventure playground and discovered Jayne's body.

The very ordinary MacDonald family found themselves sud-denly plunged into the nightmare world created by one man. Their initial reaction, like that of the victims before them and the victims that were yet to come—the living victims, that is—was, "These sort of things do not happen to people like us. They happen to folk you read about in papers. They happen to other people."

They happen to people like Wilma McCann, who lived eight doors away. Jayne had been playing in the street the night that Wilma left home for the last time. Despite the fact that Wilma had slipped out of her back entrance, the fifteen-year-old girl, carelessly playing on the Prince Philip fields, had seen her. One of the last to do so, she was able to give the police a detailed description of the clothes that Wilma had been wearing. That evening as she played happily on the grass she had less than two years to live before she was killed by the same hands.

Subsequent to that October evening, the young girl, full of old-fashioned wisdom, had said to her mother, "But Wilma did take chances, didn't she, Mum?"

Clearly, though she was walking home through the heart of the Chapeltown red light district, Jayne did not consider she too was taking chances. She knew the area well. Had grown up there. The familiar is rarely frightening. The family had discussed the other murders. None felt any fear. All the women that had been attacked were prostitutes, they reasoned. The police had not at the time of Jayne's murder revealed that women who were not prostitutes had also been very seriously attacked by the same man. The names of Anna Rogulskyj and Olive Smelt were unknown to the public.

Thus Jayne felt no fear. Took no precautions. The MacDonald girls and their mother were used to being asked by strange men if they were available for sex. The surviving women in the MacDonald family are still confronted by these men. Still asked if they are doing "business." Jayne's twelve-year-old brother was playing football on that lovely sunny Sunday morning. One of his friends came rushing toward him.

"Hey, Mackie. Your lass has been murdered!"

"Less of your sick jokes."

"No. It's Jayne, all right. They found her body in adventure playground."

There was something in the young boy's tone that told Ian that it wasn't just a sick joke.

Jayne had been murdered at two o'clock in the morning. She had been hit on the head three times with the ball peen hammer, and knifed repeatedly in the chest and once in the back. Embedded in her chest was a broken bottle top.

The following day, with the front pages of the national press headlining "GIRL 16, IN A 'JACK THE RIPPER' MURDER HORROR," another teenage girl appeared in Leeds Magistrates Court. Seventeen years of age, she pleaded "guilty" to soliciting for prostitution. Her defense counsel's plea of mitigation concentrated on the dreadful events that had occurred at the Chapeltown adventure playground.

"It is clear from the three months of murder in this city involving the violent deaths of prostitutes that the perils of that occupation are more feared now than at one time was thought possible. My client is a teenybopper of a prostitute who would be very foolhardy to contemplate a further incursion into prostitution in view of what happened last Saturday."

His client was granted a conditional discharge. At that time the police had yet to establish that Jayne was part of the series of murders, beyond reasonable doubt. Already, though, this one man had so affected thinking that even the initial very scanty information released by the police along with a wink here and a nod there to certain reporters was enough to attribute the murder to the "Ripper." Professor Gee's post mortem came as grim confirmation.

The police, clearly aware that the man responsible now represented a very serious threat to all women, decided on a change of tactics. Previously a senior investigating officer had been appointed, depending on which area a murder had taken place in. Holland had investigated the attack on Olive Smelt, Hoban the murders of Wilma McCann and Emily Jackson, Hobson had been in control of inquiries into the murder of Irene Richardson, John Domaille of the inquiry into the killing of Tina Atkinson, and Wilf Brooks from the different police authority in Lancashire was still probing the murder of Joan Harrison. Now, with the exception of the as yet unconnected murder of Joan, one man was placed in overall control, to investigate the death of not merely Jayne MacDonald but of the entire series. George Oldfield.

If the public brings any police figure at all to mind when considering these murders it is George Oldfield. He declared it a personal battle between him and the man he hunted. Assistant Chief Constable George Oldfield, a man with over thirty years of police experience, had three years previously led the investigations into the M62-coach bomb outrage. Twelve people had been murdered in yet another I.R.A. attempt to persuade Britain that they should hand over Ulster to God alone knows whom. Oldfield, who was obliged to see the injuries and mutilations in the coach, has been left with images that he will carry to the grave.

"I would certainly advocate capital punishment for terrorists," he has said. "I had the misfortune to see the terrible injuries inflicted on the victims of the M62 coach. As long as I live I will never forget the grievous injuries suffered by those two children and the other passengers."

After one of the biggest security operations ever mounted in the country, one fish was landed in the net, Judith Ward. The manner of her being caught is a salutary example of how often criminals are caught almost by accident. In Liverpool, a police dog handler chanced to see a young woman behaving in a suspicious manner in a shop doorway. She was taken to the police station merely to be questioned about whether or not she had been planning to break into the shop. Hours later the Liverpool police were astonished when she blurted out details of the bombing. She was sentenced to life imprisonment—thanks to a vigilant dog handler.

Two patrolling police officers had virtually stumbled over an inoffensive little man loitering near a sub-post office. Pulling him in for routine questioning, they found themselves facing a gun. For thirty minutes it seemed to the two policemen that they were about to die. The man was eventually overpowered, thanks to a group of miners waiting for their work bus. It was the Black Panther, Donald Neilson.

Oldfield was acutely aware that it was often that odd moment of luck which brought an investigation to a successful conclusion.

One of his first tasks was to trace, minute by minute, second by second, the last hours of Jayne MacDonald. From the moment she had kissed her father goodnight to that moment when death had leaped from the shadows in Reginald Terrace and dragged the young woman into the adventure playground, he had to know everything, know every single person whose path Jayne might have wittingly or unwittingly crossed on the last evening of her life.

One of his first decisions was to hold twice-daily press conferences. He felt he had one major ace that the men before him had not held. All the previously murdered women had either been active prostitutes or, to use police parlance, "of low morals." The public, while eager enough to read the gory details, were disinclined to assist the police in solving those deaths. Now it was different. The public were told an "innocent young woman has been slaughtered." While one can see the logic of the police philosophy, the gambit is nevertheless abhorrent. All the victims are innocent. None deserved to die. All merited precisely the same amount of concern. We cannot, must not, put a sliding morality scale on life and death. To do so is to reduce society to the level of the hunted man.

Slowly, painstakingly, Oldfield and the men and women helping him filled in the gaps in the last hours of Jayne's life. The picture that emerged was one full of "if onlys."

If only, after leaving the plastic replica of a Munich bierkeller known as the Hofbrauhaus, Jayne had gone directly home. It was then 10:30 P.M.

If only Jayne had not stopped to buy a bag of chips with her friends and not gossiped away the last precious moments of her life in the city center, only to find she had missed the last bus home. It was then 11:50 P.M.

If only she had caught a taxi home from the town center and not decided to go for a stroll with Mark Jones, a young boy she had met that evening. It was then twelve midnight.

If only Mark's sister had been in when they reached her home. Mark had assured Jayne that his sister would give Jayne a lift home in her car but the car was not there, the sister was still out. It was then 12:30.

If only they had not continued to walk about and eventually lay down in a field for a kiss and a cuddle. They arranged to meet the following Wednesday and Mark walked with her to just past the main gates of St. James Infirmary. They parted company at the

Florence Nightingale public house. It was now 1:30 A.M.

If only the two AA men who saw her walking to a telephone booth near Dock Green Pub at the junction of Beckett Street and Harehills had offered her a lift home. It was now 1:40 A.M.

If only the taxi company had been manning their phone and had responded with a car when Jayne phoned from the booth. It was now 1:45 A.M.

If only the street lighting in Reginald Terrace had not been extinguished at 11:30 P.M. she might have stood a chance, might have seen a man lurking in the bushes or hurrying across the road. It was the time that must come to us all, but surely not in such a violent, obscene manner.

Screams had been heard in Reginald Terrace at the crucial time. The listeners took no notice; as Oldfield observed, "This is an area where women are assaulted for not bringing back enough earnings, therefore another scream may not have borne much significance locally."

What an epitaph for Chapeltown.

A man with what seemed like a Scots accent was heard at about the crucial time in the area shouting.

"Fucking prostitutes. Bloody whores."

No one reacted. No one cared.

A great many people cared after the event. Nearly two hundred party-goers in the area either came forward or were traced. All gave what help they could.

Her colleagues at the supermarket where she had worked were shattered. Several had to be sent home when the news broke.

The editors of the Yorkshire *Post* and its sister paper the *Evening Post* cared. The evening paper carried an open letter on June 28. It was addressed to "The Ripper."

You have killed five times now. In less than two years you have butchered five women in Leeds and Bradford.

Your motive, it is believed, is a dreadful hatred of prostitutes, a hate that drives you to slash and bludgeon your victims.

But inevitably that twisted passion went terribly wrong on Sunday night. An innocent 16-year-old lass, a happy, respec-

table working class girl from a decent Leeds family, crossed
your path. How did you feel yesterday when you learned that
your bloodstained crusade had gone so horribly wrong?

That your vengeful knife had found so innocent a target?

Sick in mind though you undoubtedly are, there must have
been some spark of remorse as you rid yourself of Jayne's
bloodstains.

The open letter continued with an appeal to the man responsible to give himself up. It assured him that no rope waited for him,
unlike Jack the Ripper. That only understanding treatment would
be his fate. The open letter accurately reflected the mood of the
entire city.

While over two hundred detectives, often working sixteen hours
a day, collected every scrap of evidence and attempted to sift the
wheat from the chaff, Oldfield called a conference of all divisional
officers at Millgarth police station. It was hoped that the pooling of
ideas might produce the vitally needed break in the investigation.

George Oldfield went into Chapeltown and talked to the Leeds
community relations council. He visited church leaders in the
area. He went to clubs, pubs, anywhere that the Chapeltown
people gathered in numbers. To all of them his message was the
same. He was acutely aware that the largely black community bore
no love for the police. That many of them hated "the pigs." The
bonfire-night explosion of 1975 had left the line clearly drawn. He
tried to cross over that line.

"So far all the victims have been white. If I can find and identify
every person in Reginald Street between one and three A.M.—I
am looking for one person only, the one who committed this
crime. I wish to identify and eliminate all the others. This will be a
slow process. I am only looking for one person. This is a very
difficult inquiry, by reason of the reluctance in some people to
come forward and I wish to make a cry for help. There is a natural
reluctance in some people to come forward. A large number of
people in that area were West Indians and two parties were taking
place with people going between them. I am not concerned about

their activities and I don't want to know why they were there. I am only looking for one man."

The response to the plea varied. Some considered that it was a white man's problem. Others, so full of hatred for the police, would have cut off an arm sooner than help. Others put aside their hostility and suspicion and came forward. Slowly, painfully, Oldfield's list shortened. He sought 420 people. He found and interviewed 403. Among that other 17 was one man who mattered. One man who had murdered Jayne MacDonald.

As Oldfield and the other police worked and wondered, every conceivable idea was considered in their bid to catch that man.

The reconstruction of Jayne's last walk was given massive publicity. Policewoman Susan Phillips played the part of Jayne, carefully watched not only by the press but by scores of detectives. During the reconstruction they interviewed over 700 people, including one who had indeed seen Jayne walking home. Along the route Susan Phillips was photographed by a wall on which had been hastily splashed in whitewash, SCOTHALL SAYS HANG THE RIPPER.

Alongside the injunction a noose had been painted.

The police installed a free phone so that anyone could dial into a recorded message from Oldfield without the bother of placing a few coins in the box.

They made themselves freely available to the media. Police attitudes to the press, television, radio and other communicators during this entire investigation have fluctuated wildly and irrationally over the years. At the time of Jayne's death it was open house. Thus when Marilyn Webb of Yorkshire television wanted George Oldfield at the studios, she got him. When the American Broadcasting Corporation wanted to film Oldfield, he obliged. When the Los Angeles *Times* asked if they could visit the murder incident room, the doors were opened for them.

It was indeed a very open house.

The media reciprocated. They made public only what the police wanted the public to know. Thus when a Yorkshire *Post* reporter was told a curious story by a member of the public it was duly suppressed at police request. The fact that nothing appeared in the Yorkshire *Post* must have worried a perfectly respectable married couple. Perhaps now, nearly four years later, the facts may allay their worries.

A police officer had appeared at their Leeds home and asked the wife if she was the owner of a Datsun Cherry. On being told that she was, he asked if he could inspect the tires. After he had completed his examination the wife asked him the reason for the visit. He declined to tell her and left. The husband returned home to find a highly disturbed wife who recounted what had happened. He promptly telephoned his local police station, which was as unhelpful as the investigating officer. It was at this point that the couple had decided to utilize the power of the press. There was something odd in the state of Leeds, and they did not care for it.

The police were very informative when the reporter phoned. They told him it was part of elimination inquiries being made by officers investigating the "Ripper murders." But they did not want owners of Datsun Cherries to know why their cars were being checked. The police would be very grateful if the Yorkshire *Post* would suppress the story. The Yorkshire *Post* suppressed it. The reporter also agreed not to tell the married couple why the story had not been run, should they telephone and ask for an explanation.

The ripples of evil from one man were spreading ever farther.

Within one week the Scotsman who had been heard shouting obscenities in the murder area was found and eliminated. Another Celt was proving more elusive: the man thought to be Irish who from time to time had access to a Land Rover. His full description has already been given in this book. Now an artist's impression of the man was handed to the press and television by George Oldfield.

A man of similar description had been seen near the adventure playground at about the time Jayne was murdered. This time his height had shot up to "over six feet."

On July 19, Yorkshire television transmitted a thirty-minute documentary entitled "Who Is the Ripper?" Large extracts were devoted to George Oldfield showing Marilyn Webb and the viewers around Chapeltown. One particular viewer had already decided he had seen enough of Chapeltown for the time being. Indeed, nine days before the program went on the air he had struck again in Bradford. While he sat and smiled at the program he knew that another victim was in the hospital fighting for her life.

Despite the free phone, despite the public outrage, despite an artist's impressions, despite Oldfield's courageous attempt to break down race prejudice, despite the huge public response, the man responsible had claimed yet another victim. Meanwhile the other living victims, like the MacDonald family, attempted to cope. To forget the unforgettable. The investigation of Jayne's death alone was responsible for over thirteen thousand interviews and nearly four thousand statements. Before a fraction of those statements had been taken, the man responsible was prowling the streets of Bradford.

9

It was Saturday, July 9, 1977. For the past nine days he had spent most of his nonworking hours at home, brooding. Even journeys to his local pub and a few pints did not help. Even his pool shooting was suffering. They were calling him a monster, a maniac, a beast. They were enraged at the death of Jayne because she was not a whore. Just a decent lass, on her way home.

He felt he had to make amends for the "mistake." There was only one way in his mind to do that. Kill another one.

Car parked, he wandered along Lumb Lane. They were still there. Still out in the street flaunting their bodies. Selling their filth. His keen eyes saw that they were not alone.

In a side street here. A cul-de-sac there. Parked cars with a couple of men in each. They might appear to be johns to the ordinary passerby. He was no ordinary passerby. Like prostitutes, he could pick out the vice squad blindfolded. He smiled and moved on to Church Street. What he saw there gave him more problems to solve.

They were still doing business all right and in view of the fact it was Saturday night, business was flourishing—but they were being smart.

They were working in pairs. When one went off with a client the other would ostentatiously note down the car license number. They were making sure that the john saw it too.

This was going to be more difficult. He walked into the Carlisle Pub and considered the situation. Even in there he noted several plainclothes vice squad men clutching their halves of bitter. The police could have made it easier for themselves and harder for him if they had gone onto spirits. But then to have shown that degree of imagination would have landed them in hot water over expenses. Ironic, really; they'd already spent bloody millions trying to catch him. For want of a nail . . .

He sipped his pint and reflected. Obviously they had all the well known prostitutes' beats covered. No good going to any of the pubs on the Lane. He'd been shrewd enough to park his car well away. Tucked in behind the Mecca on Manningham Lane. No chance of surveillance there.

He smiled; recalling where he had parked had given him the answer to his problem. Mecca might well run the ballroom for dancers and drinkers but he knew from observation that a few of its clientele were not averse to lying on their backs for a few bob. It was part of what they considered the good life to be all about. He left an unfinished drink on the table. A glass with the most wanted set of fingerprints in Great Britain upon it. Casually washed down the drain by a very busy bartender.

Out in the street he glanced at his watch. *Only 9:30 P.M. Plenty of time yet. Go to the dance hall in a little while. Size up the talent.*

As he walked down Lumb Lane, his thoughts reverted to Jayne MacDonald. He shook his head to clear away the image. Must get a grip on himself. *Wouldn't do to go soft on the job. Might make mistakes.* He smiled broadly at the thought. As if he was capable of making mistakes. God, look at that drawing the police had given the press last week. He had nearly choked with laughter when he first saw it. If that was what they were looking for he could go on doing this for years. For a moment he was tempted to walk up to one of the vice squad cars and ask the way to Manningham Lane. He thought better of the idea. No point in being that cocky.

He walked into the Flying Dutchman. Plenty of time.

In the Mecca ballroom the Saturday evening revelry was at its height. No one was having more fun than forty-two-year-old mother of three, Maureen Long. She liked a drink and loved to dance. At the Mecca she enthusiastically indulged in both. She had previously, that evening, been to a number of Bradford pubs, so her ability to dance that Saturday evening was somewhat limited. Still, Saturday comes but once a week.

Bowie's "Sound and Vision." The Stones' "It's Only Rock and Roll." Donna Summer telling the world, "I Feel Love." One song merged into another. Maureen removed the light green jacket she had borrowed from her daughter as the pace grew more frenetic. Her long black evening dress floated in a sea of denim as she more than matched the enthusiasm of the younger people on the dance floor.

Shortly after two in the morning Maureen unsteadily left the Mecca. She planned to spend the rest of the night with her husband at Laisterdyke, a suburb of Bradford. Predictably, the nearby taxi line was a long one. She walked past it in the direction of the town center. A car pulled up and offered her a lift. You don't look gift horses in the mouth, do you? Maureen climbed into the car.

At 8:45 A.M. on the Sunday morning two women in a trailer heard cries for help; they went to investigate. They discovered Maureen Long, the woman who liked the good life, lying seriously injured on waste ground. The fact that she still lived was extraordinary. She had been attacked shortly after three in the morning. She had a fractured skull from the hammer blows and stab wounds to her abdomen and back. She should have been dead. Her attacker had certainly intended that but a barking dog had disturbed him and he had fled into the night. Nevertheless the injuries he had inflicted would have killed most people. As she was rushed to hospital, George Oldfield was being sped to the scene of the attack. If only she could remember, give an accurate description. She was placed on twenty-four-hour guard. Seriously wounded, she was able initially to give the police a few scraps of information. Perhaps after rest and sleep and medication she might have a fuller story to tell.

At the scene of the crime Oldfield, Domaille, and Holland surveyed the search operation. The entire area resembled a moon landscape. It was as though Hitler's Luftwaffe had paid a very recent visit. Horses, dogs, and cats wandered over the devastated waste grounds. The junk and rubbish of consumer society lay everywhere. Gas tanks and engineering works circled the district. Breakers yards. A railway yard. Council dwellings, some occupied, others vandalized. Most with boards where windows should have been. Gypsies in their caravans attempting to scratch a living. The local pub aptly named The Farmyard. The place is called Bowling Back Lane. At the city end of the road, as a final flourish of unreality, is a Sikh temple.

The search established that after the initial attack he had dragged her body a few yards. More important was the piece of broken sink found nearby. On it was a bloody palm print. His palm print.

A nearby night watchman gave the police something else to puzzle over. He worked only a short distance away from the scene of the attack. He was positive that at 3:27 A.M. he had seen a car speed away. He was equally positive that it was a Ford Cortina Mark II sedan, white, with a black roof.

While another incident room was established, while another three hundred police officers were drafted onto this particular investigation, Oldfield was advised by Professor Gee that the attack had been perpetrated by the man they were already desperately hunting.

The scene of the crime search also rapidly established that Maureen's left shoe, a black patent leather sling-back, and her large handbag were missing. Police established that her handbag was approximately fifteen by ten inches, imitation brown leather with large plastic imitation tortoiseshell carrying handles. Deliberately stolen or drunkenly left in the car when she climbed out? Either way, vital clues, if traced.

After an initial operation in Bradford, Maureen Long was transferred to Leeds for major neurological surgery. Oldfield was desperate for any information he could wring from the sick, frightened woman before that operation. He pleaded with the surgeons for a few minutes. In that desperately short space of time his spirits rose. He was close, he knew that, very close.

She recalled leaving the Mecca. She recalled the car that had stopped and offered her a lift. She recalled the driver.

"He was white. Big build. About thirty-five years of age. He had light brown hair. It was shoulder length. He was tall, a six-footer. Thick eyebrows. He had puffed cheeks and his hands were very large."

"The car, Maureen. What can you remember about the car?"

She strained to recall memories. It was so hard. She'd been a bit drunk. Also now her head hurt. It hurt a lot.

"It was a sedan."

The surgeon approached the bedside.

"I'm sorry, Mr. Oldfield, we can't delay the operation any longer. It's putting her at too great a risk."

George Oldfield had one more try.

"What about the color of the car, love?"

He bent close to her, this portly assistant chief constable of Yorkshire. Like an anxious father, desperate to help a sick child.

Their eyes met. Hers tightly screwed up in the effort to recall.

"It was white, or yellow, or blue."

Oldfield felt the surgeon's arm on his. No matter. If she came through the operation he could build on those fragments, flesh out the picture. Already he had something to work with. He felt elated. His conversations with Maureen, first at Bradford, now at Leeds, looked like the vital breakthrough.

George Oldfield told the press.

"Information is now coming in and the investigation is beginning to bubble. I feel we are getting nearer to the man I am looking for. If I continue to get the help from the public that I have had so far, I feel sure that we will win."

For a short while after the long operation was performed on Maureen Long, Oldfield felt sure that more information would flow from the woman. Surgeons advised him that there was no brain damage. Ultimately, however, it transpired that Maureen Long could give no further help. Her memory of the attack was impaired, either by the operation, the pain-killing drugs, or some inner sixth sense of self-preservation against insanity; the mind had blotted out the nightmare. Oldfield left her bedside after his second visit with some of the elation draining from him. It was a case of making the best they could from the fragmentary impressions given before surgery.

A week after the attack the police swooped down on the dance hall. Mick Jagger and his friends were silenced and replaced with "Were you here last Saturday night?"

"You say you saw Maureen Long here. What time would that have been?"

"Now, think carefully. This man you saw while you were in the taxi line—what did he look like? Let's start with color of hair."

Over one thousand people at the ballroom were interviewed. While Oldfield kept as a carefully guarded secret the fact that Maureen Long's memory of the events was now nonexistent, he continued to give the media the impression that a torrent of vital information was still pouring from her lips. Those closest to him knew better. It was going to be a long, hard slog without any shafts of lightning.

The police turned their attention to the Ford Cortina seen by the night watchman. That kind of car was a familiar sight in the streets of Leeds and Bradford. Many of them were driven by taxi drivers.

It had long been a police theory that the man they were seeking was a taxi driver.

Such a man would have a great deal of local knowledge. He would also know every red light district. He would know where to take a potential victim. Because of the sheer familiarity of his car he would, to a certain extent, be invisible. The mundane we ignore or fail to record. Taxi drivers were also frequently used by prostitutes after a night's work. It all fitted very neatly. All they had to do was discover which taxi driver.

After the murder of Tina Atkinson a great many local taxi drivers found themselves being "invited" for a chat at a police station. Many were rapidly ruled out as possibles. One who was not was Terry Hawkshaw. His account of his movements at crucial times left something to be desired. But then a taxi driver cruising for hire in the small hours is unlikely to have the Home Secretary in the trunk to confirm his alibi. Hawkshaw lives with his elderly mother in the center of a triangle of death; Leeds, Bradford, and Huddersfield. At the time he was first pulled in, during 1977, he was thirty-six years old. His age and general appearance could conceivably match what the police believed they were looking for.

After the attack on Maureen Long, Terry Hawkshaw was put on a twenty-four-hour watch. Everywhere he went the police followed. They watched as his white Cortina with a black roof sat in taxi ranks, picked up passengers, many times unescorted women. They kept surveillance outside his home. They followed him into pubs. Eventually they tired of the game and pounced.

The carpets were ripped from his car for forensic checks. His mother's home was searched from top to bottom. They turned out the garbage cans, checked on the tools in his uncle's nearby workshop. They pulled him in for questioning. It began with a statement from George Oldfield.

"I think you are Jack the Ripper."

They took all the clothes away from his home. They cut bits of his hair off. They took blood samples. And interspersed with all this activity there were the questions.

"How can you prove where you were on that night?"

"You must have known Tina Atkinson; how long?"

"What about Maureen Long? We have witnesses who place you outside the Mecca on the night she was attacked. What about that?"

"Why aren't you married?"

"Who does your washing?"

"What dry cleaners do you use?"

"Do you like women?"

"Do you like whores?"

"Ever been with a whore?"

One such session went on at Wakefield police station from 8:00 P.M. on a Friday until 8:00 P.M. on a Saturday. Twenty-four hours of desperation for a taxi driver named Terry Hawkshaw. Over the years at least twelve other men have shared the nightmare of Hawkshaw.

The license number of Hawkshaw's car was given to all police divisions. Other license numbers of other suspects were also circulated. While every policeman throughout West Yorkshire kept a lookout for these vehicles and carefully logged each sighting, the actual man they were seeking continued to drive into the cities and murder.

Home Secretary Merlyn Rees visited the incident room. Apart from being the titular head of the country's police force he also had another reason for his interest in the investigation. As the Member of Parliament for South Leeds he had the murders happening on his doorstep. At the end of his visit, his observation might well have been echoed by Terry Hawkshaw: "This is a new experience for me."

Maureen Long was in the hospital for six weeks. Her hair shaved for the operation, she was subsequently photographed by the national press, which informed its readers that she was wearing a black wig. She spent a further three weeks in a convalescent home before returning to her Bradford home to live on thirteen pounds a week social security. The medication helped to blur life and the nightmares. And the poverty. Her face stares out on the list of victims as the only living person in the gallery of death. Many observers have incorrectly concluded that she is the only survivor attacked by this man. Not so. Maureen had a record prior to the attack. Consequently mug shots of her, taken earlier, were widely publicized. She was presumably public property.

In March 1978, Maureen walked down Morley Street, Bradford. She strolled unwittingly into a street fight. She was hit on the back of the head with an iron bar. Yet again she was taken to Bradford Infirmary. Yet again her head was stitched. Yet again she survived.

In December 1978, she was brought before the Bradford magistrates and admitted stealing from three shops in the city center. She was fined £75 and agreed to pay at £1 per week. She told the court she was still awaiting compensation for the attack that occurred July 10, 1977. She had been granted an interim payment of £300. In April 1979 the criminal compensation board offered her £1500. Outraged, she appealed against the award, observing, "They've offered £25,000 for his capture. Surely I'm worth as much."

After a further period she was awarded an interim payment of £1250 with the promise that her case would be kept under medical review.

As part of the Ripper industry she ekes out her money charging for interviews about the night she "will never forget," except that her mind has obliged her to do just that.

This man's victim in Keighley, Anna Rogulskyj, was granted an immediate payment by the criminal compensation board of £15,000.

Maureen Long, the woman who yearned for "the good life," is "alive and well" in Bradford.

The man responsible for her appalling predicament was also alive and well and living but a few miles from her. He should include Maureen Long in his list of "victims." The fact that she happened to live is irrelevant. Many of his victims lived. Most have not been actually confronted by this man, but the ripples of evil that he first caused in long-ago 1975 are growing ever wider.

The investigation to catch this man has cost more than six million pounds, yet we offer Maureen Long less than the cost of the meals eaten by the police officers during the particular inquiry into that attack.

10

In mid-October he checked Leeds and Bradford. *No good there. Full of patrolling vice cars.* They had men in all the notorious pubs too. He considered the problem as he sipped a drink in the Gaiety. A stripper was onstage. They were as much a part of the merry-go-round as the whores and their johns. He'd seen the same woman two days before in the Bellevue on Manningham Lane. He wondered if the all-male audience were the same pack that he'd watched in the Bradford pub. *What a bloody circus.* Disgusted, he left and drove home.

He looked at his newspapers and noted with satisfaction that although the attack on Maureen Long had been given front-page coverage this time there were no moralizing editorials. If that was what they wanted he'd give them plenty more of it. *Pity that dog had barked. Would have already finished the bitch. Better luck next time.* He intended the next time to be soon. He felt the need coming on again, taking over. He had to exact vengeance, but it was lonely work. No one to plan with. No one to share his success with. He thought of the men he worked alongside. He had listened to their conversations about the murders. He'd even joined in, taking care not to express any personal opinions.

He brought his mind back to the problem at hand. Where next? He'd had a look at Huddersfield. Plenty of whores there, particularly around Great Northern Street, but they worked in such a small area. He would run the risk of being spotted. He needed a big city for the next one. Then he remembered the highways. Convenient of the government to throw tons of concrete all over the country. Why, via the M.62 he could be in Manchester in no time. Manchester. It was perfect. Plenty of prostitutes, particularly round Moss Side. Only thirty-four miles from Bradford. If he used the highway he could be there and back before the body got cold. He smiled. Really ought to write a letter of thanks to the Ministry of Transport.

Always a careful man, he decided to reconnoiter. No need to fix an alibi for the time away; he didn't plan to get back on the job in this journey, but next time. *Measure twice. Cut once.*

He cruised along the M.62, careful to keep his speed within the limits as he drove the Corsair. Useful having access to a number of cars. He was alert to the very real need to remain inconspicuous. Car was taxed. He had a license and insurance. There would be no silly mistakes. Arriving in the northern outskirts of Manchester, he moved onto the M.63, then, dropping down, he approached the southern part of the city. By Southern Cross Cemetery his keen eyes picked up a number of patrolling prostitutes. An ideal place. When he had done the job he could retrace his steps. M.63, then M.62, be back home before you could say "who's a clever boy, then?"

He pointed the car in the direction of Moss Side and the Hulme Estate. He felt the need to check this new territory over completely, just a look around, but he would be back.

The Hulme Estate had won its architects' prizes. This was to demonstrate that those who awarded such accolades had a sense of humor. Albeit a black one.

It has been said that Hulme was a nineteenth-century slum of small terraced houses. It is now a twentieth-century slum of high-rise fortresses. Some blackened by fire, others vandalized beyond repair. The small corner shop has been replaced by the overcrowded doctor's surgery. The gossip and friendly chat with Valium. Over 60 percent of its population, some fifteen thousand people, are desperately trying to dig their way out of Stalag Manchester, but there are few wooden horses. Apart from its twenty public houses, two clubs, and two betting shops there is a huge bingo hall, a cinema, several empty churches, and one library that runs a restricted service. Sports facilities are rare. There are no parks. Each high-rise block is named after a famous architect, which is fitting. The things were designed by some people for other people. Walls are paper-thin, excluding privacy. Rubbish chutes are usually blocked and elevators rarely work. Everywhere in winter there is a pervasive damp. There is nowhere for the children to play in safety. Nowhere for their mothers to socialize if one excludes pubs and bingo. In this place, violence, even murder, are commonplace. Every night, somewhere on the estate, there is extreme violence. The scientists who observed what happened when rats were placed in hostile or inadequate environments could learn a great deal from Hulme.

Truancy, vandalism, theft, prostitution, alcoholism, drug abuse. It is a sociologist's dream and a social worker's nightmare. A nightmare stamped "Made in Great Britain."

In this place six doctors prescribe over a quarter of a million tranquilizers and antidepressants per month.

Not one single policeman lives in Hulme. The patrolling black-and-white police cars are very largely ineffective, most crime being committed above the ground in the "streets in the sky." Everywhere there is a stench, often so powerful as to choke a passerby. Like the Nazi labor camps of the Second World War, Hulme is a place where only the fittest, mentally and physically, survive until they escape or are liberated.

Manchester people are rightly proud of their theaters, libraries, concert halls, and fine architecture. The man the entire nation sought does not linger at the Halle. He did not stand by the statue of John Bright in Albert Square. You would not find him sauntering into the Midland Hotel. He moved among the urban decay. Evil is comfortable and at home among the rotting.

At 9:00 P.M. on Friday, October 1, 1977, Jean Jordan left her Hulme flat. She told Alan Royle, the man she lived with, "I'm going out for a breath of fresh air."

Alan nodded as he continued to watch "Starsky and Hutch." She never returned. Instead:

"Are you looking for business?"

"Yes, how much will it cost?"

She peered at the man. He looked all right but didn't quite seem to be that elusive millionaire that she sometimes fantasized about.

"Five pounds, all right?"

"Yes, that's fine. Jump in."

It was a cold night. Jean shivered. He looked at her solicitously.

"You cold, love?"

"A bit."

"I'll switch the heater on."

He leaned forward and flicked the switch. The car rapidly filled with hot air. The engine was well warm from the run to Manchester. She glanced at him.

"That's thoughtful. Don't get many like you."

"Really?"

"No, all the bastards think about is themselves. Never give any thought to us."

"Oh, I do."

"Yes, I can see that. Where are we going? I know a few places."

"What about Southern Cross Cemetery?"

"That's fine."

In reality, Jean didn't care where it was. She'd been out looking for a john for nearly half an hour. A few minutes' warmth in the car was nearly as welcome as the fiver.

In the headlights they both saw Southern Cross Cemetery. She leaned forward.

"Go just past the gates. We can get into an open patch. It's dead quiet here."

They both chuckled at the joke.

"Now, I always say business before pleasure."

Without a word he handed over a five-pound note. He was very organized. Very prepared. He'd put it separate from the rest of his money before picking her up.

He stopped the car. It was dark. Pitch-dark. He liked that. Made him feel better. Starting the car once again, he tucked it in neatly. Getting out of the car, they clambered over the long grass.

"How do you want it, lying down or standing up? I don't . . ."

Those were the last words she ever uttered. Unseen, he had slipped the hammer into his right hand. Making a short arc, he hit her on the head. Once, twice. Again and again and again. In all he hit Jean Jordan on the head eleven times. She was dead after the first blow. He dragged the body into some bushes. He tucked her handbag under a nearby fence and surveyed the scene. Rage gone, his mind was crystal-clear. Nothing was out of place. Nothing to show that death had come to Southern Cross Cemetery that evening. Slowly he walked back to the car. Within minutes he was on the M.63, heading for home.

As the days went by, twenty-six-year-old Alan Royle, her common-law husband, waited and wondered. As he washed and put the two children to bed he recalled that Jean had always been her own woman. Always done what she had wanted.

"She's probably gone to Scotland, to see her folks," he told three-year-old Alan. "No point in fretting. We'll hear from her soon enough."

"Mummy gone away," said Alan junior.

On the other side of the Pennines there was a man who was fretting. Daily he read the newspapers. Daily he waited for the news that *he* had struck again. He thought of a trap. Wondered if the police were cunning enough to have found the body and kept quiet. It didn't seem likely. They might be clever buggers, but what about the person who had found the body? The police would have to keep him quiet too. He concluded that he had hidden it too well.

As the week progressed his wife noticed that he was preoccupied. They were busy redecorating one of the bedrooms. It was planned to be their first child's room. The child that was still a distant dream, but they were still hoping and perhaps this time . . .

On the next Friday he found her crying quietly in the living room.

"What's up, pet?"

"My period's started. I thought when it was late this time, I thought perhaps . . ." Her voice trailed off hopelessly. He put a reassuring arm around her. Inside was massive anger but the words sounded gentle and loving.

"Don't worry. It'll happen sooner or later. You know what the doctor said. Just a matter of relaxing."

Her disappointment turned to anger as well. Not at him but at the unfairness.

"Why is it? Anyone else can have children and we can't. It's almost as if we were not meant to."

"There, now. You just sit there and I'll make us both a cup of tea. You'll feel better then."

Inwardly he was angry. Overwhelmingly angry. She was right. Anyone else seemed to be able to have them whenever they wanted to. He felt the need to take his anger out on someone. On a woman. Any woman, other than his wife. He wanted to kill again. Then he smiled. He would kill again. This weekend. He would murder that slut he'd dumped near the Southern Cross Cemetery. It would be like a totally new attack. Dead bodies didn't frighten him. He'd seen quite a few in his teens when he'd worked as a gravedigger.

On Sunday, October 9, he drove yet again to Manchester.

Reaching the cemetery, he drove slowly past. There was no one in sight. No parked cars.

He ran through the long grass and after a moment found Jean Jordan, exactly where he had left her.

He dragged her dead body out. Took off the high boots and tossed them away. Her coat, blouse, skirt, all her clothes were removed, tossed like careless litter anywhere. He dragged the body toward a nearby path.

He pulled a knife from his pocket and began to stab and slash the body. He stabbed at the abdomen in anger. The sight of her nakedness arousing him to an uncontrollable fury. Again and again he stabbed her abdomen. He stabbed her back. He slashed her from shoulder to shoulder. He stabbed her back again. He stabbed her thighs. The anger within him would not subside. In all he stabbed the lifeless body some twenty times, finishing again with the abdomen. His final act was to pull out the exposed intestines and wrap them around her body.

He stood breathless. Even his horrific strength had temporarily ebbed. As he stood there he remembered her handbag. Tucked under the fence. He walked to the spot and quickly located the cheap imitation-leather bag.

"She'll have no need of my money where she's gone," he said aloud. Opening the bag, he pulled out some notes. Fourteen pounds in all. He smiled at the thought he had made a profit. Moments later he was driving back toward Bradford.

The following morning shortly before lunchtime a shocked workman telephoned Chorlton Cum Hardy police station. He was barely coherent. When the police arrived on the scene they realized why. This entire nation and many beyond its shores had for many years been asking one question with increasing frequency.

"Why can't the police catch him?"

What followed the discovery of the mutilated body of Jean Jordan provides a considerable part of the answer to that pressing question.

From the outset it was clear to the Manchester police that there was a very strong possibility that the man who held Yorkshire in thrall had crossed the Pennines. But they vacillated. Detective Chief Superintendent Jack Ridgeway, head of Manchester central C.I.D., was in charge of the investigation. Clearly, from the very beginning there was overwhelming evidence that this murder had been committed by the man being sought in Yorkshire:

1. Jean Jordan was a prostitute with a record of two warnings.

2. She had been struck on the head with a ball peen hammer.

3. Her body had been stripped. None of the knife wounds had been made through her clothes.

4. The mutilations to the body, particularly to the abdomen, were a classic indication.

All of this and much more was enough to send Ridgeway speeding to Leeds. He met Oldfield at Millgarth police station. They conferred for an hour.

Meanwhile all that had to be fed to the press was that the naked body of a young woman had been found, that police were looking for "a maniac," that there were multiple head injuries.

Admitting that there were several similarities with the "Jack the Ripper" murders, Ridgeway continued, "But there are several indisputable dissimilarities."

There always had been. There always will be.

Valuable days dribbled by as the police investigation of Jean's death followed the classic pattern, including the search of the murder area. It was here that the police committed an even bigger blunder. The biggest blunder of the entire investigation. The area was minutely searched. Yet they failed to find her handbag.

Express Message from CC G. Manchester.
12/10/2330.
Authorizing Officer Det. Ch/Supt Ridgeway.
With reference to express message nos 114/77 and 115/77 regarding the finding of the naked body of female. She has now been identified as Jean Bernadette Jordan born 11/12/56 at Motherwell, Scotland (not Royle as previously circulated). Death resulted from brain damage caused by several blows to the head with a blunt instrument (possibly a hammer). The lower body had a number of lacerations which had been inflicted after death by a sharp instrument. Neither of these weapons has been recovered. (None of the information contained in this paragraph is to be divulged to the press.) She was last seen at 9 P.M. Saturday, 1st Oct 1977, when she left her home in Lingbeck Crescent, Hulme, Manchester 15.

It is believed that she met her death shortly afterwards. When she left home she was carrying a handbag which has not been recovered. Description of missing handbag.

Vinyl leather-look handbag, color not conclusively established, but believed to be dark brown, 9 inches long, 7 inches high, 3 inches wide. It had two carrying handles and one shoulder strap made of the same material. Zip fastener and wrap-over strap which fastens with a clasp on the side of the bag, on which there are two external pockets. It contained approximately £15 in Bank of England notes, items of cosmetics and a few pieces of yellow tissue paper.

The assailant's clothing may be bloodstained and it is requested that the clothing of all persons coming into police custody be examined. It is also requested that all property records be checked regarding the missing handbag.

Any information regarding the above should be forwarded to the Murder Incident Room at Longsight Police Station, Telephone Number 061 273 5073 or 061 228 1212 Ext 8134.

Message ends.

Sender P. C. Webster Ref XW 1/0028 13.10.77.

The purse was found by a workman on Saturday, October 15. Tucked into a side pocket and therefore missed by the murderer was a crisp new five-pound note—the five-pound note that he had given her, a five-pound note that he had received in his wage envelope only a couple of days before. Her body had lain undiscovered for nine days. When he had given them the body her handbag continued to lie undiscovered for six more precious days. It was found less than one hundred yards from her body, "just outside the search area."

He may have had the luck of the devil on his side. He most certainly had the ineptitude of the police.

After the workman's discovery of the purse, police speculated as to whether that was the reason the killer had returned. How little they understood him!

Information from the Bank of England established that the note had gone into circulation, in the Bradford area, only *four* days before Jean Jordan was murdered on Saturday. The possibility of its crossing the Pennines and coming to rest in a prostitute's handbag in normal commercial transactions was remote. When one knows that it would have been in his hands only after Thursday or Friday, the two normal paydays, that possibility becomes unreal. It had come from him.

If the police in both Manchester and Wakefield had been honest with the press on Monday, October 10, if that handbag had been discovered that same day, as it should have been, the man hunted throughout the world would have been arrested in 1977. At least seven women would still be alive and at least another three would not have suffered serious attacks.

On October 25 Ridgeway returned to Yorkshire. This time he conferred with Oldfield at Wakefield H.Q. Still the police would not admit to the press what they knew to be a virtual certainty. *He* had crossed the Pennines. *He* had killed in Manchester. Oldfield told the press that his colleagues from Manchester were "following a certain line of inquiry." He also amazingly said, "We have no reason to believe at this stage that there is any connection between their murder and the ones I am investigating."

He then went back to his desk and studied the fiver that Ridgeway had placed upon it.

The chances of tracing that five-pound note were rapidly fading. The following day a team of Manchester detectives descended on the Bradford area. The press became restive. They wanted to know what was going on. They were advised, "We have a line of inquiry which is directly connected with the murder of a woman in Manchester and we are following that line of inquiry in the West Yorkshire Metropolitan Police area. There is a team of detectives from greater Manchester who are working with detectives from West Yorkshire. We will be visiting factories in the Bingley, Shipley, and Bradford areas and are interviewing all male employees. As to any links with the unsolved murders in West Yorkshire, it is far too early to draw any conclusions and Mr. Oldfield and myself are keeping an open mind."

That was from Ridgeway. Oldfield went further and told reporters the same day that he did not think there was any link between the Manchester murder and the Yorkshire murders.

Clearly this was considered clever strategy, a device to insure that they would pounce on the killer. Clearly the police considered that it was only a question of getting men employed in the area to turn out their pockets and check the serial numbers on their banknotes. This strategy fails to recognize several salient facts.

The one man who would have known exactly why they were in the area was the man they hunted. He would have rapidly known that the police sought five-pound notes that bore serial numbers close to the note he had given Jean Jordan. The murderer would have rapidly changed all the notes in his possession in case any were in the same sequence.

His vulnerability lay in his innocent colleagues. The men who worked alongside him at the same factory. If those men had been alerted when the five-pound note was eventually found on Saturday, October 15, they might still have in their possession notes that bore serial numbers close to the one found in the handbag. Yet more paydays came and went. Families bought food, paid bills, banked or spent notes from those crucial pay packets until all had been scattered to the four winds.

Why did the police vacillate? Why did they keep the serial number of the five-pound note found in that handbag a secret for twelve days after its discovery? The press do not like mass murderers running free; neither do the public. Both newspapers and their readers would have instantly responded to an appeal on October 15 that simply said: "We, the police, are investigating a murder. We are anxious to trace anyone who has a five-pound note between the following serial numbers: AW 51 121501 to AW 51 121569."

It was not until October 27 that Ridgeway revealed it was a five-pound note that was the cause of his presence in Yorkshire. But he would not release the number.

The following day he advised the press of the sequence they were interested in:

"I want to give you the first and last number of our particular run and it is sixty-nine five-pound notes, a run of sixty-nine five-pound notes, and the first number is AW 51 121501, to AW 51 121569, both numbers inclusive.

It was becoming a very morbid version of bingo. It was only after being pressed by reporters that he finally made public for the first time the number of the note that had been found in the handbag. AW 51 121565.

It would seem that if it had taken Ridgeway from the fifteenth until the twenty-seventh of October to obtain from the Bank of England the vital information concerning the serial numbers of the run of five-pound notes that included the particular note found in the dead woman's handbag, he had lost his way. Certainly a large proportion of the men he sent from Manchester lost theirs. With their Kojak clip-on lights flashing from the roofs of their police cars, half of them got lost on the journey from Manchester to Baildon, just outside Bradford. A journey that should have taken them just over one hour took nearly three hours. It was symbolic of the entire exercise: lost handbags, lost time, lost policemen.

Finally the exercise got under way. The five-pound note had been part of a consignment of £127,500 that had been delivered from the Bank of England. The money had been broken up by a receiving bank, a main branch of the Midland. Their delivery vehicle had dispersed the money in varying quantities to various branches. The important sixty-nine notes, including the vital one, were part of a consignment of a bundle of five hundred five-pound notes that had been delivered to the Midland branch at Shipley, near Bradford. The bundle of five hundred had then been paid out to various firms in the area for use as wages. As to which firm drew which notes, there was no definitive answer. What the branch could say was that thirty-five specific firms drew money from them for their employees.

With all the firms only too willing to cooperate, including setting aside interview rooms for the police, the task of identifying which firm had drawn the run of sixty-nine five-pound notes began.

Butterfields, Denbys, Drummonds, Parkinsons, and Clarks were just five of the companies in the area where workers found themselves being questioned.

Some of the companies were engineering, others textiles. Somewhere in a firm between Bradford and Keighley, one man was beginning to sweat. He knew what the police were looking for, long before it was made public knowledge. He knew that if they found the company that had taken the run of sixty-nine notes that the police would know for a virtual certainty that somewhere on that payroll was the man they were hunting. Having insured that he no longer had any notes from that particular pay packet, he waited for the inevitable. As he waited he attempted to go about his everyday work in a perfectly normal manner. One angry word out of place, a change of mood, a moment in which he showed the pressure he felt, was all that was needed to get his workmates wondering.

When the police appealed for people to turn out their wallets and asked housewives to turn spy on their husbands and go through their pockets, he joined in the general conversation about this passing excitement. He looked hard at the people he worked with. Wondered if any of them was still carrying around fivers with numbers close to the one he had given the whore. Damn fool.

Damn fool. If only he had thought. All he had to do was take the handbag. Eventually they reached the company he worked for.

He noticed that the two officers looked tired. That encouraged him. They took down his particulars. Name, address, occupation, how long with the firm. He realized that this was no more than the overture. The main work quickly followed.

"Would you mind turning out your pockets?"

"Not at all. Is this to do with the fiver you're looking for?"

"God, don't any of you read the newspapers properly? We've already a fiver. What we're looking for are notes between these serial numbers."

The detective threw a piece of paper to him. He studied it carefully.

"I'm sorry. Piece in newspaper were a bit confusing."

He emptied out his pockets, including his money. One of the police officers pointed to the notes.

"Mind if we look at those?"

"Help yourself."

The detective quickly scanned the serial numbers.

"Right, thank you. You can put that lot away now."

"We are questioning people concerning their movements on Saturday and Sunday, the first and second October. Can you tell us what you did that weekend?"

"I'll try. It's a fair time ago."

It was a response the Manchester detective had heard many times since he began this particular assignment. He nodded sympathetically.

"I know, but anything you tell us to place your whereabouts on that weekend would be useful."

"H'm, I think that was the week Leeds beat Chelsea, wasn't it?"

"I dunno. Were you at the match, then?"

"Yes, never miss a home game. I'm sure it was that weekend. I remember thinking, That's up yours, Chelsea, for beating us in the cup final."

The other detective, who had been listening quietly, began to show animation.

"You mean the final replay at Manchester in 1977?"

"That's the one. Did you see it too? Great game, but we were robbed. Should have won it first time at Wembley, let alone needing replay."

The copper had become enthusiastic.

"You're right there. Eddie Grey played them off the park."

The other policeman, not a football fan, coughed lightly. His colleague took the hint and, still smiling at the memory of Chelsea stealing the cup from Leeds, lapsed into silence.

"So you think you were at Elland Road on the afternoon of Saturday, October first?"

"That's right."

"What about in the evening?"

"Well, I would have stopped for a pint on my way home. Always do. Then telly with the wife in the evening. Rarely go out on a Saturday evening. Usually watch the Parkinson show."

"What about Sunday?"

"I usually tinker with the car in the morning. Afternoon take a stroll on moor and evening it would have been telly again, with family."

"And your wife would be able to confirm all this."

He half smiled.

"If she can remember. It's a fair time ago, isn't it?"

It went on for a while. They chatted about this and that. Eventually:

"That's fine. When would it be convenient to talk to your wife?"

A few days later he sat calmly in his home listening to his wife recalling the first weekend in October. Her words insured his freedom. Insured that he would continue to murder. When she had finished, they turned his attention back to him.

"Right. Now we'd like you to account for your movements on the following weekend. That'd be the ninth and tenth of October."

Again he had the answers. It was a bit of "I probably did" and a little of "I'm sure we went."

He'd planned for this. Planned before he'd even killed in Manchester. When it became certain that he would need an alibi he had gently broached the subject with his wife. He'd reminded

her of things they had done together on other days and quietly
asserted that they had taken place on the key dates. Just a little
autosuggestion. She agreed with his recollections. Then he'd let
the matter drop, knowing that soon the police would interview
him, then come checking his alibi with his wife. It had all been so
simple. When they questioned his wife he cleverly refrained from
prompting her.

Virtually unsolicited she had recited the events that he had
implanted in her mind.

The two detectives rose to leave his home.

"That's fine. We'll let you know if we need to see you again.
Thanks for your help. And thanks for the tea."

His wife smiled back at the tall detective. As he opened the
door to the street and showed them out he remarked, "Hope you
catch the bastard."

"Thanks. We will."

He could scarcely hold back the grin as they walked down the
garden path. He rejoined his wife in the living room.

"Why on earth should they question you?"

"Oh, they're questioning everyone that works in the Shipley/
Baildon and Bingley area. Something about a five-pound note."

She shuddered.

"I wish they'd catch this man. This Ripper."

His response carried total sincerity and conviction.

"So do I love. Like to go out shopping now?"

As he got the Corsair out of the garage he smiled.

He knew he had fooled them.

Clever to have done his homework about the football. What else
would a man like him be doing on a Saturday? Certainly not
driving to Manchester. The fact that they had not asked him about
his car lifted his spirits further. Neither had they asked for his
fingerprints. They hadn't got a clue.

As the days went by he read in the papers that "The Net Closes
On Ripper." "List shows everyone who may have given £5 note to
victim."

He read that there were "100 names left in Ripper hunt."

That the police had "a long list." That Ridgeway had stated, "I
am quite confident that we have the name of the man to whom

that five-pound note was issued. We now have the list of every person, organization, or firm to whom the bank issued five-pound notes."

He also read Detective Chief Superintendent Ridgeway's assertion, "We stay as long as it takes us to do what we have to do. There is no way I will go back to Manchester until we have interviewed the man who was given this five-pound note. If it takes a week or a month, it's as important as that."

After conducting over five thousand interviews, after tracing two hundred notes from the bundle of five hundred, Ridgeway and his men gave up. In the middle of January 1978 they returned to Manchester. Ridgeway observed, "I feel sure that the man concerned was interviewed."

11

Summer had blurred by. Flossy's A-Level exam results had been good enough to win a place at the university. The vacation with Lauris on the south coast seemed to end before it had hardly begun. It had been good to revisit Cornwall particularly. So much had happened since the last vacation with Mum and Dad. Was it really only two years previously that she had lain on a surfboard and lusted after Roger Daltry? Well, she had always been true to him in her fashion but there had been some delicious interludes with men who were actually attainable.

Now she was at the university. New doors in her life opening. Vistas expanding. Well, that's what Mum and Dad had said anyway. There didn't seem to be much of the brave new world within grasp as she sat in her room in the residence hall. As dinnertime approached on her first day she wanted to be with Ben, or Roy, or Lauris, or Mum and Dad, anywhere but this strange place.

Nervously she determined to introduce herself to her immediate neighbors on the landing. She kept telling herself there was nothing to be frightened about. They were just students like her, in the same noisy, bewildering boat. Eventually she crept from her room and knocked on the door next to hers. There was no one in. It was the same on the other side. After all that effort. She finally found someone in along the corridor. A Canadian girl named Mona. She seemed nice. But then at that moment a Martian would have appeared charming. It helped her forget that she had just heard Hot Chocolate on the radio singing "So You Win Again"; that had reminded her of her summer romance with Roy and that had made her feel sad.

Later that first day she had gone to a "party night spectacular," one of the many titles students give to getting drunk. She'd had a good time and met a few people but still cried herself to sleep that evening. Cuddling one of her sweaters helped her drift away and after a good sleep and a large breakfast she felt ready to write to Lauris. Inevitably that first letter was largely concerned with a subject dear to both their hearts:

The talent doesn't seem to be exceptional, although I have seen about five that made me look twice (or three times!).

As she wrote, her need for Lauris grew greater. They were so close. Perhaps it had been a mistake to choose separate universities. Well, she was here now. Must make the best of it. The next few days were occupied with a combination of enrolling and making further checks on the talent. Catching the mood of vibrancy of the place, she began to consider taking up orienteering and squash and volleyball and a dozen other fun things. Her excursions out into the city were initially made with newfound friends; that way they could feel collectively gauche.

Bubbling away in the first flush of it all, she wrote again to her friend: *Warden talked to us yesterday, they say no subletting rooms, they have got guest rooms which you (or rather we) can book, but I don't think they'd mind someone staying over the weekend. So if you want to come up just say the word.*

Did you find out Ben's address, and if so couldja send it—but I bet you didn't, or you would've said so before.

Her parents, laden with home-comforts, had just been to see her. It had made her feel much better. High enough to airily show off to Lauris:

Oh, yes, I finally decided (well, just about) my subjects about ½ hour before we had to give the lists in. So I'm gonna

be doing Psych, Sociology, Quantitative Techniques, Litera-
ture and the History of Ideas, English Legal Institutions, the
Nature of Scientific Activity. The books for L.H.1 look quite
good. Twelve out of *Waiting for Godot*—Beckett, *The Plague*—
Camus, *The Cherry Orchard*—Chekov. *Heart of Darkness*—
Conrad, *Murder in the Cathedral*—Eliot, two short accounts of
psychoanalysis—Freud, *The Spire*—Golding, *The Master
Builder*—Ibsen . . .

The list went on and on. She didn't know if Lauris would be
impressed. She certainly was. Her P.P.S. was more like the Flossy
that Lauris knew.
*P.P.S. Saw that gorgeous French student again today, he wears
straight leg jeans, really suit him, he's very dark with a really striking face
and dark curly hair almost Daltreyish!!!*

It was 8:30 on the night of Wednesday, December 14, 1977.
Marilyn Moore, an attractive twenty-five-year-old, was looking for
business in Chapeltown. She watched as a white Ford Corsair
moved slowly down Gipton Avenue. He was looking for business
all right. The car passed her as she walked down Spencer Place.
Thinking the driver would turn left into Louis Street and loop
back, she crossed the road and turned right into Leopold Street.
She was about to cross Frankland Place on her way to meet the car
when to her surprise she saw it parked. He was standing near the
driver's door and appeared to be waving to someone in a nearby
house. As she approached, the litany was uttered yet again.
"Are you doing business?"
"Yes," Marilyn answered.
He looked at her, then remarked, "Five pounds."
"Fine."
He opened his door and, getting in, reached across and opened
the front passenger door. She looked over at him.
"Where do you want to go?" she asked.
"I know of a right quiet place."
"Fair enough, saves me the trouble of thinking of one. It's
getting a problem these days. The amount of police about."
"They bother you much?"

"Any bother from them is too much."

She glanced at him as they drove. He was good-looking. That made a change. God, in this line of business you got all sorts. From his accent she judged that he came from Liverpool. Quite tasty. He interrupted her reverie.

"What's your name?"

Rule one of this business was never to give your right name to a john. You never knew who you were getting in a car with.

"Carol. What's yours?"

"David, but I prefer Dave."

That was probably as phony as hers, she thought, but still, what the hell.

"Who were you waving at when you picked me up?"

"Oh, me girlfriend."

"Girlfriend!"

"Yes. Haven't seen her for some time. She's been poorly."

Her right arm dangled on the back of the driver's seat.

"Shouldn't think you'd have too much trouble finding another?"

He smiled, more at his reflection in the second driving mirror than at her.

"Not too much. But who needs all that problem?"

Who indeed? He had those sleepy come-to-bed eyes and yet there was something hard, almost vicious, about him. One of the "I'm good-looking and know it" brigade. As if in confirmation of her thoughts he yet again stared at his image in the second driving mirror. She noticed that it was angled directly towards him. Vain bugger.

"Where are we going?"

"Not far, less than two miles from where I picked you up."

She giggled.

"Have you measured the distance or something?"

He had.

"No, just know my way about."

"If your girlfriend lives in Chapeltown you must know a few of the girls?"

"Know a couple. Hilary and Gloria."

"Oh, I know a girl on the game called Hilary. Wonder if it's the same one?"

"This one's got a Jamaican boyfriend."

"Don't know about her boyfriend."

"I know a Gloria too."

She was relaxed now and felt like conversation. It made a change from the grunts and groans and muttered suggestions she had to put up with from the usual clients.

"Did you read about that murder case?"

He stiffened inwardly.

"Which one?"

"Woman called Kalinda Chapman. She had two lovers. They've been accused of murdering her old man. Sounds a right-to-do."

"Bloody fools. Fancy murdering for a woman."

He stroked his beard.

Far better, he thought, *to murder the women*.

"Nearly there now."

He pulled off of Scott Hall Street and drove slowly down Buslingthorpe Lane. They were approaching some waste ground situated behind a darkened mill. Above the patch of waste land the ground rose sharply. It led to Prince Philip playing fields, where Wilma McCann had been found.

"You certainly do know your way about."

He stopped well into the waste ground. He frowned, and his keen eyesight picked up the small light of a trailer a few hundred yards away. He hadn't noticed that when he'd checked this place. She was aware of his hesitation.

"Don't worry. Those folk are used to couples coming down here. They won't give us any bother."

"Seems like I'm not the only one who knows my way about," he said.

He turned the lights of the car off.

"That'll be five pounds."

"I haven't had anything yet."

"You should know, Dave. It's always business before pleasure."

"All right, but let's get into back seat first."

I'll fix this bitch before she gets into the back, he thought.

They were about to get out of the car when that sixth sense within him urged caution. He caught her arm.

"What's the matter now?"

He'd been right to wait. In the distance the trailer door opened. A man and a woman could be clearly seen silhouetted in the doorway. They were looking towards the Ford Corsair. He tensed. A coil ready to snap at the slightest touch. She followed his gaze.

"Don't worry about them. They live here. I told you, they're used to people coming down here."

"They might be. But I'm not performing in front of an audience."

"Shy little boy, are we."

He nearly attacked her there and then. Instead he watched, ever careful as the man and the woman came down the trailer steps, the man stopping to lock the door.

"Come on. Come on."

"Oooh, getting impatient now, are we. Nothing to worry about. Look, they're going out."

The couple were indeed going out. They climbed into a car and drove slowly past. As they did he turned toward her and moved close to her to mask his face from the other car's headlights. So lucky. So lucky. Yet again the luck of the devil. If that couple had come out two minutes later he would have been caught red-handed as he attacked this bitch. The other car containing the trailer owner and his girlfriend vanished. "Well, you might as well pay me now, luv."

He was very aware that the Manchester police were still turning over Baildon, Shipley, and Bradford in an effort to trace the man who had given that Manchester whore a fiver. It had been only a few days since he'd walked cockily away from his interviews with them. No way was he giving this bitch a fiver. He might not find it afterward. It was too dangerous. He didn't know how old the notes were that he had in his wallet. *Just my bloody luck to give her a new one. If they traced that back to the same area they'd never leave until they found me.*

"Well, come on then, what's keeping you?"

"I'll pay you afterwards."

"I may look young but I'm not that young. Pay me afterwards and drive off leaving me with my panties off and you with your fiver. No, I want it before we start."

"Look, let's get in the back. We can sort it out there."

She opened the car door.

"I'm sorting it out now. Either you pay me now or you don't get it. I've had some buggers want it on credit. How do I know you've got a fiver?"

She got out of the car.

Quickly, very quickly, he got out of his side. He was around the back of the car in seconds. He swung the hammer as she stood half turned toward him. It crashed down on her head. It failed to kill. It failed even to make her unconscious. She screamed.

Shouting at her, he swung the hammer again.

"Dirty prostitute bitch. You whore."

The hammer smashed down on her again. This time she had raised her left hand instinctively to protect her head. The hammer smashed her hand and head. The scream this time was weaker as she fell to the ground unconscious.

As she lay there he shouted at the still form.

"You whore. You bitch. You dirty stinking prostitute."

He smashed her yet again on the head with the ball peen hammer.

All this noise and shouting might well have drawn attention to the bizarre scene. He thought he sensed another light go on in the trailer. He'd have to leave it at that. No time to use the knife. Jumping into the car, he reversed, then drove off into the night.

As he sped away he shouted inside the car.

"Damn! Damn!"

What really annoyed him was that he might have to shave the mustache and beard off. He'd wanted to keep them until Christmas.

An hour later a passerby found Marilyn Moore. She was still alive. Indeed, she had managed to half-walk, half-stagger to a telephone booth.

Soon police were pouring into the area. It might just be another john, they thought. But then again, it might be him.

The following morning workers in the nearby mill had something to take their minds off their boring, repetitive work. They stared as a team of police crawling on their hands and knees moved slowly forward in a carefully marked off area, while horses nuzzled into the rubbish dump and frogmen searched the adjoining inlet. The men on their knees searched the ground for traces of the previous evening's murderous assault. They didn't find any weapons. What they did find was perhaps of even greater value. A complete set of tire marks left by his car. He had an Avon Super tire fitted on the rear left, and India Autoway tires fitted on the other three wheels. The width of the tracks also dramatically narrowed the possible make of car that he had used.

Comparing these marks with those left at the scene of Irene Richardson's murder, they found that the left rear wheel had been changed before the attack on Marilyn Moore from an Esso 110 to an Avon Super tire. The right rear had also been changed during this period, from a Pneumant to an India Autoway. Like a great many other things, new tires do not grow on trees. Who had given or sold him the new tire?

Assistant Chief Constable Oldfield and the man in charge of this particular assault, Detective Chief Superintendent Hobson, were optimistic. Not only did they have yet another set of tire marks, they had another victim who had lived to tell her tale, albeit a reluctant tale. Marilyn Moore was not keen to cooperate with the police.

From Det Ch/Supt Hobson, Millgarth Incident Room.
To all divisions West Yorks, ACC Crime, police reports.
Section 18 wounding in Buslingthorpe Lane, Leeds 7, at about 8:30 P.M. Wednesday, 14th December 1977.

M.O. complainant Marilyn Moore, 25 years, a prostitute, was picked up by the below described man in Leopold Street, Leeds 7, and driven in his motor vehicle to waste land off Buslingthorpe Lane, in Scott Hall Street, where intercourse was to take place. This is a regular haunt of prostitutes plying their trade. When client refused to pay prior to intercourse she got out of the passenger side of the car. Whereupon the client also got out of the car on the driver's side. She was struck three times on the back of the head with a sharp, heavy instrument, causing severe lacerations and one depressed fracture of skull.

Complainant also suffered a severe laceration to left thumb, sustained when protecting head with hands. Complainant was knocked to the ground. Client then reversed vehicle and drove off.

Description of assailant: white male, 28 years. five feet six inches. Stocky build, dark wavy hair, medium-length beard with Jason King mustache.

Wearing: yellow shirt, navy blue or black zip-up parka, blue jeans. Said his name was Dave. Had what is believed to be a Liverpool accent. Driving a dark-colored motor car with a well kept dark-colored upholstery, manual gearbox, with some kind of box or similar object on window ledge in center of vehicle.

Suggestions as to identity of suspect to Incident Room, Millgarth St. Police Station please.

Complainant is detained in Ward 26, Leeds General Infirmary.

Condition is satisfactory.

Details of suspect not to be given to press at this stage.

The scene is being preserved and a fuller search carried out in daylight.

Crime K/11297/77 refers.

From the description of the car interior that Marilyn gave to the police, plus the tire marks her attacker had left behind, only a limited number of makes could possibly be in the frame. The hot favorites were a Morris Oxford Mark V four-door sedan or an Austin A55 Cambridge four-door sedan. Both models have what are called high tail fins. The probable date of manufacture of the car is between 1956 and 1962. In fact he was driving a Ford Corsair.

Marilyn Moore's injuries consisted of a depressed fracture on the left side of the head behind the ear, seven or eight lacerations, some nearly two inches long. There was also a four-inch laceration to her left hand and bruises to both hands. The neurosurgeon who operated was unable to say what instrument was used but told the police, "Considerable force would have been required."

X-ray examination indicated that the injuries could have been caused with her being hit on the head with a hammer-type instrument.

There was further damage too. Damage that cannot be ascertained by neurosurgery. In an echo of previous victims who had survived, Marilyn Moore said, "I can never, ever forget that night. For the first few months, all I could see when I closed my eyes was his face. Sometimes I wish that he had killed me, it might have almost been better than the nightmare he has left me."

If the police had a short list of vehicles, the descriptions of the attacker were disconcertingly at variance. Beards and mustaches can be grown or shaved off. More difficult is the ability to go from six foot to five foot seven or five foot two inches. How does one change from being Irish and forty to Liverpudlian and twenty-eight? To have tattoos and then not having them? From having puffed cheeks, yellow-stained teeth and a squashed nose to being "good-looking, with come-to-bed eyes." Pandora's box had been opened in the north of England. At no time have the police issued a composite sketch and stated, "This is the man." They have issued composites and artists' renderings of "men we would like to interview." The national press and television networks have frequently omitted that cautious qualification. After all, "This Is the Face of the Ripper" is far more dramatic.

Marilyn Moore was not the only prostitute who was disinclined to be very cooperative.

Hobson appealed for help and said, "Should any prostitute recognize the description and have been to the Buslingthorpe area with this man I would treat any information they give me with the strictest confidence. They need have no fear that I will use this information against them."

His plea for help fell on deaf ears as far as the women of Chapeltown were concerned. When your profession is by its nature against the law, when the very men who have arrested you and secured your imprisonment come asking for help, the inclination is not toward public duty. Even when it is a mass murderer being sought, even when that mass murderer has you and your friends marked down as potential victims, still the attitude remains largely hostile. This was a legacy of a law that declares that to solicit for the purposes of prostitution is a crime, a legacy of a practice emanating directly from the investigating police officers, of referring to the victims who were not on the game as innocent girls and those that were, merely as "prostitutes." Your sexual proclivity appears to determine which label the police and the press will fasten upon you, should you die at the hands of this man. Will there be an outcry and a feeling of outrage only if you are a virgin?

Even if a prostitute in one of these northern cities did feel like contacting the police, did feel she ought to help catch this man, there was often the problem of her pimp. The pimps in Leeds, Bradford, Manchester, Huddersfield, and other threatened cities took the view that it was better, far better, to let this man murder the odd whore than to get involved with the police. The supreme irony is that the function of the pimp is to protect the women who keep him in fine clothes and expensive cars. One man, one man with a ball peen hammer, a screwdriver and a few knives, one man who would look insignificant standing alongside some of those northern pimps, one man in his old cars, is living proof as many of his victims are dead, mute testimony, that the pimp is ineffectual, an unnecessary evil.

12

Most of the women on "the game" in Bradford in 1978 knew Yvonne Pearson. Several had paired up with her from time to time and worked the Lumb Lane district as a patrolling couple. One of her closest friends, a woman who worked alongside her, and who also drank with her in the predictable pubs between the predictable johns was Tina Atkinson.

After Tina's murder, Yvonne was particularly careful. She let everyone know that she carried in her handbag a lethal-looking pair of scissors. Yvonne also took other precautions. One of these was to vary her area. One week it might be Birmingham, the next London, the next Manchester. She worked on the premise that it was more difficult to hit a moving target.

Slim, with short-cut blond hair, in her early twenties she adopted a very professional approach to her occupation. Death had brushed past her when Tina had been murdered. It went close by again in November 1977 when call girl Jane McIntosh was murdered in a Bayswater hotel. Jane had moved south from Bradford because of the man with the hammer. She had urged Yvonne to do the same. From time to time Yvonne did just that, but she would always return north to her two children. Her

160

philosophy was, "You can get a nut in London just the same as you can in Bradford." In November 1977 Jane McIntosh gave that view even greater credibility when she was stabbed to death.

After the murder of a second close friend, Yvonne took even greater precautions. She was careful about which johns she went with. Careful about where she went with them. She had worked Chapeltown, had taken clients to Soldiers Field, Roundhay Park, the scene of Irene Richardson's murder, she had used the Gaiety and had met a newcomer to the ranks of the prostitutes in January 1976, a woman named Emily Jackson.

She had herself been attacked by a man in the Chapeltown area, who after hitting her, jumped into his car and drove away.

One of the precautions that she took was to take her clients home with her always. Even though acutely aware that two of her closest friends had been murdered inside, she reasoned that there was less chance of death inside. In that respect she was right.

In January 1978 she found herself in a trap. She was fearful of working as a prostitute because of the spate of murders, yet for two reasons she continued. First, there were her children. They had always been the best-dressed children on the street, always the children who never lacked for anything. Second, her pimp insisted that she continue to work. Continue to keep him in the manner that he preferred.

So she continued to pick up the johns.

The trap that Yvonne found herself enmeshed in during January 1978 had another aspect to it. She had been arrested and charged with soliciting. She was due to appear at Bradford Magistrate's Court to answer that charge on January 26. Fearful that she might suffer a further arrest if she returned with clients to her home, she resorted to the more dangerous and unpredictable car trade.

On January 21 she was living in a flat near Lumb Lane. That evening at nine-thirty she finished her drink in the Flying Dutchman and told a companion that she was going off "to earn some money." She vanished.

To Force Control for all divisions.
Police reports for publication.
ACC Crime ACC Western Area.

Murder Incident Room, Millgarth.

From Chief Supt C Division.

Missing from home, Yvonne Ann Pearson.

Although there is no evidence to suggest that harm may have befallen her she has been missing since 16:00 hours, Saturday, 21.1.78. After leaving an acquaintance looking after her two children (infant), she has not been in touch with home and this is said to be completely out of character.

On leaving home subject stated she intended to visit her mother at a Leeds address, and she would return before 1900 hours that day.

Enquiries reveal that subject has not been seen since Christmas 1977 by her mother.

Subject, a convicted prostitute, left home in possession of only train fare for Bradford to Leeds and stated that she expected her mother to provide her with some money.

Extensive enquiries in the Manningham area have failed to trace subject or any person who has seen her since she left home 21.1.78.

This woman is on bail to Bradford Magistrates Court, Thursday, 26.1.78 to answer a charge of soliciting for prostitution at Manningham. Conditions of bail are a curfew between 1900 hrs and 0700 hrs daily.

Enquiries reveal that she intended to attend court on 26.1.78 and had made tentative enquiries to arrange for the custody of her children in the event of her losing liberty, which tends to indicate that she had no intention of absconding. It is also known that she failed to keep an appointment with her defending solicitor A.M. Monday, 23.1.78.

Description:

Woman, white, born 2.2.56. Five feet five inches tall, slim build, short dyed hair (platinum blond). Wearing black turtleneck sweater, black slacks, green and black wavy-striped woollen jacket with wide sleeves, black shoes, no headgear and carried a small black handbag of the type which is carried under the arm (no handles).

It is emphasized that there is no evidence of foul play at

this stage but all the circumstances give some cause for concern.

Not to be released to the press.

Authorized by D.C.I. Wiseman.

Message ends.

24.1.78. Time now 2114 hours.

While the police showed some cause for concern, the press speculated. Had he struck again?

Subsequent investigation established that contrary to that teleprinter message she had indeed been seen after four o'clock on Saturday, January 21. She had shopped in Bradford. Returned home, asked her babysitter to stay on and had gone out to drown her impending sorrows with a friend. She fully intended to appear in court the following week. Equally she realized that as it was her third offense she faced a possible prison sentence; hence the tentative arrangements concerning her children's welfare. The clientele of the Flying Dutchman were very nearly the last to see her alive. She was seen shortly afterward on her pitch on the corner of Church Street and St. Mary's Road, Bradford. An acquaintance in a car saw a young Asian with a very fair complexion waving at someone. He looked and recognized the someone as Yvonne. He later described the Asian as five feet four inches tall, in his early twenties, with dark wavy hair, well groomed and smart. Whether the Asian subsequently crossed the road and talked to Yvonne remains speculation. He has never been traced.

The police search for the missing Yvonne gained momentum. Because of her London links it was thought possible that she might be in the capital. Despite her friends' and relations' assuring the police that it was unthinkable that Yvonne had deserted her children, the investigating officers rightly considered that it was a possibility. People have jumped bail when in far less jeopardy than Yvonne Pearson.

The press and TV were advised that there was nothing to connect her disappearance with the series of murders under investigation. The national media's reaction to this was to dismiss the woman's disappearance and to give the occurrence virtually no coverage at all. To their credit the local press, television, and radio gave the story significant exposure. At Yvonne's home her two children, Collette, aged two and a half, and Lorraine, aged five months, knew nothing of the sliding scale of media values. Despite the fact that a family friend initially cared for them, their distress at the absence of their mother grew daily more acute.

Definite sightings of Yvonne in London, Wolverhampton, and Bradford were found to be in error. The days since her disappearance crept into a week. An understaffed, overextended police force was about to be stretched even further.

In Huddersfield they speak with pride of their Choral Society, of the great days of the wool trade when the town held a premier position in the country, of their famous historic links dating back to Roman times. They are less forthcoming about Great Northern Street. If there is an afterlife and in that afterlife a hell, it may well be modeled on Great Northern Street.

An eighty-foot viaduct runs above the street carrying the main Leeds-to-Liverpool trains. At one end of the street there is a refuse dump, a short way from that a power station. A derelict school stands as a vandalized sentinel at the other end of the street. The public toilets in the street have been for many years a notorious pick-up point for prostitutes and male homosexuals. Close by that cattle market is another for four-legged animals. Opposite a woodyard is a slaughterhouse. There is a tripe works in the street. A dirty canal runs nearby, the pottery kilns and gasworks complete with a huge gas tank. Many of the houses are empty and vandalized. Nearby roads are not under city regulations and are badly maintained. Usually a dampness and a perpetual dripping from the viaducts can be heard. The road itself is scarred with potholes, while part of it is still cobblestoned. A modern Hogarth should put it all on canvas.

In this sordid place men and women sell their bodies and engage in what others call the act of love. Frequently they use the woodyard if they can find a space between the timber and the winos who sleep there.

On Tuesday, January 31, 1978, two of the prostitutes looking for business in Great Northern Street were Helen and Rita Rytka, attractive 18-year-old twins. At 9:10 P.M. Helen was picked up by

The many faces of the "Yorkshire Ripper." The media gave him a face for every day of the week. When newspapers published the composite picture *(bottom left)* and asserted it was the killer, A.C.C. George Oldfield attacked them bitterly. It is, however, rather an accurate likeness.

Wilma McCann, mother of four, on October 29, 1975 told her children she was "going to town again." At 10:30 p.m. she was at The Scotsman. The following morning her partially stripped body was found on a Leeds playing field.

Emily Jackson turned to prostitution because of mounting debts. Every evening she drove to the Gaiety public house, and while her husband sat at the bar, Emily sought clients in the nearby streets. On January 20, 1976, she met her last customer. The following morning her body was found, with over fifty stab wounds.

Irene Richardson, twenty-eight years old, mother of two children, unemployed and virtually homeless. Her body was discovered at the Soldiers Field, Leeds, on February 6, 1977. Yet another murder investigation was opened, led by the man nearest the camera, Detective Chief Superintendent James Hobson.

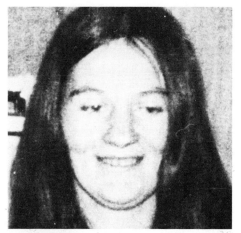

Patricia Tina Atkinson, last seen alive leaving the Carlisle Hotel in Bradford on April 23, 1977. The following evening her mutilated body was discovered in a middle-class apartment complex. No one had seen or heard anything to cause alarm.

Sixteen-year-old Jayne MacDonald walked to her death from a Leeds pub. Her body was later discovered by playing children in an "adventure playground."

Jean Jordan, also known as Jean Royle. Her murder should have resulted in the arrest of the killer.

Elena (Helen) Rytka, eighteen. Her twin sister Rita shows A.C.C. George Oldfield precisely where she last saw Helen alive in Great Northern Street, Huddersfield. While Rita waited for her sister to return, Elena was murdered less than fifty yards away.

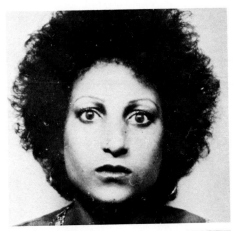

Murdered ten days before Helen Rytka, Yvonne Pearson was last seen a few minutes after leaving a Bradford pub. Her body remained undiscovered in nearby Arthington Street for over two months. During that time the murderer returned to the scene and shifted the body.

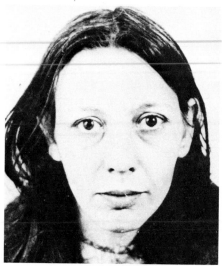

Vera Millward left her Manchester home on the evening of May 16, 1978. Investigating officers survey her body the following morning.

Josephine Whitaker, who was slaughtered while returning to her Halifax home. Her body was discovered in Saville Park on April 5, 1979. She was nineteen.

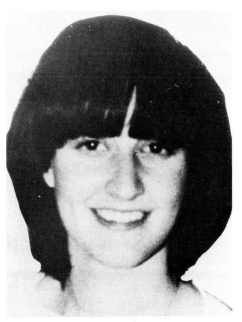

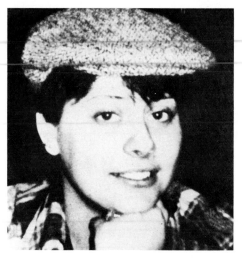

Barbara Leach, a twenty-year-old student who was murdered in Bradford on September 2, 1979.

Marguerite Walls, a forty-seven-year-old civil servant who was murdered in Farsley in August, 1980. James Hobson asserted that she was not killed by the mass murderer. He was wrong.

Jacqueline Hill, a twenty-year-old student who was murdered in Leeds in November, 1980.

a client in his car. A few minutes later Rita acquired a customer. After they had finished he returned Rita to Great Northern Street. The sisters had an arrangement that after each customer they would return to the spot and await the other's return before soliciting new business. Rita had returned to the rendezvous at 9:30 P.M. Helen was not there. Eventually after waiting for a while in the freezing cold, Rita returned to their room half-expecting to find Helen there. The sparse, dingy room was empty. After a bad night and an even worse morning, Rita, although reluctant to go to the police, felt she had little alternative. Neither of them had ever spent an entire night with a client. She knew it was foolish to worry; after all Huddersfield was nearly fifteen miles away from the nearest prostitute murder.

Rita hesitated. She reasoned that to go to the police and virtually admit that they had been soliciting prior to Helen's disappearance was tantamount to saying "please arrest me." If Helen were then to appear, a great deal of aggravation would have been suffered by both for no reason.

It was not until Thursday evening of February 2, that Rita notified the police of her missing sister. Now the West Yorkshire police had two missing prostitutes to find, Yvonne Pearson, last seen in Bradford, and Helen Rytka, last seen in Great Northern Street, Huddersfield.

At 3:10 P.M. on Friday afternoon a number of police officers, several with dogs, arrived at the woodyard in Great Northern Street. One of the dogs, unleashed, immediately found Helen Rytka.

The teleprinter signals had by now taken on a nightmare quality.

From ACC Crime, West Yorks.
To All Divisions and Road Traffic.
Area ACC's.
Area Chief Superintendents, C.I.D.
Copies to chief constables North Yorks, South Yorks, Humberside, Notts, Lincs, Derbyshire, Lancashire, Greater Manchester, Chester and Merseyside.
At 3:10 P.M. on Friday, 3rd February 1978, the naked

body of Helen Rytka born 3/3/59, a half-caste Jamaican
woman, was found partially concealed in a timber yard off
Great Northern Street, Huddersfield. The body had severe
injuries to the head with a blunt instrument and stab
wounds to the body. Neither instrument has been found. It
has not yet been established whether the deceased had
been subject to sexual interference.

The deceased, who was an active prostitute, had only
lived in Huddersfield for the past two months but it is
known that she took clients to the woodyard where her
body was found. She formerly lived in Bradford.

She was reported missing from home on the 2nd February, 1978, having been seen by her sister, also an active
prostitute, at 21:10 hours on Tuesday, 31st January, 1978,
in Great Northern Street, Huddersfield, at which time she
was seen to get into a dark blue colored sedan, possibly an
Audi 100LS, driven by a white male about 35 years of age
and of smart appearance. Attention is drawn to previous
offences of murder of prostitutes which have occurred in
the West Yorkshire metropolitan police area since 22/7/75,
details of which have been circulated in police reports 634,
case 1 (23/7/75—McGowan)
703-1 (31/10/75—McCann)
758-1 (21/1/76—Jackson)
1021-1 (6/2/77—Richardson)
1071-1 (24/4/77—Atkinson)
113-1 (26/4/77—McDonald)
1123-1 (10/7/77—Long)
1234-1 (14/12/77—Moore)

Attention is also drawn to West Yorkshire metropolitan
police criminal intelligence bulletin dated 9th May, 1977,
and police report 1189, case 1, dated 13/10/77, relating to
the murder of Jean Bernadette Jordan at Manchester.

It is urgently requested that special attention be paid to
the clothing of all persons coming into custody since the
31st January, 1978, as the clothing of the assailant may be
bloodstained. It is also requested that collators' records,
offense reports and traffic wardens' records be searched
and the details of any dark blue Audi 100 motor vehicles

which have come to notice during the past 12 months be passed to the Incident Room at Huddersfield Police Station. Telephone number Huddersfield 30955, extension 201, or Huddersfield 30955 and 31353.

It is especially requested that details of the injuries suffered by the victims in this series of attacks *should not be released to the press.*

Authorizing officer ACC (crime)

Message ends.

It is indicative of the pressure the police were now under that the above list of victims does not differentiate between prostitutes and nonprostitutes. It was clearly coming at the West Yorkshire police from all sides.

The addition of Mrs. Renee McGowan to the teleprinter list is particularly curious. The unsolved murder has never been publicly linked with the other crimes. Mrs. McGowan was found strangled, partly clothed, with her wrists tied behind her back on a bed in her high-rise flat in Bradford on July 23, 1975. Police stated at the coroner's inquest that they considered a possible motive was jealousy. A member of a Lonely Hearts Club in Bradford, fifty-five-year-old Renee had been planning marriage at the time of her murder. Why not include the murder of Debra Schlesinger, an eighteen-year-old woman found stabbed to death a few yards from her home in Leeds on April 22, 1977? The murder is still unsolved. Or the murder of Mrs. Mary Gregson, strangled on a canal towpath at Saltaire, Shipley, on August 30, 1977? Murder still unsolved. Or the murder of prostitute Barbara Booth and her three-year-old son, Alan, on January 7, 1976? Both murders still unsolved. Or the murder of Mary Judge, a forty-three-year-old prostitute found battered to death near Leeds Parish Church in 1970? Murder still unsolved. Exactly how many murderers are on the loose in Yorkshire?

George Oldfield and the men working with him moved into Huddersfield in droves. As always, the police were initially evasive or noncommittal. With snow falling heavily, the area was cordoned off, leaving the media outside the cordon to speculate as to exactly what was going on in the woodyard. They noted the arrival of

Oldfield, of Domaille, and subsequently the chief constable of Yorkshire, Ronald Gregory. Another arrival allowed through the cordon was Professor Gee, about to carry out an initial post mortem on the murder site. The following day at a packed press conference George Oldfield was in one of his less candid moods.

After telling the media of the circumstances leading up to Helen's disappearance he appealed via the press, television, and radio reporters to anyone who lived, worked, or who was in Great Northern Street area between 9:10 P.M. on January 31 and 3:10 P.M. on February 3, 1978, to get in touch with the police, whether or not they thought they might have seen something of significance. He told them of the client in the Datsun who had taken Rita off at 9:10 P.M. and gave his audience a description of the man. He advised the media, "As yet the post mortem has not been completed but we hope this will be done later today by Professor Gee."

In fact Gee had completed his initial post mortem on the murder site on the previous evening. There was little doubt in his mind or in the minds of the men who watched him, who was responsible for the murder of Helen.

At his morning press conference on the following day, Oldfield continued, "The indications at present are such that I cannot discount the possibility that the man we are looking for is the one responsible for other similar attacks."

That same reluctance on the part of the police to be totally honest with the press and public is a hallmark of this entire investigation. Previously, invaluable time had been lost from Tuesday, January 31 to Thursday February 2 while Rita Rytka wondered and worried what to do. Now, on Saturday the fourth, more time was being lost.

Helen's body had been found naked with the exception of a brassiere, a sweater, and a pair of socks. It was partly concealed under a pile of timber.

The post mortem revealed that she had received five blows to the head, caused by a hammer-type instrument. There were multiple stab wounds to the abdomen.

None of these details were given to the media. Nor were the reporters told that Helen had not died where her body had been found. She had been attacked and murdered ten yards away.

Either on the next night or the night after, her murderer had returned and carried her to the place of concealment. Marks on the dead girl's body clearly showed that he had worn rubber gloves to move the body.

The Sunday press had to content itself with HAS THE RIPPER STRUCK AGAIN?

Memories dim quickly. People leave areas, even countries, in that space of time.

If Rita had reported her sister's disappearance on Tuesday, the murderer would almost certainly have driven into a police road-block upon his return to the scene. How did he know that it was safe to come back and move the body? Was it luck or knowledge? It was a question that occupied the senior officers a great deal.

While the hunt for Yvonne Pearson was stepped up, the murder incident room at Huddersfield was working a twenty-four-hour day. If the client who had driven off with Helen while her sister watched at 9:10 P.M. was not the killer, the need to find him was just as desperate. He should know how long he had spent with the murdered woman, should know what time he had returned her to her beat.

Equally urgent was the hunt for the man who had then taken Rita off. He would at least be able to confirm the time he dropped her back. He might also have other vital information.

The sisters had operated their own security plan, which did not merely entail going back to the rendezvous and awaiting the other one. They agreed that their clients would get only twenty minutes. So in theory, if both left at more or less the same time, both should return simultaneously.

On January 31, 1978, the security plan had gone horribly wrong. Helen's 9:10 john was traced. He had returned her to the spot at 9:25. Five minutes later, when Rita had returned, her sister had gone. In those bare five minutes the killer had appeared out of the dark and persuaded Helen to go with him. A few minutes and Rita would have seen him. Would have noted his license number. At a moment between 9:25 A.M. and 9:40 P.M. while Rita stood just a few yards away, Helen was murdered.

On the morning of Thursday, February 2 a driver delivering

timber to Garrard's woodyard found a pair of women's panties. They were blood-stained. They were hung on a fence to "give the lads a bit of a laugh." On the same morning, the foreman, Cyril Emmerson, noticed a bloodstained piece of plastic on the ground. This was the spot where Helen had been murdered. Demonstrably, then, the killer had returned on the evening of Wednesday, February 1, and hidden the body.

Neither bloodstained panties nor bloodstained plastic had stimulated any unease in the men in the woodyard. It speaks volumes about what passes for the norm in Great Northern Street.

George Oldfield drove himself and the people working under him hard, very hard. The cost of the investigation into this series of murders had already reached awesome proportions by the early months of 1978. Over half a million man-hours had been worked, over forty three thousand people interviewed, statements taken from over eleven thousand, one hundred and twenty thousand vehicles checked. There had been over sixteen thousand house-to-house checks. In fiscal terms the investigation had already cost over one million pounds. In human terms the cost was incalculable.

Oldfield had begun to build a greenhouse in his garden at about the time Anna Rugolskyj had been attacked in mid-1975. Now, in February 1978, the half-completed greenhouse lay long forgotten as he worked on average a fourteen-hour day. If the quality of the information he provided the news media was heavily edited he nevertheless made himself freely available to journalists. By now the murders were gaining a worldwide notoriety. One night after collapsing into his bed he was awakened by yet another reporter.

In answering his questions Oldfield grew somewhat terse, but checked the impatience when he remembered he was being broadcast live via an Australian radio station. On call twenty-four hours a day, working a seven-day week, he dramatically demonstrated his commitment to his own words.

"I am determined to get this man. I only hope we get him before he can strike again."

If the majority of the victims had not been prostitutes—had been Sunday school teachers or schoolgirls or nuns or men—then public outrage would have swept the country, but as Oldfield observed, "The public couldn't care less about the fate of these prostitutes."

It was difficult, damned difficult to persuade the prostitutes' clientele, shuffling, furtive johns, to come forward. Petrified that their little night excursions might become known to their families, they hid behind their front doors and doubtless lamented the state of the country's morals. And while these men kept their own counsel, he was still at large. The man with the ball peen hammer, screwdrivers, and knives was in effect being given a seal of approval by the silent "don't want to get involved" brigade.

Even while the police were still camped in Great Northern Street, the prostitutes returned. The oldest profession in the world dies hard.

Oldfield had to fight a long uphill battle as he sought evidence. His appeal to all people who were in the area between 9:10 P.M. on Tuesday and 3:10 P.M. on Friday to come forward, fell largely on deaf ears. It might possibly have produced some results if he had asked all people to come forward who were in the area on the night *previous* to the murder. Clearly the man responsible does his homework. Clearly he visits each potential murder scene a number of times before he strikes.

Terry Hawkshaw, the taxi driver from Drighlington who had previously been shadowed, interviewed, and house-searched was pulled in again. Carloads of police emulating Starsky and Hutch descended on Hawkshaw's home at seven o'clock one morning.

Questioning him at the police station, Oldfield again stated, "Look, I know you are the Ripper. Why don't you confess?"

Unfortunately for Oldfield and fortunately for Hawkshaw, he had an ironclad alibi for the night Helen Rytka was murdered. The police had been so convincing that they even had Hawkshaw himself wondering if he had a "Jekyll and Hyde" personality.

On February 6 Oldfield was relieved to hear that Yvonne Pearson had been seen in London; the sighting, however, was not confirmed. While most available personnel were fully occupied investigating the murder of Helen Rytka, other officers were still attempting to locate Yvonne Pearson.

The murder incident room at Huddersfield police headquarters began to resemble Greenwich laboratory as large cards breaking down the time between eight and midnight into fifteen-minute sections were pinned to the walls. All the cards showed a large blow-up of the Great Northern Street area. Colored tickets on the cards represented sightings of either people or vehicles at salient times. The hundred detectives assigned to this particular investigation were broken into teams, each with specific lines of inquiry to follow up. Any new lead, every scrap of information, was fed back into this incident room. Gradually the large cards began to fill with colored tickets. A john here was traced. A passing truck driver there came forward. Upstairs the police sports bar and club was packed with pressmen. On the murder site itself police generators hummed as the floodlights relieved the wintry gloom.

Posters showing the face of Helen superimposed on the body of Rita wearing identical clothes to those worn by her sister on that fatal night stared sightlessly from a thousand sites. The posters—in English, Punjabi, and Urdu—appealed for information.

The media began to show a frenetic interest in the surviving twin, Rita. Research indicated to the waiting reporters that if they could not fill the airtime and pages with pertinent facts about the murder, there was considerable mileage in the previous histories of the Rytka girls. They begged, demanded and cajoled Oldfield in their attempts to get interviews with Rita. Oldfield was equally adamant that in the early days of the investigation no one was getting to the girl. She was a key witness, and further, the man responsible for her sister's death might, in the view of the police, return to murder the surviving sister. Frustrated at not getting the Rytka story on a plate, some of the reporters left the police bar and ventured out in search of details.

Born of a Jamaican father and an Italian mother who subsequently had another set of twins, Helen and Rita were put under official outside care at a very early age—four months—when their parents separated. After five years they were back home, then after a further five years went back to outside care again. Helen, whose name was Elena but who preferred the less exotic version was, so her mother told reporters, "Always my favorite daughter. She would always come to talk to me and tell me her problems. She cared for me and I cared for her." That must have done wonders for the petrified Rita's morale in the days shortly after her sister had been murdered.

A school friend recalled Helen's "love of dancing." It made a human-interest story. A previous employer described her as "a nice kid," referring to the time when she had worked in a Heckmondwike candy factory. The headlines those articles produced were in odd contrast with:

SEX DIARY SHOCK. RIPPER MURDER SQUAD CHECK LIST OF LOVERS.

And

RIPPER SLAYS TOWN PROSTITUTE.

By now the circus was well under way. The factual story of the Rytka girls was too poignant, too important, to need tarted-up headlines. To trivialize the life of the girl in this manner was to insult the dead.

Having been rejected by their stepfather, all four Rytka children found themselves in a children's home, St. Theresa's in Knaresborough. Four children of multiracial parentage, the nuns discovered, were not what potential foster parents were seeking.

In May 1974 the then fifteen-year-old twins read a series of articles in the Yorkshire *Post*. The articles dealt with adoption and foster parents. Rita wrote to the newspaper.

I am a child in care and have been for twelve years. If my twin sister and I got fostered out together it would be like winning £1,000 in the football pools. But money is not involved, LOVE is.

I have enclosed a poem called "Lonely and Unloved" just to give you a good idea of what it is like to be lonely and unloved. I did not sit down for hours on end composing this poem, but I just wrote it down, changing only a few words to make it rhyme. I wrote it not from my head, but from my heart, because only from the heart can the feeling of loneliness be expressed and only from the heart can the feelings of being unloved lie deep within.

To get fostered out together means to us a place of love and care and it is then that you feel wanted, because someone somewhere realizes what love really is and to get fostered out is part of love itself.

We can only wait, hope and pray to get fostered out together, but someday I hope we will.

*   *   *

One verse was a grimly accurate prophecy of what lay waiting in a Huddersfield woodyard.

> No one cares if I was lured
> Lured into the deepest hole
> Cast aside by those so cruel
> And treated like a mule.

Shortly afterward those prayers were answered. The two girls were given a home by a married couple living in Dewsbury. For two years they had a healthy, normal, happy home life in an ideal environment. At eighteen years of age they no longer fell under local authority. The girls were free to go and do what they wanted. Within nine months of leaving a home full of warmth and love they were in Huddersfield, patrolling Great Northern Street and selling to the johns what passes for warmth and love in that area.

Oldfield kept the press away from Rita for over a week but, necessity being the mother of a great many things other than invention, two freelance reporters persuaded the police to pass on a note they had written to Rita. Essentially it was a request for a new poem. Rita obliged and the result was duly published in the *Sunday Mirror.* One verse ran:

> In innocence she lived,
> In innocence she tried,
> In innocence she walked the streets
> Simply to survive,
> In innocence she died.

Whatever the general public thought of this form of journalism, the rest of Fleet Street were not amused. They hadn't got the poem. Reporters redoubled their efforts to get an interview with Rita. Eventually Oldfield agreed. It was announced on Saturday, February 11, 1978, that there would be a press conference the next day and that the reporters would be able to question the surviving sister.

The Catholic church felt that enough was already far too much. The church had been responsible for the girls during their time in care. There was little they could now do for Helen, but clearly they considered Rita was in need of further protection. Having kept the media dangling for nearly two weeks, George Oldfield now discovered that there is a higher authority even than that of assistant chief constable.

The church instructed a Dewsbury lawyer, and acting on those instructions he made it plain to Oldfield that under no circumstances was the church going to be a party to the exploitation of Rita.

The wrangling continued on the Sunday selected; indeed, the press conference was delayed for forty minutes while Oldfield pleaded with both the lawyer and a representative of the church's children's protection society. Ultimately it was agreed that Rita would read a short prepared statement and that the photographers could have their fill.

All of this was going on in the middle of the biggest manhunt England has ever known. It was going on while the mutilated remains of Helen Rytka lay unburied. It was going on while Rita and the other members of the Rytka family were in shock.

In her prepared statement Rita expressed the hope that "the public would not forget Helen. I am helping the police all I can and I hope that the public will do likewise."

Rita's hopes have been in vain. Both press and public have forgotten her sister. She has become a mere statistic, one face in a macabre gallery. Yesterday's news, it seems, is no news at all.

The police continued to make headway with the investigation. Oldfield was acutely aware that this was the closest he had yet come to catching his quarry. Again headlines informed readers of the "Net Closing on Ripper." This time the headlines had a measure of credibility.

The massive effort initially reduced the search to 104 vehicles and 118 people who were seen in the area between 8:00 P.M. and 9:45 P.M. The numbers began to fall. Clients were traced. Those who desired to remain uninvolved found themselves involved. Despite the massive publicity that this particular murder had been given by press, television and radio, the public response was never overwhelming, just a steady trickle. But trickles do eventually fill the cup.

The Yorkshire *Post* and its sister newspaper the *Evening Post*

offered £5,000 reward for information leading to the conviction of
the murderer of Helen Rytka. Local businessmen offered to
double it to £10,000. This was in response to the initial Home
Office refusal to approve a £10,000 reward from public funds—
they considered the sum "far too high."

The public responded with over six hundred phone calls and a
hundred letters within a week, all claiming to have "vital
information."

Oldfield went onto "The Jimmy Young Show" and between the
pop and the corn appealed to the public.

Prostitutes discovered they could earn more money being
interviewed than intimate. Reporters hastily scribbled down their
innermost thoughts for consideration at the nation's breakfast
tables.

Through all of this, missing pieces were being found and put
into place. Vital seconds were being eliminated from the crucial
time. By February 25, Oldfield knew he was on the brink. He had
actually succeeded in reducing the key time to "a minute or two."
A witness who drove his car along Great Northern Street twice
between 9:25 and 9:30 had seen Helen standing by the toilets.
Rita had arrived back at their rendezvous very shortly after 9:30.
She had missed her sister by seconds. From over one hundred
vehicles the police had reduced the list to four.

The list of 118 people that had to be traced and eliminated was
also reduced to four. It was at this stage, with the investigation at
its height that Oldfield received the disconcerting news that the
sister of the late Jayne MacDonald, sixteen-year-old Debra, was
missing from her Leeds home. For two days he lived with the
nightmare thought that while he had kept a twenty-four hour
watch on one victim's sister another's had been murdered. To his
relief she was discovered alive and well with her boyfriend in
Blackpool.

Oldfield got back to the main item on the agenda.

From ACC (crime)
To All Divisions and Road Traffic, Area ACCs, Area Chief
Superintendents, C.I.D.
Copies to Chief Constables North Yorkshire, South York-
shire, Humberside, Nottinghamshire, Lincolnshire, Der-

byshire, Lancashire, Greater Manchester, Cheshire, Merseyside.

Murder of Helen Rytka at Huddersfield between 31 January and 3 February 1978.

It is now desired to trace urgently the driver of a white Datsun sedan 160B or 180B model which is alleged to have been driven from Great Northern Street into Hillhouse Lane, Huddersfield, about 9:30 P.M. on 31 January 1978 by the following described man, with a half-caste female passenger who could have been the deceased.

The description of the driver of the Datsun car is as follows. 45 years of age, clean shaven, sallow complexion, sunken cheeks. Fair or graying hair, combed forward and cut with fringe over forehead, fairly long at sides over ears.

Wearing light colored jacket, shirt and tie, wristwatch on left hand. A composite photograph of the man will be published in reports.

It is also desired to trace and identify the following vehicles and drivers which are said to have been seen in Great Northern Street, Huddersfield, between 9:30 and 9:40 P.M. on 31 January 1978.

1. Morris Oxford sedan motor car series 6, believed dark green in color. Registered between 1962 and 1971, suffix letters up to "J".

2. Ford Cortina MK 1 sedan white or light pastel color. Registered between 1962 and 1966, suffix letters up to "D."

3. A Datsun 160B or 180B sedan mid-blue color.

Forces may consider keeping observations in areas known to be frequented by prostitutes and maintaining an index of the registered numbers of cars seen curb-cruising. Such an index has proved invaluable in the present investigation in tracing males, and their vehicles, who have been using prostitutes.

From such an index all clients of the deceased's sister for the 31st January 1978 have been traced and eliminated from the enquiry, including one refusal. Also the last known client of the deceased that night has been traced and eliminated. It has also proved advantageous for prostitutes to be encouraged to note the registered numbers of

vehicles used by their clients. Should forces set up indexes
of vehicles curb-cruising in their area on the lines suggested, it is asked that details of Morris Oxfords series 6,
Ford Cortinas Mk 1 and Datsuns, white 180B and mid-blue
160B, be passed immediately to the Incident Room at
Huddersfield. Suggestions regarding the identity of the
man referred to above would also be appreciated.
    Message ends.

To reduce the list of potential vehicles to four was a remarkable
achievement, particularly when one is aware that Rita's information concerning the cars that both sisters got into at 9:10 P.M. was
hopelessly inaccurate and the witness who saw one of the Datsuns
referred to was color-blind, which was not established until
sometime afterward. Whatever the color of this car, the "white"
Datsun driver has never come forward. This may not be significant
in view of what happened when George Oldfield released the
police composite to the press and television reporters. The man
was wanted merely for the purposes of elimination, no more. If the
composite is an accurate representation, this man must have got a
considerable shock when on February 28 newspaper after newspaper throughout Great Britain carried the image with captions
that read FACE OF THE RIPPER and IS THIS THE FACE OF THE
RIPPER? Admitting to being a john is one thing; admitting to being
a mass murderer is something else.
    The owner of the blue Datsun also vanished into the hills.
Known to local prostitutes as Joey, or Joy, he was a regular
customer. Aged about 47, graying hair on which he sometimes
used cream, height five feet ten inches, he was believed to live in
the Huddersfield area. Joey has subsequently been traced and
eliminated.
    Police considered the most significant sighting that of the Morris
Oxford seen parked by the toilets in Great Northern Street at 9:30.
    Its owner was also seen lurking in the shadows of a woodyard.
He quickly turned his face into the shadows as a car went by, but
he was not quite quick enough.
    The description the witness gave was: "He was aged about
thirty, medium build, five feet eight inches tall, wearing a dark
jacket and trousers."

He was also seen by three other people in the area between 8:15 P.M. and 10:00 P.M. Still he had lingered, waited his chance. He had been particularly interested in the Rytka sisters. Shortly before 9:30 P.M. he had approached Helen. They had entered the woodyard. Five minutes later Helen Rytka was dead.

Helen was buried in Bradford, after a Requiem Mass at St. Anthony's Catholic Church. The date of her funeral was March 9, six days after what would have been her nineteenth birthday.

He was restless. Unable to relax, he paced the floor. He returned to the table and, standing, poured out a cup of tea. Stirring the two spoons of sugar, he felt the anger rising from within. He had followed through the press and television and radio the police investigation of Helen Rytka's death. He had laughed when he read that the net was closing in on him. He'd found that bit funny over the years. Now in early March 1978, when he should have felt a peace, there was within him an energy that desired him to take some form of action.

As he paced the room once more he relived the interview he had had with the two police officers about the fiver. If only they had known. He stopped stock-still in the room.

He had the answer. He wanted to give the police a little present. Something to help them in their work. And he knew exactly what that something should be.

He walked out of the room, down the hall and into the kitchen. Opening the cupboards beneath the sink, he carefully moved the variety of tins and boxes of floor polish and cleaning agents. After a moment he found them. The pair of rubber gloves. Unrolling them, he recalled the last time he had worn them, the night after he had murdered Helen Rytka.

He remembered how on the previous evening he had stood in the woodyard and watched the pair of them parading up and down the street, watched as they had both been picked up just after nine o'clock. As he waited for one of them to return, cars continually went by, some cruising, some members of the public bent on less exotic entertainment. It was more like Piccadilly Circus than a quiet backwater of Huddersfield. Despite the cold he had begun to sweat, begun to wonder if he had picked the right place.

He had rechecked the woodyard where he intended to bring the first of the two who returned to the rendezvous. There was the entrance and over near the back of the yard broken fencing, beyond that the land beyond led under the viaducts. On the other side a mere hundred yards farther on was the Bradford Road. The spot he had chosen was perfect from that point of view. Two exits.

After he had killed Helen he'd been disturbed by another john who was on the prowl. Quickly he had vanished into the dark, but he hadn't liked the idea of leaving her near-naked body out on the cold ground. Hence the rubber gloves.

On the next night, Wednesday, February 1, he had returned to the woodyard. The johns, the cruising customers, the prostitutes were all still there. Couldn't see that other half-caste girl, though. He knew he could have been walking into a trap, but he had to take that enormous risk of discovery. He returned to the body. It was exactly as he had left it. Putting on the rubber gloves, he had moved her to somewhere decent. Somewhere out of sight.

As he recalled all this the excitement within him flowered. An index finger played over the distinctive pimpled pattern on the palms and lower finger joints. He traced his finger along the ribbed linear longitudinal patterns on the fingertips and thumbs. The excitement within him grew even more intense. He smiled at the thought of what he intended to do—return to the still undiscovered body of Yvonne Pearson.

On March 10, 1978, a letter postmarked Sunderland and addressed to George Oldfield arrived on the Chief Constable's desk. It read:

Dear Sir

I am sorry I cannot give my name for obvious reasons. I am the Ripper. I've been dubbed a maniac by the Press but not by you, you call me clever and I am. You and your mates haven't a clue that photo in the paper gave me fits and that bit about killing myself, no chance. I've got things to do. My purpose to rid the streets of them sluts. My one regret is that young lassie McDonald, did not know cause changed routine that nite. Up to number 8 now you say 7 but remember Preston '75, get about you know. You were right I travel a bit. You probably look for me in Sunderland, don't bother, I am not daft, just posted letter there on one of my trips. Not a bad place compared with Chapeltown and Manningham and other places. Warn whores to keep off streets cause I feel it coming on again.

Sorry about young lassie.

Yours respectfully
Jack the Ripper

Might write again later I not sure last one really deserved it. Whores getting younger each time. Old slut next time I hope. Huddersfield never again, too small close call last one.

Forensic tests established that the writer had taken care to avoid fingerprints. The paper outside the margins had been cut off after the letter was written and there was no trace of fingerprints on the page or the envelope.

Crank letters. Lunatic communications. Claims to be the mass murderer, none of these were a new experience in this investigation. In the first four weeks after Helen Rytka had been murdered, the Huddersfield incident room had received nearly two hundred anonymous telephone calls and over fifty anonymous letters. Just one comment in the letter stopped the police from putting it in the "nutters" file. The reference to Preston '75.

The odd similarities between the murder of Joan Harrison and some of the victims in Yorkshire had already been noted.

Alert, therefore, to the possibility that the person hunted by Lancashire and Yorkshire police were one and the same, the reference in the letter to Preston '75 gave the West Yorkshire police food for thought. How could the letter writer have linked the Preston murder with the others unless he was responsible? The answer was, very easily. In an article in the Yorkshire *Post* dated March 9, 1977, the following appeared. It was a quote from Chief Superintendent Jim Hobson.

"We are also following up a possible link with a similar type of murder in Preston in November 1975, when a prostitute was found stabbed to death in the town center."

That article appeared almost exactly one year before the letter was sent to the police.

There is in fact a curious mistake in that quote from Hobson. Joan Harrison was not found "stabbed to death." She had been struck on the head with what first was thought to be a shoe heel and later considered to be consistent with a "hammer-type instrument." All her other injuries were consistent with violent kicking. There was not a single stab wound. Now, the murderer would know that. Why, when writing a gloating letter to George Oldfield claiming responsibility for that murder, did the letter writer not give a detail or two that only he could know?

A further possibility that the letter writer had gleaned his information about the murder of Joan Harrison being linked with the others was a report in the *Daily Mirror* of April 12, 1977 that told its readers that the West Yorkshire police were exploring the possibility of a connection.

The pros and cons were tossed back and forth by the detectives. The debate was still raging when the Northern editor of the *Daily Mirror* contacted the West Yorkshire police. He told them that he had received a letter purporting to come from "Jack the Ripper," which was duly sent to George Oldfield. Like the first, it had been posted in Sunderland, this time on March 13, 1977, five days after the first. It was quickly established that both letters came from the same hand. It read:

Dear Sir

I have already written to Chief Constable George Oldfield "a man I respect" concerning the recent ripper murders. I told him and I am telling you to warn them whores I'll strike again and soon when heat cools off. About the MacDonald lassie, I didn't know that she was decent and I am sorry I changed my routine that night. Up to murder 8 now you say seven but remember Preston '75. Easy picking them up don't even have to try you think they're learn but they don't. Most are young lassies, next time try older one I hope. Police haven't a clue yet and I don't leave any I am very clever and don't look for me up there in Sunderland cause I not stupid just passed through the place not a bad place compared with Chapeltown and Manningham. Can't walk the streets for them whores. Don't forget warn them I feel it coming on again. If I get chance sorry about lassie I didn't know.

Yours respectfully
Jack the Ripper

Might write again after another week gone maybe Liverpool
or even Manchester again To hot here in Yorkshire. Bye.
I have given advance warning so its yours and their fault.

The view within the police ranks at that time was divided.
Some considered the letters a hoax, others were convinced they
were genuine.

Less than two weeks later the West Yorkshire Police found the
woman they had been seeking for two months.

From ACC Crime, West Yorks Met Pol, Bradford
To CC South Yorks
CC North Yorks
CC Greater Manchester
CC Lancs County
CC Humberside
CC Derbyshire
Police Reports
AT 12 noon Sunday, 26th March, 1978, the body of
Yvonne Ann Pearson, 22 years, a convicted prostitute, was
found secreted under an old settee on waste ground off
Arthington Street Bradford.
A post mortem has been carried out by David Gee and
death was due to massive head injuries possibly caused by
a heavy blunt instrument. It is thought that death occurred
some weeks ago and the body is partially decomposed. The
dead woman was living with a friend off Lumb Lane,
Bradford, until 21st January 1978, when she left home
saying she was going away for a few days. (She was in fact
due to appear before Bradford Magistrates Court on 26.1.78
on a charge of soliciting for prostitution.)
On 23.1.78 Pearson was reported as missing from home
and in view of the recent state of prostitute murders a
large-scale search was carried out and enquiries made
regarding her whereabouts, all of which proved negative.
There have been no positive sightings of Pearson from her
being reported missing until the discovery of her body.
It is probable that the clothing of the assailant will be
heavily bloodstained and it is requested that laundries and

dry cleaners be checked for the period from 21st January to 3rd February 1978 inclusive.

It is thought from the pattern of the injuries that this death is *not connected* with the other circulated prostitute murders publicly referred to as the "Ripper Murders."

An Incident Room has been set up at the police H.Q., the Tyrls, Bradford. Telephone Bradford 23422 exts 219 and 686.

Orig: D/Supt Lapish
Message ends.

For the pimp who had forced her to continue prostituting herself despite her fear, there would be no more pound notes put in his hand by Yvonne. Her "protector" would have to seek out other women to exploit.

For two small children who had waited for her return, there would be no mother.

For Yvonne, a bright, vivacious, intelligent young woman, life had been snuffed out. With less concern than a normal person would show at running over a dog, her murderer had quite literally smashed her to death.

Yvonne had left the Flying Dutchman at 9:30 P.M. on Saturday, January 21, 1978. Her last words to her friend were, "I'm going to earn some money." She had walked to the corner of Church Street and, standing exactly where her friend Tina Atkinson had stood on the last night of her life, had met her first client. He was also her last. By 10:00 P.M. she lay dead on a piece of waste ground near Arthington Street. Her killer had hidden her body under an abandoned settee. He had then piled grass sods and debris over the settee. But he had not erected this grim mound immediately after the murder. When her body was discovered her left arm was entangled in the springs of the settee, indicating that he had placed it on her body after rigor mortis had set in, a period of at least four hours after death. For over two months the remains of Yvonne Pearson had lain there. While children played close by, while people went in and out of the nearby Woolpack pub, while workers clocked on and off at the Punjab Cloth House, Mesra Textiles, Iqbal Knitwear, Rai Cloth, while immigrants negotiated loans at the Kalyal Finance Co. and while the newsagents across the road had sold papers that told of her disappearance and then of Helen Rytka's murder, while mundane daily life went on, a mother of two children lay and rotted under an old couch.

Many weeks after she had been murdered her killer returned to the scene and lifted the couch to survey what he had done. Yet again he moved the body. A copy of the *Daily Mirror*, dated February 21, was found under the right-hand side of the body. It could not have blown there. It had been deliberately placed there, then the body moved on top of it.

She was discovered by a passerby who saw her right arm protruding from the couch. The post mortem revealed massive head injuries probably caused by a boulder. He had then jumped on her chest, causing broken ribs, which ruptured the liver. There were no stab wounds. Her brassiere had been pulled above her breasts and her panties pulled down to the pubic region. Her slacks which had been removed were found under her body. She had been killed some distance away from where she was found. He had then dragged her by her collar to the settee. Her handbag and its contents were found not far away, but after two months it was impossible to establish if the murderer had taken anything. Toddling children or the casual passerby might easily have wandered away with some of her possessions.

Detective Chief Superintendent Lapish, the man in charge of this particular murder investigation, displayed extreme caution when questioned by reporters. While the newspapers ran headlines linking the murder to "The Ripper," Lapish took an agnostic position. It seemed to him even less likely to be one of the series of murders when Professor Gee had reported his findings. Smashing women on the head with very heavy boulders was not part of the pattern that had been established. *The Guardian* headlined, RIPPER IS "CLEARED" OF NEW MURDER BY POST MORTEM.

This inevitably led to speculation that she had been murdered by someone attempting to emulate the mass murderer. As Lapish observed, "We did have a fellow who set out to beat the Black Panther's record." This was a reference to Mark Rowntree, who immediately after the Black Panther's arrest stabbed four people to death.

As the investigation progressed, Lapish and his colleagues

continued to assert that this death was not the work of the mass murderer. But they knew that over in Preston, Joan Harrison had also died without knife wounds, had also been kicked brutally. They also knew that the displacement of Yvonne's brassiere and panties had occurred in at least five of the series of deaths. Contrary to popular myth, this man did not leave a unique mark on every victim. He did not kill in precisely the same way each time.

Part of the reluctance of the Bradford police to admit the strong possibility that Yvonne was a victim of the mass murderer was apprehension at the public's reaction to the knowledge that he had murdered twice within the space of ten days: Yvonne Pearson on January 21, 1978, Helen Rytka on January 31, 1978.

Yet again the police faced the task of finding the dead woman's regular customers. From Yvonne's address book it was established that they were seeking over thirty-six clients who were regulars. Lapish warned, "Come and see us, before we come and see you."

Some did. Most didn't. Like the investigating officers before him, the detective superintendent was confronted with a wall of silence. An attitude of indifference. While her colleagues and friends continued to solicit business within yards of the murder site the police attempted to make progress with an investigation that was two months old before they started. It was an impossible task, made more difficult by the mobility of the victim. Yvonne had worked the circuit in so many towns from Glasgow to Southampton. Like most prostitutes, she had been shrewd enough to move from a town after two convictions. A third normally means imprisonment. Moving to a new town and using a different name is one way the women retain their liberty. Each town where Yvonne had worked had to be checked, prostitutes in a dozen cities questioned, all in an attempt to find the most difficult and dangerous of murderers, the random killer.

Police officers had to be drafted from other areas because of the enormous strain on the West Yorkshire police. Incident rooms were now going full blast in Huddersfield, Bradford, and Leeds. In an attempt to find the murder weapon used on Yvonne the police moved nearly a ton of stones to the forensic laboratories.

Police carefully examined the file on yet another unsolved murder, that of twenty-year-old Carol Wilkinson. She too had been battered to death with a boulder or coping stone. Police admitted publicly that the two murders had disconcerting similarities. Carol had been murdered in the same city in November 1977.

Like Yvonne Pearson, Carol Wilkinson had also been so badly battered about the head and face that identification was effected only with great difficulty. Carol's father was able to identify his daughter by the engagement ring her fiancé had given her the previous year.

The major differences between the two murders were that Carol worked as a salesclerk in a bakery and that she had been murdered at nine o'clock in the morning. At first the police had feared that Carol was a victim of the mass murderer. They dropped that view very early in their investigation and considered that the respectable young woman had, like Yvonne Pearson, been murdered by "someone else."

The confusion and doubt surrounding these two murders—police confusion and doubt, that is—warrants very close examination, particularly in view of subsequent events with regard to both murders. And particularly in view of the fact that there is a young man serving a life sentence for the murder of Carol Wilkinson.

Police beliefs on exactly who did and who did not kill particular persons are sometimes alarmingly flexible. On April 1978, the *Daily Express* reporter, having talked to George Oldfield, had a headline front-page story: 9 TIMES A KILLER. MORE VICTIMS AS MURDER HUNT POLICE SAY: THERE IS NO COPYCAT.

Lapish told the press later the same day that he had spoken to George Oldfield, who had told him, "I've been misquoted, in fact I told the *Express* I was still keeping an open mind on the Pearson murder."

Subsequently the murder of Yvonne Pearson has always appeared in the list of killings attributed to the mass murderer.

Should the murder of Carol Wilkinson also appear in that list?

As the police investigation into Yvonne's murder began to falter against a wall of suspicion and indifference it became clear to the investigating officers that some basic monitoring work would have to be done in the future.

*　　*　　*

From Detective Chief Superintendent Hobson for ACC Crime.

To All Divisions, West Yorks Met Police.

Officer in charge of Incident Rooms at Leeds, Huddersfield, Bradford.

Also for information of Deputy Chief Constable.

The series of murders in the force area currently being investigated have all occurred in places where prostitutes have taken their clients for intercourse. Divisional officers should identify streets or spare ground in their divisions where prostitutes actively frequent for this purpose. Usually it is a cul-de-sac or spare ground not overlooked by houses. Officers of divisional vice squads are usually aware of these places. A full list should be available in each division and divisional officers should ensure such places are visited daily, repeat daily, particularly late evening time. A daily log should be kept at each division and reports of all clients' cars seen at these spots forwarded to the respective area incident room at Leeds, Bradford, or Huddersfield. Incident Room staff will examine files currently held and all such places mentioned in prostitutes' statements will be sent to the respective divisional officer to enable him to prepare a comprehensive list as outlined.

Message ends.

It had taken nearly three years before this very basic, fundamental, and obvious action was initiated.

Yvonne Pearson, like the eighteen-year-old who had died at the same hand in Huddersfield, was buried at a Roman Catholic cemetery. Professional Yvonne, the one who had been prepared, with her long scissors and her careful choice of johns. The girl who worked the circuits all over the country was gone, and far too quickly forgotten.

Forgotten too were those two letters purporting to be from the mass murderer. They were filed with the many other communications from unbalanced people and time-wasters. The police reasoned that the writer, if he had been genuine, would hardly have ignored the murder of Yvonne Pearson *if* it was one of the series. True, he had referred to the murder of Joan Harrison, not by name but by "Preston 75"; maybe he had read one of the press items on that killing. The police reasoned that they were too generalized and that there was nothing that specifically linked the writer with the murders. True, he had threatened to kill again and this time an older woman "maybe in Liverpool or Manchester." Time would tell if any credence should be given to that threat.

One communication, to Huddersfield C.I.D., that in the long run bore considerable fruit was not filed in the "nutters" box.

In May 1978 the police received information from a former member of the Argyll and Sutherland Highlanders. He'd read about the murder of Helen Rytka. The few details given of exactly how she had died particularly disturbed him.

For the ex-soldier her death seemed frighteningly familiar. Similar to some appalling events that took place on a farm in Fermanagh, Northern Ireland. A young farmer and his assistant had been brutally murdered. The two men, both Catholics, had been stabbed again and again in the heart and the chest. The ex-soldier, speaking quietly on the telephone, told the murder squad at Huddersfield of his fears that men in his own regiment had committed the murders in Fermanagh, of his fears that possibly the same men were responsible for the "Ripper" murders. He was just able to recall the names of the soldiers he suspected.

The information was duly passed to the Belfast police. As a result three soldiers are now serving prison sentences for the murder of the two men. For once a ripple of good had emanated from the deeds of the mass murderer.

13

With her first two terms at the university and her nineteenth birthday behind her, Flossy was discovering that a lot of play and little work made for a great deal of apprehension about her approaching first-year exams.

Somehow studying mock exam papers, earnestly reading *Sons & Lovers*, cramming sociology, paled when the competition was a live concert with Be-Bop Deluxe or The Clash. Disco dancing at the local Mecca or watching "Poldark" on TV were much better ways of spending an evening than curling up with a statistics paper or an Encyclopaedic Concordance. D. H. Lawrence was all very well, but Clint Eastwood was better.

It was a constant mental battle between the course work that had to be done and the excitements that simply could not be missed.

During her first term a friendship with a fellow student named Tim blossomed into an affair. Flossy did not consider that the pair of them made the earth move, but as she observed in one of her many letters to Lauris, "It helps me through the homesickness and the friendsickness." She daydreamed about Robert Powell, Andy Gibb, Elvis Costello, and Ben. Continually her thoughts returned to Ben. Their love affair had not ended happily—few do—but theirs had been finished by Ben's father. Concerned that the brilliant career he envisaged for his son was being distracted in its early stages by the romance, he brought pressure to bear on his son, who followed his father's wishes.

While Flossy's relationship with Tim was on and off and interspersed with other friendships, her thoughts invariably returned to Ben.

Had Lauris heard from him? Should she send him a Valentine card? Should they visit him in London when they went down for the David Bowie concert?

For Lent 1978 she had tried to give up swearing and had begun to indulge in the occasional cigarette, as an aid to dieting—the theory being that it would stop her eating. *Seems a bit daft substituting one vice for another*, she remarked to Lauris, in yet another of her many letters. It was good having Lauris to write to. Something of value from her youth to hold onto.

All of the others here have great accents. Wish I did. Everyone has to ask me where I'm from cos they can't tell. Just put my plate into soak cos I can't get the dried Weetabix off it. Tim's still fine. Rob, Ann, Phil, Tim and I went to see *Saturday Night Fever* last Sat. I think it is really good (a bit *Shampoo*-ish in a way, lots of people seem to have missed the deeper theme). When we got back I went to Tim's for coffee and we were perfecting his John Travolta up and down the corridor. We had a really good talk and I think he's the nearest person I've found here who thinks like us (words in the wrong order but you know what I mean). F'rinstance, he gets restless, would like to go somewhere where it's all happening, e.g. London, gets fed up with the restrictions on dress here (you know what we were talking about, wearing really modern clothes, e.g. gold blouse or similar and being ostracized because of it).

I'm gonna try and get Rob to tape Patti Smith's new one for me. I really love the single now. Did you know that Kate

Bush wrote "The Eyes of a Child" when she was fifteen? Where did we go wrong?

We're doing Eysenck today, you know, that obscure psychologist that no one's heard of. I keep panicking about exams but can't seem to really settle down to work properly. The last day or so I've felt really homesick, not so much for home but just to be houseyish and listen to Radio 4 without feeling guilty cos I ought to be reading Kafka. Know what I mean. Was feeling really desperate on Sunday. Nearest I've come to taking my checkbook and going off. It'll pass I spose.

Might be going to India next Easter. Got to get ready for lectures now so I'll write later.

Tell you what, get a bank loan, start your own riding school, and I'll come and do the paperwork in the morning and help with the grooming, mucking out and of course exercising in the afternoon. If you do that I'll leave university as well. Wouldn't it be fantastic. Oh well, back to statistics. Do you get the idea I've gone past the stage of caring for my stats? (I think the stage of caring is "Measure of location or central tendency"!)

Love, Flossy

P.S. My cheese plant has got a lovely big new leaf, a properly holed one.

P.P.S. Love Carly Simon's new one as well. I'm into female vocalists again.

By early April 1978, the chief constable of West Yorkshire, Ronald Gregory, was confronted with a major crisis. A crisis very largely, if not totally, created by one man. The mass murderer. Gregory had resisted press demands that Scotland Yard be called in to take over the investigation. He had defended his investigating officers at every opportunity. Now, with the statistics outstripping any murder investigation in the entire history of the police force, a solution had to be found to a number of ever-increasing problems. The crime rate for West Yorkshire had increased frighteningly. Figures for 1977 showed an increase of over 17 percent. The detection rate had dropped by over 4 percent. Since the man they hunted had commenced his attacks in 1975, hundreds of police officers had left the West Yorkshire force; the force, already nearly one thousand under strength, had to absorb, train, and attempt to hold onto the recruits who came into the service. There were severe financial restraints on Gregory. There were local councilors, including one mouthing nonsense about wanting the killer "dead or alive," who had clearly seen too many western movies. There were unsolved murders in many parts of the area that could not be attributed to the mass murderer and at the heart of the murder investigation was George Oldfield, a man who was obviously struggling.

George Oldfield had run the gamut of emotions during the hunt. His high optimism had produced "The Net Closes on the Ripper" headlines. His frustration moved him to observe, "Life's become very cheap in this civilized country of ours. There's a general state of apathy, of unconcern at violence. Fifteen or twenty years ago we'd have been holding the public back, so many would have been anxious to give us information. We'd have wrapped up this one by now."

It was very fair comment on the nation, but it also clearly illustrates that Oldfield was at the end of his tether. We are not all apathetic and indifferent. Perhaps if Oldfield and his colleagues had shown a greater degree of honest frankness with the public, had advised the nation of the facts of the murders and the trail of clues the killer had left, the public might have responded.

Clearly, even as early as 1978, catching the man responsible had become an obsession with George Oldfield. Obsessions can often be dangerous, blinding the obsessed to certain aspects, excluding highly relevant probabilities.

Oldfield's emotional need to be deep in the heart of the investigation had insured that his other duties as one of the area's assistant chief constables had been cared for by others. There was now a crucial need for him to be at his desk rather than out in the field. On April 14, Gregory chaired a meeting at Wakefield at which a number of his most senior and experienced men were present.

The result of that meeting was the formation of the Prostitute

Murder Squad. A team of one dozen hand-picked men, chosen by their leader, Detective Chief Superintendent John Domaille. Domaille had been involved in a number of the inquiries and had led the investigation into the death of Tina Atkinson. The squad would report to Oldfield, and their main task was "evaluating what had already come out of previous inquiries, coordinating and supporting any future investigation." It was not the intention that this squad should assume responsibility for any specific murder; rather that they should very carefully analyze all that had been done, check all the information that had come to hand, suggest further lines of investigation. Personnel would be assigned to the squad as and when Domaille felt necessary. This meant that many of hundreds of officers could turn their attentions to solving other crimes while, in the broadest sense, the squad would attempt to involve every serving officer in West Yorkshire in their own very specific hunt.

A month before the formation of this murder squad the then Home Secretary, Merlyn Rees, said, "I have no reason to believe that there need be fresh minds brought into this matter."

Now Chief Constable Gregory was creating a squad that very largely consisted of fresh minds.

Gregory and the officers serving underneath him had from the very beginning of this series of murders attempted to avoid the name that the press had given to their perpetrator. They very rightly felt that to describe him in that manner would be to elevate the man in some way and possibly help create folk legend; hence the popular title for Domaille and his hand-picked men, "the Prostitute Murder Squad." Excluding the fact that Jayne Mac-Donald was not a prostitute, the reasoning behind the choice was excellent. Alas.

"Domaille's Dozen Hound the Ripper"

"The Ripper's Deadliest Foe Goes into Action"

"Pledge from the Man Set to Snare the Ripper"

"Ripper Squad"

"Twelve Just Men Will Track Down Ripper"

He read the headlines with interest. He studied the photographs of Domaille striding down Chapeltown streets, of Domaille playing chess. He felt flattered that "an elite squad" had been created to catch him. He read Domaille's statement, "I will not rest until he is caught."

He spread his maps out on the table and considered the possibilities. Chapeltown, Manningham, Great Northern Street were out. On recent visits he had noted that vice squads were very active in all three. No good parking miles away and walking into one of these areas. He needed to have the car close by when he was working. *Couldn't borrow the Oxford again, have to use the Ford.* He smiled as he recalled how easy it had been in Manchester. He'd even gone back and done more work on that one, totally uninterrupted.

He'd have to check the car. One of the tires needed changing. He thought of the vast Hulme estate, known locally as "Lubyanka." Plenty of whores there.

He recalled reading about Manchester's chief constable, a man called James Anderton. The chief constable had been going on about Britain being an immoral country. It seemed that the chief constable was particularly enraged about prostitution and pornography and had launched massive drives in the Greater Manchester area against both elements. He laughed again as he addressed his map, his eyes narrowing as he concentrated on Manchester.

"Perhaps the chief constable would like a little help?"

From the Chief Constable, Greater Manchester police.

To all divisions, crime squads, crime areas, records office, the Chief Constable of West Yorks Police for the attention of Det. Ch. Supt. Domaille, Millgarth Police Station, West Yorkshire.

Murder

At 8:15 A.M. Wednesday 17.5.78 the body of a female was found on waste land in Livingstone Street, at its junction with April Street, Brunswick, Manchester. This junction is situated at the rear of the Manchester Royal Infirmary.

The deceased has been identified as Vera Evelyn Millward, born 26.8.37, alias Anne Brown, alias Mary Barton. She was a convicted prostitute.

The area where she was found is an area known to be used by prostitutes and their clients.

Death was due to blows to the head with a blunt instrument, a severe abdominal wound and a stab wound to the back. It is believed that death occurred between 12:00 midnight and 2:30 A.M. 17th May, 1978.

The deceased was wearing a reversible coat, blue/brown, checked on one side and all blue on the other, a short-length floral dress, blue canvas shoes, a pink cardigan, white panties, white underslip, and a blue and white bra.

The clothing of the assailant will be heavily bloodstained. Inquiries are requested at dry cleaners. All returns to the incident room at Longsight. Negative returns are required. No handbag or any other personal property belonging to the deceased has been found.

It is desired to trace any person who knew the deceased, or her present address, especially any persons who may have seen the deceased during the 24 hours preceding her death.

Details of the injuries are not to be released to the press. Any information to Det. Ch. Supt Ridgeway, Incident Room. Longsight Police Station.

Vera Millward had left her Hulme flat at 10:00 P.M. She had told the man she was living with that she was "just popping out for some cigarettes." He was later to deny that she was a prostitute. Her last conviction had been in 1973, but she kept it a secret. They had two children. He knew nothing of a previous five. Neither did he know that she worked the car trade. In fragile health, Vera at forty-one looked fifteen years older. She got her cigarettes that night. She also picked up one client with a car. They had gone not to the Southern Cemetery but to another spot favored by Manchester prostitutes, the rear of the Royal Infirmary. This was no darkened deserted field. Although the particular piece of land was a quiet place, they were still very close to the massive hospital, floodlights, nurses, doctors, emergency room, and nearly eight hundred patients. Certainly by the early hours of the morning most of the hospital activity would have ceased for the night but there was still the risk of someone coming to park a car, someone going to emergency.

Indeed, Vera, unlike the majority before her, had not only had a chance to scream, but her cries of "Help! Help! Help!" were heard by a man taking his son to the emergency room for treatment. The man assumed it was a patient having a nightmare.

The man who murdered her struck her on the head with his hammer three times. He dragged her some four yards, then threw her body on the ground. He opened her coat, her cardigan. He lifted her cotton dress and slip. He pulled down her tights and panties to expose her abdomen and back. Turning her body over he stabbed her in the back, then he struck with his knife with such verocity at her abdomen that her intestines spilled out. He carefully pulled her tights and panties up, pulled down her slip and cotton dress and closed her coat. He rolled the body hard onto its right side and stabbed at the right eye, causing the lid to puncture and bruise, but Vera would never feel a bruise again. He straightened her legs, folded her arms, and removed her shoes. He placed the shoes on the dead woman's body, where they half rested on a close-by fence. Then he drove away, leaving a perfect set of tire prints.

He had indeed changed his tires. This time the front left was a well worn India Autoway the rear left an Esso E110, the front right an Avon Super Safety in good condition (this had been the rear left tire when he had attacked Marilyn Moore) and the rear right had remained the same for the attack on Marilyn and the murder of Vera, an India Autoway, now well worn.

This Bradford killer had also left the mutilated body of a woman behind at the Manchester Infirmary, a mother of seven children.

The number of children motherless because of this man had now reached twenty-three. If he had not panicked while attacking Olive Smelt, Maureen Long, and Marilyn Moore, the motherless would have numbered thirty-one.

This time at the Manchester coroner's inquest all the above significant details of the injuries this man had inflicted were suppressed. The previous coroner's inquest on this side of the Pennines had resulted in some of the injuries suffered by Jean Jordan being made public. It was the only occasion during the entire series of murders that such details were given. The West Yorkshire police, who had no control over that particular inquest, were furious. Now that all details on all victims are being made public knowledge it is the turn of the public to be furious. Furious at the man who calmly roamed seeking to kill and maim to murder and wound, furious that the police would have his doings remain secret on the assumption that they know best. Who guards the guards?

Soon after, the Prostitute Murder Squad under John Domaille, Domaille's "Dirty Dozen," as they were known by their police colleagues, came to a fundamental realization. If the public in general were indifferent to the series of murders, the surviving prostitutes were not only indifferent but positively hostile to police requests for help. They resented what they regarded as the enemy's asking for cooperation.

In the first quarter of 1978 the police had conducted an energetic drive against the prostitutes of Bradford, Leeds, and Huddersfield. Chief Constable Anderton of Manchester had not needed the stimulus of a mass murderer in his attempts to clear the streets. The Greater Manchester police have had for years very clear instructions on how to deal with anything outside Anderton's concept of morality. Thus nine police officers kept a round-the-clock observation on the home of one prostitute. When their efforts eventually resulted in the woman's being brought before the court, Judge Zigmond observed, "With the crime rate that we have today they would have been better employed patrolling the streets."

Certain forms of publication have also incurred the wrath of Manchester's chief constable. Large amounts of "pornographic material" have been seized. One bookshop that has been raided thirteen times still awaits its first prosecution. Homosexuals in Manchester have fared little better. One of their clubs in the city center, "Napoleon's," has been visited a number of times by the police and the manager warned, "We are contemplating a prosecution for "licentious dancing."

Lay Methodist preacher Anderton stepped out of his pulpit in 1978 to scourge the city's motorists. Police could be seen at every traffic light in the city checking that the motorists were making the "right" signals.

By his own admission, Anderton has "connived" with National Front leaders when they plan their marches in the area. There is a notable absence of sex shops, saunas, and massage parlors in the city of Manchester.

There are still more than two hundred prostitutes working full time despite the zealous James Anderton—perhaps, more pertinently, despite the fact that two of their number no longer work. Their bodies are rotting in graves.

The view of Anderton's opposite number in West Yorkshire about prostitution is markedly different. When announcing the formation of John Domaille's squad, Chief Constable Ronald Gregory said, "I would not be against legalized prostitution but not in its present form. I think these girls are exploited and the prostitute industry as it is today I am against. In a different form I think it could be regularized. It could be legalized, I think, in some way. That would eliminate a lot of these vicious attacks that there are on prostitutes but I don't think a lot of them would want that sort of thing anyway. They prefer private enterprise."

The newspapers of Yorkshire were divided in their response. Self-appointed leaders of our morality were predictably scandalized. One, a Dr. Janet Cockcroft, had just returned from New York, where she had chaired the United Nations Status of Women Commission. Choosing her words carefully, as befits a chairperson, she said, "I think the suggestion to legalize it is nuts. It is barmy."

The people who had to cope with the reality behind the debate, the public, supported Gregory.

Three hundred housewives and mothers from the Bradford Branch of the National Housewives Association called on Home Secretary Merlyn Rees and all local M.P.'s to back the call for legalization. The citizens of Leeds were equally in agreement with their chief constable.

Throughout the furor, prostitutes in all these cities continued to work. Righteous indignation, controversy, police raids, editorials, even the series of murders by a man who was apparently singling them out—nothing stops such an old profession.

However, Domaille and his men discovered that many of the amateur prostitutes, housewives, students, teachers, had crept back to their homes. Contact magazines started to go out of business. There were more vacancies for those little cards in newsagents boards. There was less "activity" in certain pubs, clubs, and dance halls. A little pin money on the side was one thing, a ball peen hammer on the head something else.

Other women who were professionals decided to try different locations. They became the "away day girls," catching a cheap day return trip to London, working all day and catching the last train home to Bradford or Leeds. There were others who, with the right pimp, found they could continue by working some of the highly respectable hotels in the north. But that kind of woman, with a certain style, good looks, and the right connections was not what this murderer was seeking. He sought his victims among the working class and often that section of the working class that was poor, inadequate, uneducated, and trapped in the slums where they sold their bodies. The high-class prostitute, with the luxury flat, the car, and all the trappings was not for this man. He sought the most vulnerable. And as he stalked them they nerved themselves to continue working. Some carried safeguards as Yvonne Pearson had done. Mace, knives, scissors. They took to working in pairs, one taking the license number of the car that the other went off in. The Rytka sisters had tried that. Others determined they would do business only in their own homes. Tina Atkinson had used that routine. Others thought the best form of safety lay in always working near either their pimp or a male friend. Emily Jackson used to solicit within yards of where her husband would sit with his pint.

There seemed to be no way to avoid this man who hunted them, other than to retire from "the game." Some would have liked nothing better. But pimps and poverty make hard masters, so Manningham Lane and the surrounding area—an area that had been the chief promenade for the city when Jack the Ripper was carving his way into criminal history in London—was still in 1978 the chief promenade for the prostitutes.

Domaille's squad began to take the women down to nearby Queens Road police station. They were taken in small groups, never more than six at a time. The purpose was not to charge them yet again. This time it was tea and sympathy. The women found to their surprise that they were being called by their Christian names. That no one wanted to play the heavy with them. In fact the police not only wanted aid, they were also offering it.

It was an official attempt to make the women adopt a more professional approach to their jobs. To refrain from getting a belly full of drink and staggering out looking for a client. Never to go with a john in a car unless an associate had definitely taken the license number. To use only certain police-designated areas when actually earning their fee. To make note of all unusual requests, of any customers who turned violent.

The women listened mainly in bemusement. After all, these police had been arresting them left, right, and center for months. They'd even raided a few brothels that had sprung up as protection against this one man. They had driven some of their friends to cities throughout the United Kingdom and now here they were calmly patting the girls on the head and telling them how to be more efficient.

It was an absolute reversal of tactics. Another of the changes of police philosophy was to put these women in very real risk from the mass murderer. With regard to Manningham the police created a situation in which they were virtually conspiring with the killer, inviting him, tempting him to walk along Church Street and pick his next victim. Whose body is it, anyway?

It's Joan's body. One of her clients demanded sex on credit. He was desperate for it and had no money. He did have a knife. He got his sex. Joan has thirty-three convictions. She also has three children and a husband who vanished many years ago.

It's Betty's body. She is doing a three-year course at a northern university. Father dead, mother poor, grant inadequate. "A lot of guys virtually forced me to do it when I was straight, before I was eighteen. I thought sod this, I'll make the buggers pay."

It's Veronica's body. With her large poster of the Fonz looking on in her one-room Bradford flat she indulges the whims of her clients. Schoolmistress, mother, butch, Fem. A woman for all reasons.

It's Sandra's body. So jumpy now because of *him* that she sleeps with an axe under her bed but still maintains "it's a living."

It had been Yvonne Pearson's body. One of her clients had liked to be burned with cigarette ends and matches. Another had insisted that she treat him as her slave and force him to do her housework. He would then insist that she humiliate him and make him reclean everything. This "man" is still cleaning the homes of a number of women in Bradford. Still giving the women the little presents that they "insist" upon, at his insistence. Still putting on frilly panties and a little pinafore at their "command." This captain of industry then returns to his place of work and publicly moralizes about the scandals of the prostitutes on the streets of Bradford.

There are young girls who have been forced onto "the game" at the age of twelve or thirteen by a pimp. The technique is to seduce the young girl, then threaten to tell her parents or the police what she has done. This threat is invariably accompanied by violence. Many, surprisingly, fall for this blackmail and go with a few of his friends, "just for a laugh, you know, baby," then the occasional stranger. Then all strangers and no friends, not even the pimp—he can't be bothered.

There are the older women, like Jane in Bradford. Jane has been giving money to her pimp for eleven years. Recently because her earnings have dropped he has started to attack her seriously. Torturing her with electric wire, plugging it into the main current and pushing the live wires inside her genitalia. The Bradford police know all about this man. They are powerless to act unless Jane is prepared to make a complaint and then follow through with evidence in court. She is not prepared to. She does not want her arms broken by the pimp.

There are Christine and Susan, again from Bradford. Like the Rytka sisters, they work closely together. Christine is sure that the mass murderer kills while the women are bending down performing oral sex, that he hits them on the head while they are in that position. Neither she nor Susan will perform this act, whatever fee is offered. Both knew Yvonne Pearson and Tina Atkinson. On the night Yvonne was murdered, Christine was working a few yards from her. She was arrested by the vice squad. If the officer had chosen to arrest Yvonne, Christine would have been the rotting body in Arthington Square. These two have coped with a young man who said he was vice squad "and demanded free fucks. He also stubbed cigarettes out on me." He wasn't vice squad. He is now doing time.

They have coped with johns who had knives. "One pulled a knife on me when I refused to fuck without a condom."

Christine is nineteen years of age, with a young child. Susan is twenty-one years of age, with three children. Like all of the other women's fees, it is five pounds for a short time. Ten pounds for the same short time in the privacy of a house. They work very closely together. If a john wants one of them he is obliged to take the other in the car as well, otherwise "no business." When one has her period the other does all the work and shares the money. Both have been on the game since they were sixteen years old. Both have been through the hands of pimps.

There is Nancy, well known in Lumb Lane. Aged thirty-eight. Looks nearly sixty. Last year Nancy was pregnant. She continued to work. She was still working when her waters broke, over her client.

Some prefer the Asians. "They enter, shoot their wad, and that's it. The job's finished. Ten seconds' work, if that."

Others incline toward Irish johns. "The Irish are buggers for it over here. Go mad to get sex. Can always charge them an extra fiver to suck a nipple."

These women come in all shapes and sizes. All colors, all attitudes. Some, a very few, have a positive aim. To save money to buy a home. "Just until my husband comes out of the slammer." To get a new car.

Some, far too many, appear to have no alternative. No choice. They are on a treadmill that is without exit. Many are very poor. Most have families in which they are the only earner. Many are trapped by the ever-lurking pimp, that appalling creature that drains the very life force from them. When Yvonne died and her body was eventually discovered, one of her friends as a mark of respect refused to work that night. She got a beating from her "protector."

Others do it because they like doing it. They consider the pay and hours they work to get it preferable to clocking into a factory at eight in the morning. Most have at some time experienced other forms of work and concluded that opening their legs was easier.

The British method of dealing with all these women is to state: "Prostitution is not a criminal offense but most ways of attempting to practice it are."

The women take the view that the police are interfering with and frequently stopping the prostitutes from doing a job of work. The murder squad approaches to the Bradford prostitutes in May 1978 represented therefore a bizarre change in official policy. A change caused solely by police anxiety to trap one man.

The murder of Vera Millward caused Oldfield and his support team to reconsider the two letters posted in Sunderland. They were pulled out of the crank file. Yet again the police read the threats. Particularly pertinent was the statement contained in the second letter, "next time try older one I hope" and the threat that it might be in either Liverpool or Manchester. Just two months later forty-one-year-old Vera was murdered in Manchester. Police opinion now heavily swung to the view that the letters were indeed from the killer. Domaille discussed the murder of Joan Harrison with the Lancashire police.

Then there was Yvonne Pearson's murder. Publicly the police maintained their view that the man they were hunting had murdered eight times.

Secretly the majority believed it was at least ten. In June 1978 a secret dossier was circulated by the West Yorkshire police to their colleagues in other parts of the British Isles. It was headed: MURDERS AND ASSAULTS UPON WOMEN IN THE NORTH OF ENGLAND.

It gave details of the murders, *ten* murders. It gave details of the attacks where women had survived, *four attacks*. The public had been told of *eight* linked murders and *one* linked attack where a victim survived. Why? In mid-1978 it was generally assumed throughout the country that this man attacked only prostitutes. The murder of Jayne MacDonald could be rationalized on the basis that a young woman, walking home through the heart of the red-light area in the small hours died by mistake. Indeed, the police fostered this view. They of course had the advantage of the unpublished letters, with the "apologies" for the death of Jayne.

Thus any woman who was not a prostitute would have been perfectly justified in concluding that she was safe. Maureen Long had discovered differently, yet somehow the fact that she was not a prostitute was glossed over. Anna Rogulskyj and Olive Smelt had also discovered differently, yet the fact that both had been attacked by the mass murderer was suppressed.

While Domaille organized a slide show of the appalling injuries the dead women had suffered, a slide show by the police for the police, the public was kept in total ignorance. Rumor and legend became public substitutes for the truth.

In September of 1978 the chief constable of West Yorkshire quickly increased the number of murders to ten and survivors to four.

Olive Smelt had been told privately by the police after the murder of Helen Rytka that her attacker was the mass murderer. Had it really taken the West Yorkshire police force from 1975 to 1978 to work that one out?

In March 1978 Chief Constable Gregory had stated that the net was closing on "Ripper," that the police had never been closer. When publicly stating in September that the man was responsible for even more murders, even more attacks, he did not mention any nets closing. He did venture the view, "We will be pressing on, and we will get this man in the end."

As autumn gave way to winter many of the general public in the north of England relaxed. There had been no significant publicity for many months other than the Chief Constable's isolated statement in September—a deliberate press blackout. The last murder had been in May 1978 and many felt that the man responsible was dead, either by suicide or natural causes. It was a dangerous belief that had crept in once before in the fifty-four-week gap between the murders of Emily Jackson and Irene Richardson. Now as Christmas 1978 approached, the public understandably took an optimistic view. If more people had been able to read a story that received very little coverage, they might have had greater cause to worry.

Two detectives assigned to the murder squad were suspended, and subsequently tendered their resignations when the story became public—resignations that were accepted with alacrity.

Their crime, and crime it was indeed was: fraud and dereliction of duty. Many thousands of statements had been taken over the three years of the investigation. John Domaille's men had set about the task of double-checking and verifying those statements. The two suspended police officers had not double-checked or verified their allocated quota of statements but had claimed substantial overtime and expenses for the nonexistent work. Fraud is a crime which the public in general will find themselves in court and possibly prison for committing. If you are a police officer you can obviously just resign from the force.

Beyond that there was the appalling possibility that one of those unchecked statements might well have contained crucial evidence, vital information that could have led to the capture of the notorious mass murderer. Reporter David Bruce of the Yorkshire *Evening Post*, having been tipped off, got in touch with Deputy Chief Constable Austin Haywood, the man responsible for the department that controlled the force's discipline and complaints department. Haywood observed, "I view this as a very grave matter."

David Bruce may care to know exactly what concerned the Deputy Chief Constable.

From Deputy Chief Constable.
To all ranks. To be read out on parade for the next 24 hours.
Each tour of duty.
It has been my unpleasant duty to suspend certain detective constables for grave dereliction of duty and irregularities connected with the series of prostitute murders. This fact has received substantial publicity and I know that detailed information has been given exclusively to Mr. David Bruce of the Yorkshire *Evening Post*. I have had no option but to confirm this information, which is of a type never voluntarily released.
The damaging effect on police and public morale needs no explanation from me. If any officer has any reliable information leading to the identity of the police informant concerned I should be pleased if this could be passed to any

officer not below the rank of superintendent under confidential cover.

If any officer has had any contact with Mr. David Bruce
during the last 48 hours I should be glad if he would
inform the appropriate A.C.C., who should pass details to
me as soon as possible under cover. It will of course be
useful if any officer is seen talking to Mr. David Bruce in
the near future.

Message ends.

Never mind about the mass murderer getting away because of
corrupt policemen, let us ascertain who tipped off the press. Two
weeks later two more detectives were suspended for the same
reasons.

14

Genesis at Knebworth, David Bowie at Earls Court, part of her summer vacation spent with Lauris in Greece and Italy—the year had certainly had a number of high moments for Flossy. After returning to the university in September she had gained greater independence by leaving the residence hall and moving in with seven other students. The large Victorian house with its uninvited tenants of mice and the occasional rat provided each student with her own room as well as shared communal areas. Flossy surprised herself more than the others when she became quartermaster, organizing the house budget and chore schedule.

In November, Lauris came from Nottingham to spend a weekend with her. Upon arrival, Lauris found herself being rapidly taken to her friend's "inner sanctum."

"It's good to see you, Lauris."

"Oh, I thought I'd never get here, Flossy."

Lauris looked with surprise at her best friend, who stood with her finger across her lips.

"What is it?" Lauris whispered.

"No one here calls me that. They all use my real name. Would you mind awfully? I think they'd tease me for weeks if they knew."

Lauris laughed.

"Of course not, Barbara. After all, we're grown-up women of the world now."

"Sure you don't mind? I just know that Rob and the others wouldn't give me a minute's peace."

"Forget it. Now that we've sorted that out, do I get to meet them?"

"Yes, of course."

Lauris followed Barbara Leach out of her Bradford "inner sanctum."

The weekend was a great success. Particularly memorable was the Indian dinner on Saturday night. The left-over Indian water bread *japatis* quickly froze in the winter air. The group hurled them up and down Great Horton Street like Frisbees; the remnants served as ashtrays.

30th Nov. '78

Dear Lauris,

How's this, then? Real writing paper—I think this Christmas idea is going to my head; well, actually I don't feel very festive at all. I did last weekend but that's another story! I thoroughly embarrassed Phil by reading out the bits about him in your letter, in the kitchen at dinnertime when most of us were in there! He was really chuffed, although he made a flippant comment and suddenly became very interested in his baked beans!

It was fun seeing you. S'good that we can just pick up again as if we haven't been away from each other. "I'm Free" just came on the radio. I still love that song, he sounds so "free," doesn't he? Cor, baby, that's really free! Was Penelope Keith good? Silly question really, and what about the Caretaker?

Well, I also had my haircut and decided that it's too severe for winter and doesn't look half as good without the fuzzy permed bits. In other words I don't like it. Got another essay today—well, we have a "choice" of about seven, all on different aspects of Bernstein's work (Basil B, that is).

Well, it's beddy-byes for me now. I'm absolutely knack-
ered, God knows why, 'cos I haven't really done anything
today.

Love and hugs,
Barbara

He walked slowly along Lumb Lane. It was late January 1979.
He was puzzled. There was something odd going on. Something
unusual. He hadn't seen a single whore all along the lane. Yet here
it was Thursday evening, one of the city's paydays, nine in the
evening and not a prostitute to be seen.

The fact that the murders he had committed had sent many
prostitutes into early retirement and others to safer towns did not
occur to him. If it had he would have brushed it aside. He was now
so steeped in blood that, like Macbeth, it was easier to go forward
than to turn back from further bloody deeds. Now he *had* to kill.

The anger had grown over the years, had surged at each of his
disappointments in life, whether real or imagined. That anger was
now a constant factor. Someone somewhere had decided that he
should not know the joy of fatherhood. Those continual disappointments had been the initial driving force that had sent him out
to hunt and strike down women. At first it had been any woman;
then, with the realization that prostitutes were far more vulnerable, presented far easier targets, he had concentrated on them. He
still would if given the opportunity. It was so easy to kill them. No
problem. But now that initial anger was fueled with a new
explosive factor. His mother had died.

He'd always been the closest to her. The other children had all
had their share of her love and attention but his relationship with
his mother had been very close, very special. Now suddenly, at
the age of sixty, on the day she was due to retire from work, she
had died. The doctor said it was a heart attack. All he knew was
that he grieved for her, missed her, needed her. His fine house,
his good job, his car, even his beautiful loving wife, none of them
could compensate for the loss. Now he didn't care a damn who
paid for that loss. He was deeply determined that someone,
anyone, was going to pay.

As always, he planned. His were not the acts of the aggressive psychopath. No sudden bursts of rage that led inexorably to violence. What was within him was far worse than violence under control. What was within him was a hatred. That had always been the motivation. Since his mother's death the hatred had increased tenfold.

Externally gentle, charming, kind, and considerate. Inside, total evil. An evil in which he luxuriated. He had the inner knowledge and full control to be able to pick a night completely at random. Months in advance. Like making a long-term business appointment.

He walked up to the top of Lumb Lane. His puzzlement grew. Across Marlborough Road, at the top of Church Street, he found what he had been seeking. There were not just one or two patrolling Church Street. He rapidly counted fifteen women. It was like a bloody circus. His bemusement grew as he began to stroll down Church Street. There were several cars parked. Not johns but plainclothes police officers. Several prostitutes were calmly chatting with the police officers. Other whores, he noted, were being picked up by cruising johns, yet the police made no attempt to arrest, caution or stop them. There were far too many women in the small street too. Far too many to work it gainfully. He had over the years become something of an expert on the profession. He knew more about the street habits of these women than the police did. He had to know, it was his work.

Something very odd indeed was going on. There had been nothing in the papers for ages. He watched as a group of about six girls began to approach the traffic lights prior to crossing into Lumb Lane. One of the watching detectives came running out of a car and approached the group. He was close enough to overhear the conversation.

"Now, come on, girls. You know the rules. Not past the lights."

They roared with laughter as one of their number responded.

"No, lad. We're going off bloody beat for a while. Give some of the others a chance. You've got us packed in like bloody sardines."

The detective looked skeptical.

"Where are you going, then?"

"To the International Club."

The detective relaxed. The management at the International

got very heavy if any of their clientele attempted to solicit
"business" on the premises.

"Right, then."

"Why don't you come and buy us all a drink?"

"What, on my expenses?" Half waving an arm he returned to
his colleague in one of the parked cars.

*What did the policeman mean about knowing the rules? What was that
about "not past the lights"?* He decided to follow the girls and have
a bottle of beer at the International.

When he quietly entered the club it seemed as if a union
meeting had just begun. Some ten prostitutes were at the bar. An
attractive woman behind the counter was vainly attempting to
keep the girls to the principal item on the agenda, ordering drinks.

"Please, girls. Now, is it three gin and limes or four? Is it one
Scotch and orange or two?"

She clapped her hands and the class promptly came to attention.

"Sorry Lorna, we're just a bit steamed up."

"Then let us throw some fluid on the heat and cool down a
little. Now, who is having what, girls?"

Eventually they were all served. So was he. Unobtrusively
sipping a light ale and affecting a total lack of interest in all about
him, he listened.

"It's all very well police giving us amnesty, but what's the
point? How can we work? We're falling over each other."

"You know, the word's getting around. The girl from Nottingham said all her mates had heard. The word's gone right round
the circuit that you don't get nicked in Manningham."

"Scotch, Jean? Look, there's another. Buggers off from Bradford years ago with her pimp and, sod me, there she was last night
chatting up my weewee man."

"Your weewee man?"

"You know him that pays me forty pound a time to piss on him.
I can't afford to lose business like that. My weeweeman's the rent
for a month every time I see him."

"Well, why didn't you tell her to bugger off?"

"Don't worry, I did. But time I'd got rid of her, he'd buggered
off too. He's shy."

Lorna, sitting behind the bar, had been listening intently to the
complaining prostitutes.

"I told you this would happen. Didn't I tell all of you? If brains were drains you lot couldn't hold a teardrop between you. It's one thing the police deciding to make it legal in a small part of Bradford. But nobody thought it through. Of course you're all going to be falling over each other. Of course girls on other parts of the circuit are going to come pouring into Church Street. Christ, gold-diggers of 'seventy-nine."

"Well, we were here first, Lorna."

"Course you were, love. I know that. Time you told the vice squad. Get them to move these bloody invaders back to their own towns. Right?"

A black girl in her late teens smiled.

"Right. We'll tell the fuzz if they don't get rid of this foreign competition we'll spread our wings again. Right down Lumb Lane."

The others clapped and laughed.

Lorna spoke to the young black girl.

"Sonia, remember it needs a group of you to go to the station. Not just one. Let them see that you're organized."

"Organized!" said a brunette with a shout. "Let me tell you about *their* bloody organizing."

"Right, Jean," said Lorna, "tell us."

"First night of this amnesty. Few weeks back. All very top secret. All very hush-hush. Murder squad's new plan to catch Ripper. Legalize being on the game but only legalize it as far as the traffic lights on corner of Church Street. Restrict hours of business from seven P.M. to one A.M. Any girl working outside those hours or that little area gets arrested. Move out the vice cars and bring in the murder squad, low profile, invisible, make them look like johns or just members of the public. Tell them to sit there and make note of all license numbers. Sooner or later the Ripper will come for one of us and, bang, out of nowhere the invisible men of the murder squad will have the bastard. Right? First night I was on that beat with you, Sonia, right?"

"That's right, love."

"Little old man and his wife cross over to where a detective constable and a policewoman, both plainclothes of course, are pretending to have a kiss and cuddle while they note license numbers. The little old man bangs on the window.

"'I want to hand this in,' he's shouting. D.C. winds down his window. The old man is wanting to give him a wristwatch. 'I found it on pavement.' 'Well, why do you want to give it to me? I'm not police. Just stopped to have a chat with my girlfriend.' The old man looks at him and laughs. 'Don't be bloody silly, lad. 'Course you're a policeman. You're waiting to get Ripper's license number, we all know that.'"

Lorna called out amid the laughter.

"Because we already know the police license numbers. Sonia give me one of their numbers."

"Take your pick. SUM or AKY."

Jean joined in. "Or XWX."

"Nice to know they take such good care of their live bait."

Quietly, he bought another beer. It was indeed live bait. The young whore was right, she would never know how right. Strung out down Church Street in the hope that he would come looking and pick one. Obviously they had no idea of his license number, therefore the plan must be that after he had picked one up and murdered her they would check out all licenses of cars that had entered the area in the previous twenty-four hours. They were conspiring with him, to murder. Presumably they thought it was worth losing another whore to catch him. He looked across at the laughing, drinking group of women. *Bloody fools.* He'd always known they were stupid but surely they could work out that the plan was for one of them to die. Official police policy. If they had told the whores to just take their clients to certain spots, ones specified by the murder squad, they must damn well know that if a john suggests somewhere else, nine times out of ten the woman will agree, rather than lose the customer, particularly when business was bad and he had insured that it was bad. His head shook silently in wonder. Lorna mistook the movement.

"Another drink, love?"

"Oh, yes. Why not?"

"Same again?"

"Please."

He noticed an enormous bottle of champagne near him on the counter. There appeared to be various signatures all over the label.

"What's that? Raffling it for charity?"

"That? Oh no, that's very special. Double magnum of champagne. When Ripper's caught we're popping that. We've got balloons, streamers. Party will be a cracker. Come in if you're in the area."

"Right, thanks."

He waited for her to rejoin the group of prostitutes. For the moment the group were quietly sipping their drinks and Lorna always believed the management should make new customers feel welcome.

"You from round this way, then?"

"Yes. Not far."

He sipped his drink; then, making a gesture toward the group of women, continued, "Couldn't help overhearing. I always thought these girls had blokes who protected them. Didn't think they needed police."

Lorna laughed.

"You mean their pimps?"

"Ay."

"Best part of the day the pimps are in the betting shops. Best part of the evening in the pubs. They're very good at breaking a woman's arm, or putting a bottle over her head when her earnings are dropping off. They slow down a bit when it comes to dealing with a man, if you get my drift."

He smiled.

"That girl, there, Sonia. Her pimp's line to her was, 'You're too good to be on the game in Bradford. Stick with me and I'll get you into the London bigtime.'"

"And how long ago was that?"

"Nearly four years. Must be a bit of a tail back on the M.1., wouldn't you say?"

They shared the joke, then Lorna was called back to the group of prostitutes. He grew thoughtful. *Have to check out the other areas.* Leaving most of the last drink, he moved quietly toward the exit. It was clever how he had developed this talent for coming and going like a will o' the wisp. Lorna was holding forth as he made for the door.

"So all right, homosexuality is legal. It's legal. Thank God it's not compulsory, but at the moment it's legal. So why do these women have a problem?"

* * *

He grew more thoughtful in the weeks that followed. He drove to Chapeltown, Great Northern Street, Moss Side, and Hulme in Manchester. Everywhere it was the same. Leaving his car well outside the red-light areas, he would enter by foot. Always there were watching police cars, but with the exception of Bradford it was business as usual—if the whores were seen doing business they got arrested. Clearly they were being driven from the streets in these other cities in an effort to drive him to Church Street. He thought of the live bait dangled there. He was tempted, felt almost churlish not to accept the police gift. He considered using a different car. No trouble getting hold of one for a night. Getting on the job in Bradford with a different car and false license plates. *That would have them running about.*

At the factory his preoccupation went unnoticed. He had never been a great mixer. He was friendly enough with the others, but he didn't go out of his way to seek their company during off hours. Just quietly kept himself to his family, to his home, his wife, his brothers and sisters and his father. None of them saw any change within him. They never had. They never would. He had not changed. What he was he had always been.

It helped that most of his working life was spent behind the wheel of a truck. Alone on the road with just his thoughts he would indulge himself, let the mask slip, relive the murders, enjoy the memories. Alone in the driver's cabin during the early months of 1979, he decided quite calmly that it was time to murder again. His mother was dead, that was reason enough.

15

Dear Lauris,

Gave Phil your note, and he asked for your address, which I gave him, so expect some poison-pen letters soon.

I'm not too bad—well, I don't know, I wasn't. More of that later. Well, done, (sorry, that comma shouldn't be there) for the good conduct in potentially harassing situations (i.e., meeting Mark on Wed.). If you do fall for Mark again, don't jump out of your window, come up here and jump out of mine, then you can be found in a back alley, which sounds better, or you could just hang around and wait for the Bradford Ripper (yes, he's operating again, he got one in Huddersfield).

I don't think I'd have to give Phil a knockout drop to get him to Nottingham, more like stopping him taking over the train to get there faster. Back in a mo. Gotta listen to at least some of this lecture.

Later. I now know all about research methods. Finished *Tess of d'Urbervilles* today—I want to read it again! I'm still ½ way thru *Gunner Rommel who* (or something like that) and

Plague Dogs; think I'll start *St. Mawr* or 'praps *Madding Crowd* (being in a Thomas Hardy sorta mood).

Bit of trouble with Steve—he says he loves me! Said it twice now and then he pins me down to what I feel—I say just friends; he goes off being subdued, etc. and makes me feel guilty. Aaaaaagh!!

Ah well, must get on with my D'alerbert and post a load of pornographic films off (I lie about the porno films).

Lotsa love,
Barbara

March 23rd 79

Dear Officer

Sorry I havn't written, about a year to be exact, but I hav'nt been up north for quite a while. I was'nt kidding last time I wrote saying the whore would be older this time and maybe I'd strike in Manchester for a change, you should have took heed. That bit about her being in hospital, funny the lady mentioned something about being in hospital before I stopped her whoring ways. The lady won't worry about hospitals now will she. I bet you be wondering how come I hav'nt been to work for ages, well I would have been if it hadnt been for your cursered coppers I had the lady just where I wanted her and was about to strike when one of you cursing police cars stopped right outside the lane, he must have been a dumb copper cause he didnt say anything, he didnt know how close he was to catching me. Tell you the truth I thought I was collared, the lady said don't worry about the coppers, little did she know that bloody copper saved her neck. That was last month, so I don't know when I will get back on the job but I know it wont be Chapeltown too bloody hot there maybe Bradfords Manningham. Might write again if up north.

Jack the Ripper

PS Did you get letter I sent to *Daily Mirror* in Manchester.

The police policy of a press blackout on the investigations into this series of murders had functioned from mid-May 1978. The thinking had been to force a reaction from the man they hunted.

Prior to May 1978 it had taken only a telephone call to arrange for George Oldfield to take a television interviewer and camera crew on a midnight tour of Chapeltown. Chatting to prostitutes at the request of the TV interviewer, discussing the case, no angle refused. Film and television crews, reporters, all readily obtained access to the murder incident room at Millgarth, Leeds. Indeed, so many TV crews went there to film that one senior detective observed, "Isn't it about time we stopped playing at Starsky and Hutch and caught this bastard?"

In mid-May the shutters had come down. Apart from Gregory's statement in September upping the total of murders that the police held the killer responsible for to ten, and the number of attacks to four, there had been scant coverage. What should have been a front-page story about the four criminal police officers, criminals who remain unconvicted, was tucked away in most papers in a half column.

They had wanted to provoke the killer. To their delight the third letter written by the same hand had arrived on Oldfield's desk near the end of March. Like the other two, it had been posted in Sunderland. Unlike the other two, it yielded vital forensic information.

Before the police had an opportunity to evaluate that information they were obliged to consider if the press blackout had provoked a great deal more than a letter.

From A.C.C. Crime, West Yorkshire Metropolitan police.

To Chief Constables Northumberland, Cumbria, Durham, Cleveland, Merseyside, Lancashire, Greater Manchester, Cheshire, Nottinghamshire, Derbyshire, Lincolnshire, South Yorkshire, Humberside.

Not to be disclosed to the press.

Murder of and assaults upon women in West Yorkshire and Greater Manchester since July 1975.

With reference to previous circulations and crime intelligence bulletins about the above crimes, at 6:30 A.M. today, 5th April, 1979, the body of Josephine Anne Whitaker, 19 years, a Building Society clerk, was found in Saville Park, Halifax. She was not a prostitute nor was her moral character questionable. She was last seen alive when she left the home of her grandmother at 11:55 P.M. on the 4th April to walk to her own home, a distance of about 1 mile. Death is believed to have occurred between 12:15 A.M. and 12:30 A.M. on the 5th April. There are several similarities between the circumstances surrounding the death of Josephine Anne Whitaker and the deaths of and assaults upon other women in West Yorkshire and Greater Manchester in recent years but, as yet, it cannot be positively connected. However the possibility cannot be overlooked and forces are advised to give special attention to areas where prostitutes are known to solicit and to areas where they are known to take clients for sexual purposes. An incident room has been set up at Halifax. Telephone numbers: Halifax 64421, 64422, 64423.

Authorized by A.C.C. Mr. Oldfield.

Message ends.

It was him all right. The post mortem, yet again performed by Professor David Gee, confirmed that. Josephine's murder could not be brushed aside with that extraordinary hypocritical moral double standard of the British, with "they're only prostitutes" or "they ask for it, you know" or "he's only after whores." The enemy for this man had been, from long before the first attack, women. Any woman. All women. All in jeopardy. All had been in jeopardy from the very beginning. Now for the first time this basic, fundamental fact began to percolate through a few minds.

Police strategy had been to maintain a very high profile in all red-light districts, to observe all known places where clients were taken for business. This strategy, again reiterated in that tragic Telex, the Telex that also contains the sad confirmation that the strategy had gone appallingly haywire, was fatally flawed.

For months they had sat and waited in their familiar cars. Balked and deprived of risk-free access to women in the red-light areas, he had merely returned to the city where in 1975 he had launched a murderous attack on Olive Smelt. Olive Smelt is first and foremost a woman. That is why she was in danger. That is why she was attacked. That is why Josephine Whitaker was murdered. No possible mistake because of locality. There is no red-light district in the city of Halifax. This city is tucked close to the Pennine range. In summer the surrounding countryside displays a charm and beauty hard to imagine during winter. In the first few months of the year the wind rips down from the surrounding hills, cutting through the thickest overcoat.

When Josephine Whitaker said goodnight to her grandparents at their home in Huddersfield Road, they had been a trifle anxious. It was sleeting and dark, and about twenty minutes short of midnight. They urged her to stay overnight. She looked at her new cocktail watch on her wrist and reminded them she would be home with her parents just after midnight. The watch, a self-bought present, had been the particular reason for the visit. It had arrived from the mail-order company that day and she had proudly come around to show it to the elderly couple.

A ten-minute walk across Saville Park held no fear for the nineteen-year-old girl. There was no reason why it should, even at night. The park, set in a good-class residential area, was well lit, there would still be plenty of people about, and apart from that, she was a strong, healthy girl who enjoyed dancing and horseback riding. Local discos were fun but horseback riding up on Norland Moor was better.

He struck Josephine twice on the head with the hammer. She was only three hundred yards from home and safety when he pounced. Mercifully she died instantly. He dragged her dead body twenty-five yards into the park, away from the lights. On the way one of her smart tan shoes with their stacked heels fell off. Unheeding, he continued to drag her body. He stabbed the lifeless body twenty-five times, mainly in the abdominal area. He repositioned her clothes. Her other shoe had also fallen off, this one near the body. He looked around for its companion but could not see it. He stuffed the one he had between her thighs, then, covering the dead body with her own jacket and clutching the four-inch knife in one hand and the ball peen hammer in the other, ran to his car. A moment later and Saville Park was free of wild animals once more.

Josephine, like so many before her, lay on the wet grass throughout the night, waiting to be found.

An early-morning bus driver had seen "the bundle of rags" as he drove by. He reported it when he arrived at the depot. Metro Calderdale took no action. An hour later, at 6:30 A.M., one of the many workers on their way to Rowntree Mackintosh, Mrs. Jean Markham, also saw the bundle of rags, and noticed a shoe some distance away. She crossed the road and was about to pick up the shoe when she realized the bundle was something more than rags. She bent down to help the young girl. Josephine was long past help in this world. Mrs. Markham staggered in traumatic shock to a phone.

Shortly afterward the police activity attracted the attention of a young newspaper boy. Curiously he strolled across the park. He saw a body partially covered. Then he saw a shoe. This thirteen-year-old boy recognized the shoe. It belonged to his sister Josephine.

A photo of what that teenager saw is contained in this book. Originally it appeared in the local Halifax *Courier*. There was a storm of protest. People wrote to express "disgust, horror." The editor was subsequently reported to the press council, which rightly rejected the complaint. One of the reasons the editor gave for publication was, "It may help in speeding justice."

While certain citizens of Halifax were being disgusted and horrified, George Oldfield and his fellow officers were again working a sixteen-hour day as they struggled to catch the man responsible.

Alongside Oldfield was another veteran in the hunt, Detective Chief Superintendent Holland. He had been involved in many of the specific murder investigations after his first brush with the entire case when he headed the investigation into the serious assault on Olive Smelt.

Now the burly policeman had taken over control of the murder squad, Domaille's dirty dozen. Domaille, who had rashly stated when assuming command of the squad, "I will not rest until he is caught" was now being rested. He had been promoted to the position of commander of the Police Academy at Wakefield.

It was beginning to seem as if the man they hunted had enough determination to exhaust the most tireless of policemen.

They probed the young girl's background. Employed at the Halifax Building Society as a clerk, recently promoted, happy in her work and well liked by workmates.

They looked at her love life. Engaged at sixteen to local youth,

Craig Midgley; this was broken off in 1978 by mutual consent. Since then had formed no serious relationships.

Could her killer have known her? Known that she always crossed Saville Park at a certain time on a certain day? She rarely saw her grandparents during the week, usually visiting them on Sundays. Her stepfather, Hayden Hiley, observed, "This man's timing could not have been more precise if he had planned it. But he could not have planned it because she did not regularly go out on a Wednesday."

Even when David Gee had removed all possible doubt and confirmed that this young woman in Halifax had died at the same hand as the mass murderer, these routine inquiries had to continue.

Prior to the confirmation from the pathologist, Assistant Chief Constable Oldfield was still clearly indicating his total failure to grasp the essential nature of the man he hunted.

"If this is connected with the previous Ripper killings, then he has made a terrible mistake. As with Jayne MacDonald, the dead girl is perfectly respectable. . . . It appears he has changed his method of attack and this is concerning me, i.e., now in a non-red-light district and attacking innocents. All women are at risk, even in areas not recognized as Ripper territory."

The response from the people of Halifax to police appeals for information was outstanding. *This* had been the motivation of the local editor when using that photograph.

Sightings of people, scraps of information about cars, all the flotsam and jetsam of a murder investigation that is absolutely vital to its success began to flow into the Halifax murder incident room.

As pieces went into the formless puzzle they often indicated that bigger, more important pieces were still missing.

At about 9:00 P.M. on April 4, just three hours before Josephine was murdered, a man driving a dark-colored Ford Escort attempted to pick up a woman in the center of Halifax. Described as "about thirty years of age, with dirty blond collar-length hair, which was greasy and curly and worn over his ears, he had a Jason King mustache which ended halfway between the corners of his mouth and chin, square face and jaw, and his general appearance was scruffy. Wearing a heavy brushed cotton shirt with a tartan check, open-necked. Also wearing a tartan lumber jacket with a light fur collar.''

A later sighting of the same car saw it drive along Saville Park at midnight and park in the entrance of the Saville Park Lodge, a cafe, long closed at that hour. The Ford Escort was made between 1968 and 1975, suffix letters G to N.

Marilyn Moore, who had survived a vicious attack in December 1977, reacted sharply when she saw the composite the police released to the press. "That's Dave. That's the man that attacked me."

The second sighting of the car in Saville Park, very close not only to the place where Josephine was murdered but also close to the time of her death, had a curious postscript. The owners of the cafe, tucked up in their beds, heard the sound of footsteps near their outside toilets at about 12:10 A.M.

No woman ever came forward to eliminate that puzzle. No man with a Ford Escort solved the riddle of the sightings.

There was another curious sighting at 11:40 P.M. A young woman of Josephine's age and general description and apparently wearing very similar clothes was seen walking close to the park and in the direction of Josephine's home. Walking quite naturally alongside her and with her was a man described as aged nineteen to twenty-two, height five foot eight inches, medium build, mousy-colored greasy hair brushed right to left and a little wavy; appeared not to have shaved for three to four days—stubble on face, prominent cheekbones, sunken cheeks; believed to be wearing a three-quarter length dark-colored coat and jeans.

Did Josephine meet and walk with someone on her way home? If it was not the killer, why did the man not come forward? If it was not Josephine and her killer, why have the couple not come forward?

A new tan- or orange-colored Rover 2.5 or 2.6 liter was seen near the same Park Cafe at about midnight.

A dark-colored Datsun sedan, possibly station wagon, was seen parked without lights very close to the murder spot at about 12:10 in the morning.

These could not all be shy johns, or uncooperative prostitutes. This was *not* a red-light district, but the heart of respectable Halifax where people took offense at the reality of death being shown over their tea and toast. Surely such sensitive people would be the first to rush to the police and eliminate the Datsun that was theirs, or the Rover that they had stopped while they popped into the toilet.

Fortunately the mass murderer himself was a damn sight more forthcoming.

He left some very clear footprints near Josephine's body. The imprint of his size-seven industrial-type boots is there in Wakefield, waiting for him. Boots he could throw away; the size of his feet should prove more difficult to hide.

Quite suddenly information and evidence were pouring in to George Oldfield.

Forensic at Weatherby advised him that the stamp on the third letter received shortly before Josephine's murder had been licked by a person with blood type B, that rare type of 9 percent of which only 6 percent secrete in their semen and saliva. Blood type B, the same type that had been found in the semen traces taken from the dead body of Joan Harrison in Preston.

It was all starting to fit together. The police were now totally convinced that the letters came from the mass murderer.

In letter two he had threatened "next time try an older one I hope"—that was after the murder of eighteen-year-old Helen Rytka. The next victim had been forty-one years old, Vera Millward. Now with that small trace of dried saliva the writer had linked himself with the particular murder that he had referred to twice: the killing of Joan Harrison.

If further proof be needed the police considered they had it. One of Joan's boots had been stuffed between her thighs. Now, one of Josephine's shoes had been placed in the same position.

Lancashire's Head of C.I.D., Wilf Brooks, had remained skeptical for four years about the links between the murder of Joan and the series of murders. Now he was quoted as believing that the likelihood that the same man was responsible had moved from "possible to probable."

When Professor Gee had made further tests he was able to advise Oldfield that he had found traces of oil on Josephine's body. It had been left inadvertently by her murderer. Gee and police forensic established that it was a machine oil. It indicated that the man who had left it could well have engineering or mechanical connections, perhaps be a machine-tool fitter or an electrical or maintenance engineer.

Detailed study of George Oldfield's relationship with the various news media leads one to the inevitable conclusion that they are, in Oldfield's view, merely something to be used, a weapon that is at police disposal. The dictum would seem to be, "tell them what you want them to know, not what they want to know."

Thus on May 17, West Yorkshire's assistant chief constable (crime) gave the press a few of his inner thoughts. Speaking of the man he was hunting he said:

> I believe him to be white, between thirty and fifty-five years of age, at least average to above average height, an artisan or manual worker either skilled or semiskilled, with engineering or mechanical connections. Possibly a skilled machine-tool fitter, electrical or maintenance engineer.
>
> I believe he lives or works in West Yorkshire or in close proximity to that area and in all probability lives alone or with aged parents or a parent and that he has some connections with the northeast area.
>
> I would like the management of firms engaged in machine-tool manufacture, engineering, including electrical or marine engineering, plant and machinery maintenance or similar trades, to examine their records and let me know whether they have any business connections with the northeast. Also whether any of their employees skilled, semiskilled or unskilled were engaged in work in the northeast or Tyneside on any of the following dates: seventh or eighth of March, 1978, twelfth or thirteenth of March, 1978, twenty-second or twenty-third of March, 1979.

He also asked if northeast firms would let him know whether employees from firms in Yorkshire were engaged in maintenance, repair, or installation work on their premises on the respective dates.

He was asking a great deal of a great many people. He was not giving much away himself. Only after another of those leaks that annoy the police so much was it confirmed that all those dates referred to letters, letters thought to have been written by the mass murderer. Information about blood types, shoe size, machine oil, etc., were still in the top-secret file.

There are more than two million engineering workers in the country. The number of engineering firms in Tyneside alone is more than ten thousand.

While the preponderance of the inquiries swung to the north-east, the investigation in Halifax continued. Many of the local people had come forward, had attempted to help. Regrettably those missing pieces of the Saville Park puzzle stayed off the board.

The coroner's verdict on the happy, pleasant nineteen-year-old woman who had died a few minutes from her front door was "Murder by persons unknown."

16

Dear Lauris,

Got your letter this morning with a little green stamp on it saying "6p. to pay." Fraid they don't accept Co-op stamps.

Do you realize that it's gone up to 40 pence a load? (I'm writing this bit in the launderette.)

Rob is still not talking about his split-up with Ann, wish he would, might help him. I noticed though that he puts "Feels Like the 1st Time" by Foreigner on the Mannerville jukebox and he keeps singing that bit, "And I guess it's just the woman in you that brings out the man in me." Oh dear.

I've just about managed to get those stats done!! Only a term late!! Only got my discussion bit to do now.

I've gone all wistful again. I keep listening to nice tunes on the radio and playing Pink Floyd and things. Find a nice man for me at Nottingham ('cos there seems to be plenty there) and persuade him to do a post grad course at Bradford . . . now!!

Easter weekend at home was lovely. The vacation job book has arrived—from the look of things we'll have to aim at

Two of the cities that lived in fear of one man for over five years. *Above:* a street in Leeds. *Below:* Bradford.

Many of the victims still live. *Above:* the four children of Wilma McCann—Richard, Sonje, Angela and Donna. *Below:* Emily Jackson on vacation with her children, Neil, Christopher and Angela.

David, Beryl and Graham Leach at the funeral of Barbara.

Mrs. Irene MacDonald with family friend Mrs. Birnberg.

Jayne, Janet, Debra and Ian MacDonald.

These women survived the Ripper's attacks:

Olive Smelt

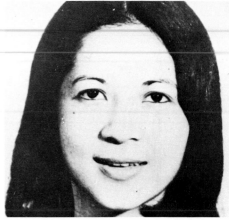

Upaehya Banbara

Anna Rogulskyj

Marilyn Moore

Marcella Claxton

Maureen Long

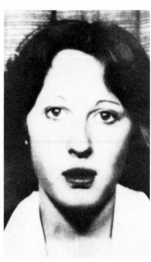

Teresa Sykes

Above, left to right: Dick Holland, George Oldfield and Jack Ridgeway listen to the "Ripper" tape. It fooled the police and led to one of the greatest wild-goose chases in the history of crime. *Below:* James Hobson and Chief Constable Ronald Gregory, two men at the heart of a police investigation riddled with errors.

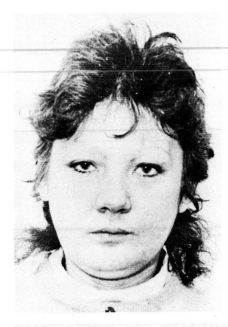

Joan Harrison, murdered in Preston on November 20, 1975. Again and again, police have asserted that this woman was killed by the Yorkshire Ripper. She was not. Her murderer is still at large and is probably responsible for the letters and tape that fooled the police. *Below:* extracts from two of the letters.

Dear Officer,

March 23rd 79

Sorry I haven't written, about a year to be exalt, but I haven't been up North for quite a while. I wasn't kidding last time I wrote

was last month, so I don't know when I will get back on the job but I know it wont be Chapeltown too bloody hot there maybe Bradford, Manningham. Might write again if up North.

Jack the Ripper

P.s Did you get letter I sent to Daily Mirror in Manchester.

About the McDonald lassie I didn't know that she was decent and I am sorry I changed my routine that nyght.

Sutcliffe and his wife, Sonia, at their wedding reception in 1974. Eleven months after these photographs were taken he held a different knife with quite a different purpose in mind.

A far cry from the squalor in which he preyed, Sutcliffe's Bradford house. After his arrest, a handwritten note was found among the maps in his truck. It reads: "In this cab is a man whose latent genius, if unleashed, would rock a nation. His dynamic energies would overpower those around him. But let him sleep?"

strawberry/raspberry etc. picking. I'll bring it with me if I come down next week.

If you don't wear underwear at that party just remember not to get too drunk and start parachuting.

Lots of love
Barbara

P.S. Thought as I'll be in Grove Terrace next year, of having an extra key cut for you, no need to worry about being out on Friday nights then.

P.P.S. Going to a new riding school now, bit like Orton in its heyday, only better. They've got 50 horses! Millions of dogs, cats, geese, donkeys (the dogs come out with us on rides). Helen who runs it is really nice. Gaye and I were chatting away to her as if we'd known her for ages. It's only £2 per hour and this Thursday we're going for a 2-hour one for £3. Saw *Deerhunter* on Monday. V. good.

They came from all parts of the globe. Their theories were as varied. American crime psychiatrist Dr. Arnold Lieber told the West Yorkshire police that the man they were hunting was influenced by the moon.

Clairaudient Doris Stokes declared that his name was "Ronnie or Johnnie, he lives in a street named Berwick or Bewick, his surname begins with 'M,' he is of slight build, about five feet eight inches."

Occulist Billy Watson said, "I find him at some time working on a building scheme between Sunderland and Gateshead. He has neat, dark ginger hair."

Map dowsers put him in Sunderland or Cumbria.

King of the Witches, Alex Sanders, said that while in a trance he had made contact with the killer's spirit. "He lives alone in a flat in South Shields, overlooking railway arches."

Hypnotists offered their services. In fact the police had already had survivors, Marilyn Moore and Maureen Long, hypnotized. The results were not impressive.

A former nurse using a method she called radiesthesia (it involves swinging a needle over a map) said her efforts indicated the murderer lived in the Barnsley/Sheffield area.

Astrologers predicted he would strike on certain specified days.

He didn't. Others confidentially asserted he would not kill again. He did.

Clairvoyants. Spiritualists. Faith healers. Private detectives. Pyschic detectives. Armchair detectives. Criminologists. Sociologists. Psychologists. All offered their views, theories, and opinions.

The criminal underworld in Manchester vowed they would catch the killer, one of their number stating, "All this police action is screwing up our business."

Suddenly, dramatically, Assistant George Oldfield received help from a totally unexpected quarter. Help of such a nature that Oldfield and the officers around him felt that now the net was indeed drawing very close on the mass murderer.

A small package was posted from Sunderland on June 17, 1979. It was addressed in labored capital letters to ASST. CHIEF CONSTABLE OLDFIELD. LEEDS C.I.D., LEEDS CENTRAL POLICE HQ., LEEDS, WEST YORKSHIRE. Also scrawled on it was "From Jack the Ripper." Handwriting experts were in no doubt that the writing was from the same hand that had sent the three letters. The contents removed any last remaining doubts because some of the information contained cross references to the third letter.

This time there was no letter inside the envelope. This time the police listened to the voice of the letter writer, on the cassette he had sent.

I'm Jack.

I see you are still having no luck catching me. I have the greatest respect for you, George, but Lord! You are no nearer catching me now than four years ago when I started. I reckon your boys are letting you down, George. They can't be much good, can they?

The only time they came near catching me was a few months back in Chapeltown when I was disturbed. Even then it was a uniformed copper, not a detective.

I warned you in March that I'd strike again. Sorry it

wasn't Bradford. I did promise you that but I couldn't get there. I'm not quite sure when I'll strike again but it will be definitely sometime this year, maybe September, October, even sooner if I get the chance. I am not sure where, maybe Manchester. I like it there, there's plenty of them knocking about. They never learn, do they George? I bet you've warned them, but they never listen.

At the rate I'm going I should be in the book of records. I think it's eleven up to now, isn't it? Well, I'll keep on going for quite a while yet. I can't see meself being nicked just yet. Even if you do get near I'll probably top myself first. Well, it's been nice chatting to you, George.

Yours, Jack the Ripper

No good looking for fingerprints. You should know by now it's clean as a whistle. See you soon. 'Bye.

Hope you like the catchy tune at the end. Ha. Ha.

The "catchy tune" was a fragment of a pop song by Andrew Gold called "Thank You for Being a Friend."

The accent of the speaker was clear and unmistakable, what is popularly called "Geordie." He spoke as calmly of death and slaughter and mayhem as if he were reading the weather forecast. The voice was controlled, very controlled. On the original tape one can clearly discern the stops and starts, the clicks on and off from the mike switch. Not all the clicks are caused by the man making the recording. The police edited out one particular segment. They have never revealed what it is—never made this extract available to anyone outside a few very senior police officers.

The extract is yet another reference to one particular murder. *The murder of Joan Harrison.*

Also suppressed is the fact that in the view of many speech experts who heard the edited recording that the police did make public, the speaker is masking a speech defect. Probably a stammer.

At times the tape runs on. After "but they never listen" the tape runs on for thirteen seconds of silence while the speaker gathers himself to read the next passage of his prepared speech.

There was none of the rich rise and fall of cadence that one usually hears in a Wearside accent. Flat, unemotional, a voice from the grave. In ordinary circumstances it would be a frightening recording. Under the present circumstances it chilled those who heard it, men accustomed to the violence of our society, familiar with death. Men who had frequently been obliged to view appalling, shocking, disgusting sights, men who had been obliged to stare at the victims that this speaker claimed as his. It is easy to feel deep shame at belonging to the same world that could breed such a creature.

On June 26, 1979, George Oldfield called a major press conference and exploded the tape upon the assembled media and thus upon the nation. Among the men seated alongside Oldfield were Detective Chief Superintendent Jack Ridgeway from Manchester, hunting the killer of Jean Jordan and Vera Millward, Detective Chief Superintendent Wilf Brooks, who sought Joan Harrison's murderer, and Assistant Chief Constable (Crime) Brian Johnson from Northumbria.

The three-minute-thirty-second tape was not all that Oldfield had for the press that afternoon. He had also decided that the time had arrived to release some handwriting samples. Photographs of the four envelopes were handed out to the reporters.

Oldfield went on with his press conference.

All newspapers have deadlines. The biggest scoop of the century is utterly useless if it arrives on the editor's desk thirty minutes after the edition has left the building and is being sped throughout the city in vans.

The two o'clock start to the press conference was cutting it close for the local evening editions. When Yorkshire television interviewer Marilyn Webb persuaded George Oldfield to give her an exclusive interview before the general press conference it was the turn of the press reporters to be enraged. The delay insured that some newspapers could not carry the story on June 28. One of those to miss out was the Bradford *Telegraph and Argus*.

Their retaliation was swift and stunning. On July 12, after the acrimony between the paper and Oldfield had reached extraordinary proportions, the *Argus* revealed to its readers these clues. The murderer, they said,

"Kills with an engineer's ball peen hammer.

"Wears size seven boots with distinctive molded soles that police have described as 'Army style or industrial boots.'

"Leaves traces of machine grease from his fingernails.

"Has a rare blood type, having left traces behind during one of his frenzied attacks.

"Drives an old van or car."

They were accurate on every count but one. Though his blood type is indeed rare he has never left traces of his blood. The pique of the Bradford paper made interesting reading, particularly for the mass murderer.

Having parked his car in the garage, he went indoors. *No one about. Good opportunity to sit down and study that article in the* Argus *again. God, they were right about so much. How did they know?*

He began to rationalize. *There must be thousands and thousands of ball peen hammers knocking about. Size seven? Well, plenty of men had small feet. Machine grease? In Bradford? In the north? Whole bloody area was awash with machine grease—have to be more careful in future, though.* The blood type comment puzzled him. *How had they discovered that? As for the old van or car, so what? That hardly described the Rover.*

Glancing at his watch he realized he would have the house to himself for some time. He needed cheering up after that lot. Needed a laugh. Now, what was the number you could dial? He'd made a note of it somewhere. He found what he was looking for and began to dial. "Dial a Ripper," the papers were calling it. He rang. It was busy. He rang again. Still busy. He'd read in the papers that thousands and thousands were dialing it. That it was more popular than the talking clock.

In between many attempts he made a cup of tea. Thousands of people had not only phoned and listened to the recording, apparently thousands had also subsequently phoned the police and asserted they recognized the voice. Police had received nearly three thousand phone calls in the first couple of days, the papers had said. Experts were all over the papers and TV going on about the handwriting and what it told them about the writer. He'd found all that very interesting.

He'd heard the tape played on TV and the radio. He had read every newspaper he could lay his hands on. Massive front-page coverage. Finally he managed to get through; as the voice began he mouthed the words along with the recording, he knew them so well.

"I'm Jack. I see you are still having no luck catching me. I have the greatest respect for you, George, but Lord! You are no nearer catching me now . . ."

His mouth began to twitch.

"I reckon your boys are letting you down, George. They can't be much good, can they?"

He started to laugh. He tried to choke it back so that he could hear more.

"I warned you in March that I'd strike again. Sorry it wasn't Bradford."

He could listen no longer. His laughter filled the empty house. On and on he laughed. Every time it began to subside the voice on the phone triggered more hysterical response from him.

"Maybe September, October, even sooner if I get the chance."

Helpless, he put the phone back on the hook. He had the greatest difficulty listening to the recording when in company. Alone it was always impossible.

They were pouring men into the northeast. Hundreds of officers going around with bloody tape cassettes of that recording.

They had voice experts diagnosing exactly where the speaker came from, psychiatrists giving considered opinions on the state of the killer's mind, based on the tape.

It was causing a worldwide sensation. And it was all so very, very ironic.

It was not his voice. He had not made the recording.

God knows who this man was. Written three letters to the police, sent them a tape. All a hoax. Somebody out there was on his side. He just hoped whoever it was kept up the good work. "Sorry it wasn't Bradford." He started to laugh again, then grew thoughtful. He hadn't murdered in Bradford since early 1978. He'd planned to but vice cars were everywhere, that pantomime on Church Street. Well, just suppose, just suppose the next murder was in Bradford? Oldfield was quoted as saying the tape might be a hoax but that he was convinced that it wasn't. Something to do with those letters. Well, of course the same nutter had sent the lot. No doubt of that. If he killed in Bradford, in September, that would clinch it, would remove any doubts they had. He would have fulfilled the threat heard by the nation. The nutter had talked about maybe doing the next one in Manchester as well.

He considered the two alternatives. There would be no doubt massive police surveillance in Manchester particularly in September or October. But the situation might have eased off in Bradford. Apart from anything else, he was already here in Bradford. Why bother to drive to Hulme?

The more he considered the possibility, the more the idea appealed to him.

13th July
12 noon

Dear Lauris,

Got your letter this morning and as I'm struggling with some boring research work I thought I'd start a letter back.

Just think how good we are being, 'stead of going off and having fun during vacation. There you are in Nottingham and here I am in Bradford both being good little girls (well, most of the time) and getting down to work (well, some of the time).

Just waiting for Gaye to come round then we're off to the Manville for a pint. I went to the Mecca last Friday and about one o'clock I suddenly remembered Pete (Sheffield) and it didn't bother me at all—even if he'd been there I think I'd have ignored him unless he spoke to me 1st. Good step forward, don't you think?

5ish. I think this is going to be yet another day late as it's pouring down outside, it's 5 o'clock and I'm rather damp from wandering around town with Gaye. I was v. naughty and bought some new earrings (how's your hair, have you got your ears pierced yet?)—one is a feather pair (pastel pink) and t'other little beads n'things (long thin ones 1½ inches I'd say) only just cost £3 for the two, not that I could afford it, but after a dinnertime in the Manville . . .

Got to mend my trousers today cos I'm going riding tomorrow and two weeks ago I split them at the thigh. I tried wearing my jeans last week but they were so tight I felt as if I was perching on the saddle all the time. I'll send this now. See ya.

Love, Babs

George Oldfield released an extract from the third letter on June 29, 1979. Not surprisingly, the response from the release of merely the four envelopes had been very poor. He hoped for a better reaction from the heavily censored extract.

From press blackout to massive publicity. The attitude of the West Yorkshire police toward publicizing details was as consistent as a weathercock. Now they had gone full circle back to massive publicity.

At bingo halls the caller's shouts of "legs eleven" was interrupted for "I'm Jack."

Customers of public houses left their drinks on their tables and listened quietly to the tape.

Some of the hundreds of thousands dialing the free phone number to hear the automatic message succeeded in misdialing to an elderly couple living in Pontefract who had the misfortune of having over two hundred people demanding to hear the tape.

Factory workers downed tools. Machines were switched off while the police played the cassette recording.

Nightclub acts found they went onstage with their patter and songs to audiences chilled by the tape.

Miners found police with a cassette waiting for them instead of a shower when they came up.

Strippers held onto their underclothes for an extra three minutes while the tape was played.

Prisoners found welcome relief from their regime when the tape was played to them.

It had become a bizarre panel game, played by the entire nation: "Catch the Killer."

This extraordinary and unique attempt to catch the killer was initially concentrated in the northeast. A proud people, already devastated by many years of economic depression, on a scale that the south of England cannot comprehend, now had an additional weight to carry. If the police were right, then the Wearside had spawned the most horrific murderer of the century in this country.

Villages like Hylton Castle with its three thousand low-rent housing units suddenly found a police van in their midst with the voice of a boasting Wearsider shaming them all.

Tyneside, with an unemployment figure nearly double the national average, heard the threats of this hoaxer booming in its streets. While they waited for the new boat orders to come in, the unemployed listened to a lunatic on tape.

Suddenly the women of the northeast shared the gripping fear that had become a way of life for their sisters in Yorkshire and Lancashire. It could not be shrugged off with an "it doesn't affect us" attitude. It did. This man was one of them. They might argue about which village he came from, which town had left its mark on him. But there was no mistaking the cold fact that it was indeed a genuine Wearside accent.

Brothers, sisters, mothers, fathers, all now found themselves in a nightmare as they pointed the finger and said "It's him." God alone knows how many marriages, friendships, relationships have been destroyed by the man who sent that tape. He most certainly did not destroy the dead women who littered the north but destroy he most certainly did. His victims still live. Or most of them. He has murdered but, with one exception, not the women that he claims are his victims.

Many a man in Sunderland went through bloody hell after the finger had been pointed. They were taken in for questioning, sometimes for hours, sometimes for days. Even after they had been cleared by the police there would still be friends who now avoid them, neighbors who crossed the street upon their approach. Salem had come to the northeast of England.

Reporters wrote that the reason that the killer had not struck in Sunderland was that prostitutes there do not solicit in the street. Presumably there must be another Sunderland in another country. The one in the northeast of England has street prostitutes in abundance. One of them, a girl named Sandra, told the police, "I recognize that voice. I have had sex with the Yorkshire Ripper three times."

The obsession that enveloped George Oldfield in his hunt for the mass murderer became even more marked after the tape recording had become public property. The assistant chief constable's comments clearly illustrated that to him it had become that most dangerous of things for a policeman, "my case."

"It is a personal challenge. I suppose it is very much him against me."

"I would like to talk to this man and I feel he wants to talk to me. If he wants to phone me that would be fine. . . . This has become something of a feud. He obviously wants to outwit me but I won't pack it in until he's caught."

"I'll meet you anywhere, anytime. *Alone.*"

"The voice is almost sad, a man fed up with what he has done, fed up with himself. A man who feels he knows me enough almost to take me into his confidence."

On August 13, 1979, Oldfield's body declared that it was time to take a rest. He suffered a heart attack and was ordered to take sick leave. In his absence Dick Holland took temporary command. Holland, like his superior, is also on record as stating his firm conviction that the man who sent the tape was the mass murderer.

17

"No good looking for fingerprints. You should know by now it's clean as a whistle.

"See you soon. Bye.

"Hope you like the catchy tune at the end. Ha. Ha."

For a moment they all sat mesmerized, then David Leach turned the radio off. There was quite a gathering. Graham had come over from Cambridge. Lauris was down from Nottingham and Barbara from Bradford. Graham was the first to speak.

"Must be fun up in Bradford, Babs?"

"Because of him, you mean?"

"Yes."

"You just try not to think about it all the time. Can't live in constant fear, can you?"

Beryl came into the room carrying a parcel, which she handed to her daughter.

"What's this, Mum?"

"From your father and me. Thought it might stop you nagging us to buy them."

She rapidly opened the parcel.

"Oh! New riding boots. The ones I wanted. Oh thanks, Mum. Thanks, Dad."

Her father spread his hands expansively.

"Could be worse. You might have seen a Mercedes you fancied."

"Look, Lauris. Look."

"They're great. Pity we're not at the same university, I might get to borrow them."

Beryl began to set the table for tea.

"No, Babs and I will do that, Mrs. Leach. They teach us how to at Nottingham."

"Thank you, Lauris. What were you talking about just now, Barbara? About living in fear?"

"Oh, just the Ripper, Mum. They played the tape again on the radio."

Beryl gave a shiver of disgust.

"Thank God nothing like that happens here in Kettering."

"Or in Nottingham, Mrs. Leach. Do you remember, Babs, when I wrote to you about walking around town in the middle of the night with Noreen? You were amazed."

"Yes, I was. It's absolutely unheard-of for a couple of girls to walk around Bradford at night. At night no girl in her right mind will walk anywhere by herself, not even from the university halls."

"Should have gone to Bath or Birmingham, sister. They offered you places."

"You can talk, Crow. You went to Cambridge and had to cope with their rapist. Oh, it's not so bad, Mum. I mean in our street we've only got two brothels and that nice Mr. Sing who lived a few doors down and went to jail for knifing two people in a nightclub."

David shook his head, bemused.

"Well, the sooner this fellow's caught the better."

"Don't worry, Dad. P'rhaps I'm lucky. Never had any trouble. Does make you wary though, walking about by night. I find I jump at anything and always suspect the worst of everyone."

She caught her mother's worried look.

"It's all right, Mum, I'll always be on my toes. Crow, can we play some of your records while you're all scoffing?"

"Sure. But no chewing gum on the records, right?"

"Right."

"Don't you want anything to eat, dear?"

"Mum, I'm trying to lose weight. So's Lauris. That's why we

can't bear to watch you all. Come on, Lauris."

A moment later the house was filled with the sound of Roger Daltrey telling everyone that "We won't get fooled again."

He parked the car well out of the red-light district and after carefully locking it walked toward Lumb Lane. He was hoping that perhaps things had quieted down—that the whores were no longer confined to Church Street. He was disappointed. The same bizarre scene met his eyes. Lumb Lane without a single prostitute. Church Street overflowing with them and with murder squad cars. *Eight months now they had been at this nonsense. They had a bloody cheek making it legal, even in the small congested area.* He wandered into the Carlisle, ordered a pint of bitter and quietly made his way to the far end of the bar. The pub was full of them. It was like a bloody bus service. This lot waiting to take over from those outside. He'd made up his mind the next one was going to be Bradford and nothing was going to change that.

13th Aug.
11:30 Monday night

Dear Lauris,

Yes, I know I saw you at home yesterday but I've just had a brilliant idea, well I think it's brilliant. Hope you agree. How about you borrowing some of my grandma's money to go to jolly old Hellenic places with? I know how much you don't like being in debt, but it wouldn't be like that 'cos you know there'd be absolutely no pressure for paying it back (Paul's just told me what bad grammar this is but you know what I mean, don't you, besides, it wouldn't be like one of my letters if it wasn't, would it?!) Anyway, it wouldn't matter at all (you know that) and I doubt if ever you can guess how much I want (or need?) to go away. Mum said I could have £200 so I thought if you praps borrowed £100 even, we could have a couple of reasonable weeks 'cos we could split the money down the middle (as usual), then we could both enjoy ourselves, what d'ya think? Please agree 'cos I don't think I can get thru till finals without cracking up if I don't get away!!?

A bit later in my room.

Oh, to have a relationship like the one I had with Ben!
'Spose that was bound to come up 'cos I'm playing lots of Jeff
Airplane at the mo, especially today—that track that I played
a lot last summer, remember? But it does seem at the mo that
it was rather idyllic, I want—oh, what do I want? Talk about
writing down your thoughts as they come into your head,
even ½-finished thoughts!

I suppose (understatement) another reason why I'm depressed is 'cos of Paul—he thinks he'd going to get a "Dear
John" type letter from Melv any day now and he's rather
down about it, which puts me in a bit of a position, what do I
do? I feel really sorry for him but at the same time pleased
but if he's down about her, he's not going to think of any
kind of relationship with me unless of course its purely
sexual—and you know where they lead (Rob?). We have
been getting on well, very well in fact, friendwise. Should I
seduce him and hope it sparks something off or leave it till he
makes a move (if he's going to?!)?

Now I've read that bit again, and it sounds really calculat-
ing but you know what I mean and how I feel don't you?

Anyway, I'll finish here and send this off tomorrow
morning so that I'm not in suspenders for too long (about
Greece). Here's hoping.

Lots love,
B.

P.S. My new room in the attic here looks great. The shelves
that Dad bought last weekend and fixed up when he brought
me back up are a treat. Have half adopted a white kitten and
called it J.C. ('cos of T.C. and J.C.C., John Cooper Clarke).

In the middle of August he yet again checked out the Lumb
Lane area. The situation was as before. Again he went to the
Carlisle.

From the moment that he had decided to oblige whoever had
sent that tape and letters to the police, the urge to kill again and to
kill in Bradford had grown daily.

Again he considered using false license plates on the car. He'd done it before, after that other visit from the police. They'd logged his car in a couple of the red-light districts. Yet again he had fooled them. Again his alibi had stood the test of their questions.

He had conned them again when they had paid yet another visit to the factory, checking out companies that used ball peen hammers, checking companies that used certain kinds of machine oil. Either he was the most brilliant murderer ever or the police were all bloody fools. He smiled. Not once, not twice, but three times now he had fooled them. Three times he had been closely questioned. You'd think they would be able to put one and one and one together and get the right answer. So much for all these bloody cross-referenced index files they were always going on about. So much for all those little cards he'd seen on TV when the cameras went into the murder incident room in Millgarth. *Inefficient bastards.*

He was strongly tempted to use some false license plates again but there was always a chance of a random check with their bloody computer. Well, even if they did a routine search of his car, he could hardly be doing his kind of work without his hammer, screwdrivers, chisels, and knives. That'd take some explaining away, yet he'd fooled them so many times. Perhaps he could fool them again?

Frowning, he sipped his drink and weighed the pros and cons in his mind. Perhaps there was somewhere he could leave the tools? Pick up the prostitute and stop on the way to collect what he needed. They'd still have his license number, though. Those buggers sitting up in Church Street. If he used false plates that might draw even more attention.

Deep in thought, he strolled out of the Carlisle. The car was safely locked and he felt like a walk.

Preoccupied, he walked the length of Lumb Lane and turned into Manningham. It was a warm summer's evening. People about in the city enjoying themselves. Suddenly he stopped stock-still. *Must be losing my touch. Should have thought of it before.* That one he'd dumped at Bowling Back Lane. That's where he'd picked her up. He was staring at the dance hall on Manningham, the spot where he had offered Maureen Long a lift home. There were no police cars in sight. It wasn't one of the beats used by the prostitutes.

Have to be careful, though. They might bring the cars down to this area when the dance hall closed and the people turned out.

He walked back quickly to the spot where he had parked the car. As he started the engine he checked the time. *Half past ten. Plenty of time to pop home, pick up the tools, and be back outside before they came out of the Mecca. Christ, time to have a bath and a meal and watch TV as well.* No, tonight, he decided, was for checking out the possibilities. Wouldn't do if the police were on surveillance and he was stopped with hammer and knives in the car. In fact, rather than wait outside he now had a better idea. Why not go in and check?

The surging sound of Donna Summer singing her McArthur Park medley swirled around the disco. On the packed dance floor a hot sweating clientele were getting their money's worth.

He stood outside the crowd, as was his custom when checking. The music was good and he felt the inclination to join in but thought better of the idea. Low profile was basic when he was checking. His eyes were drawn to a group of young people leaping and jumping about to the music. Obviously students. One girl in particular caught his attention. Good looking, about five feet four inches, bit too much weight but still very attractive. He noted her dark brown hair, cut medium length. She had a good figure inside that blouse. He moved closer to the dance floor. She was wearing tight jeans and as she swung her shoulders away from him he saw a brass badge on her bottom. He was too far away to make out what was written on it. He looked at her long legs as she moved in her own private world. She was a very good dancer. Then he saw her shoes. Not shoes but boots. Red high-heeled boots. He felt the excitement surging through his body. He had to physically restrain himself from walking onto the dance floor and joining this young woman. He knew now. Knew for a certainty whom he was going to kill next. It was only a question of where and when. She swung back toward him and noticed he was looking at her. She smiled at him warmly. Quickly he turned away and melted into the background.

"Who are you smiling at, Babs?"

"Dunno. Just some guy. He looked nice."

Later he followed the group home. Noted the road she lived in—Grove Terrace. The number of the house was of no importance. He decided to check the area. The whores of Lumb Lane and Church Street were a good mile away. The university where she probably went was just across the way on Great Horton Road. About three hundred yards away, going into town, he saw to his amusement the city's central police station.

Good to do one on their doorstep. Retracing, he walked up Great Horton Road. Past the Deutsche Evangelische Kirche. Past a restaurant called The Last Pizza Show. Past a board that proclaimed that the building behind it was The Association of Ukrainians (Bradford Branch). Past the pub that would be her local "The Manville Arms." It was a mixed area and not one he had previously checked. He saw with interest that many of the Victorian houses in the side roads running off Great Horton Road were owned by the university. Others by Asians. Shops on nearby Morley Road with their "Khan Brothers Hardware and Electrical" and "Mugal Electric" signs showed the influx.

Back and forth he walked. Down Ash Grove and then left into Morley Road, then immediately left again into Back Ash Grove, a cobbled alleyway that led back to Great Horton Road. He made mental notes of various possible spots. He checked on entrances and exits.

This was not a red-light district where no one gave a damn what was going on. This was like the last one in Halifax. *Need to be careful. Need to be sure. Measure twice. Cut once.*

20th August
'bout ten p.m.

Dear L,

Suddenly remembered tonight that I hadn't written back to you, so thort I'd start a letter in bed.

Never mind 'bout Greece. Praps we can get there during Xmas vac. Don't worry, I do understand 'bout exams. *Do* I understand about exams!

We took J.C. to the pub tonight, she's been once before and doesn't mind, she's a real favorite, the punks kept coming up saying, "Ah isn't she lovely"! One has demanded that we take her in tomorrow night as well!

She seems to be fairly OK now, got over her flu and is as lively (and as pesky at times) as a cricket!

Just had an amazing weekend. The Manville's been done up now and it was the kind of celebration on Friday, so was in there Friday, Sat, and Sun dinnertimes (latter with parents who'd come for the day, it was good to see them) and also at night, usual finish drinking time was 2:30 A.M. then went for a curry and consequently on Monday I was a bit ill—not booze, just generally run down I think 'cos I hadn't been to bed before 3 for the past week, most times it was 4:30 A.M. or after. Blows yer mind, man!! Really been having a great time. Got tangled with Tony over the weekend (remember the punk barman who looks a little bit like Mark? Geordie?). Don't know quite what's happening now, he was a bit off yesterday (well, v. off, he virtually forced himself to say hello to me it seemed) but tonight he was the same as usual, with a special wink for me. Oh, I don't know, we slept together a couple of times but strictly slept—last night kinda turned me upside down, Paul came up 'cos he couldn't sleep and— well—how could I resist? Mind you, I really don't think there's any possibility of much there except friendship and I'm not quite sure how I feel about that.

Had my left ear pierced again today—a bid to catch up on Tony 'cos he's got three in each. Did I mention that he was one of the 1st three punks in Bradford? He's amazing fun and v. interesting for someone with three O-levels!! Spot the intellectual snob! No, honestly, I don't mean it but he seems to have led a really hard life. Hope nothing goes wrong there to spoil anything that there is—if you see what I mean!

Was going to have my hair permed back at Kettering this week but Sue's on holiday so I thought I'd leave it. It's looking really scruffy now.

D'ya know it's been really nice with Rob away—I haven't missed him at all. I know it's an awful thing to say but I haven't. Spose it'll be good to see him again but to face the prospect of rows in the house about anything and everything, well, you can imagine.

I still haven't done much work. J.C. and the Manville keep

taking up my time (Roy is trying to get me to work there now, but I'm a coward!) I started a bit of Ideas today, but it was so frustrating (the reality of beauty, it was about?) that I gave up after ¾ hr.

To get back to Tony, we went around town together on Sat afternoon and all the way round he was trying to embarrass me (he didn't succeed), he was doing Third Reich impressions and passing comments at virtually every female he saw—it was really entertaining! He's got amazing muscles as well, s'funny, obviously he's got a reputation for being hard but he says no one in Bradford has ever seen him fight, no one challenges him. S'funny how people can build impressions isn't it—he's really quite an insecure and gentle person.

Ah well, must get to sleep now, praps write a bit more tomorra.

Tomorra. Going to sign on now so I'll post this.

Love,
B.

The following day, to her parents:

Well, here it is, the long awaited epistle, although I'm not guaranteeing (doesn't look right but Paul doesn't know either) it'll be the same length as St. Paul's (no, I haven't canonized Walter, I meant t'other one).

Well, what's happened recently: We've been in the Manville quite a lot. On the Sunday when you'd gone, we stayed late in the Manville and consequently I was ill on Monday. Not due to excess alcohol as you might think but I think I was generally run down, lack of sleep and all that sort of thing. My head was spinning and aching. I had a terribly sore throat and swollen glands, oh yes, and my body was aching all over like before you go in for a heavy cold. My tongue looked as if it was coated in ermine (without the black spots). What fun, ay? I was more or less OK by Tues altho' I still had swollen glands and a sore throat. Walter had dumped JC in my room in the morning 'cos he'd gone off to Harrogate and she kept pouncing on, and fighting my feet all afternoon

(I stayed in bed till 5 p.m.!). She's a right little pest at the mo 'cos she's so lively! Oh yes, she got a clean bill of health from the vet—during conversation he found out that I was a student and then he didn't charge me for the consultation— it didn't cost a penny! That was nice, wasn't it? 'Specially for me.

I had my left ear pierced again last week, a lovely little diamond stud. So I'd caught up with Tony (you remember he bought us a drink) on one side, then on Friday night in the Manville he got a bit drunk (as per usual for everyone in the M on a Fri night) and Debbie (a friend) pierced his ear (again) and nose, with a hypodermic syringe. Just went outside and came in a minute or two later with ear and nose pierced. Apparently it doesn't hurt that much to do it yourself—I don't spose it would 'cos now professionals don't even freeze your ear, do they? Rob enjoyed his hol, and is in a much better mood now. He burst in last night (Tues) (he came back on Sun) and pulled the lounge door off its hinges, so we can't close it now! So J.C. has the run of the house, now which is OK as long as she doesn't meet any rats. I think they only come out in the kitchen though, so we close that door.

Sorry my writing's so scrappy but I've already written to Guy, Phil and Tim to tell them about the gas bill so I can't be bothered to keep it tidy—and it's readable isn't it, just about!

Got the Apocrypha vol. that I wanted yesterday—about a third of it is all apocalyptic writings so it's really valuable, and introductions saying how early Xian differs from Jewish and late Xian. Mind you, there's a fair old bit there to plough thru.

You'll be pleased to hear that they're cleaning that bit of alley above us as well, although they've put all the burnable stuff at the end of our garden and it stinks to high heaven.

Vegetables are going well. We usually cook the potatoes with their skins on so they don't mash up. Works quite well. Only discovered the cabbage yesterday so haven't tried that yet.

Can't think of anything else at the mo so I'll drink my cup

of coffee and put this in the post (not at the same time, you understand).

See ya.

Love
B.

Barbara yawned and blearily climbed out of bed. Thursday morning, she thought, then her face brightened. It was signing-on day at the local Labor Exchange. The money from social security was more than welcome. The small white kitten observed her bare feet as she padded about the room. Suddenly it launched an attack.

"Oh! J.C., that's no way to treat your mother."

Barbara moved around the room picking up her cosmetics. She checked her diary. There was an entry for the day, August 30. She had written "Going home?" Well, there wasn't much point, couldn't get her hair done until Sue came back from her holidays. She made a mental note to call home on Saturday and ask Mum to book an appointment for the following week. She bent down and picked up the kitten.

"Right, J.C., let's see if those louts are out of the bathroom. You can come and play with my toes in the bath. But no biting."

The following day she met Gaye for lunch at the Shoulder of Mutton. Gaye was the nearest she had come to finding a replacement for Lauris during term time. They had grown close over the past two years. Comparing notes on the various men in their lives. Horseback riding together outside Bradford. Lunchtime chats during term when they skipped off together for a drink and a bite. In the evening they were invariably joined by some of the men who roomed in the same house as Babs. Both women much preferred the lunchtimes. At least then she could have an uninhibited moan about the people at 20 Grove Terrace. She always felt better after talking to Gaye, and of course they were both taking the same degree. It was that aspect that brought them together for lunch on Friday.

"You see, Gaye, if we share the research like we did last year, we can get twice as much done. Remember that personal construct grid?"

Gaye laughed.

"Only too well. I remember how hard we found it clarifying our thoughts about relations and friends. Until we had that little chat in your room. Said we'd chat for an hour—"

"And ending up talking all day. Do you want another drink?"

"In a minute, Babs. I think you're dead right about working together—"

"Thought I'd find you two here waiting for me."

The interruption had come from Rob, who had appeared unheralded and uninvited.

"Rob, we're talking about work."

"Makes a change. Let's change the subject, then."

"Rob, will you go away and play with someone else, please."

"You are joking of course."

"I am not joking of course."

"Oh, all right. Be like that, then."

The pique that he stormed off in was incongruous. The two young women looked at each other, then spontaneously laughed. Gaye gripped her friend's arm.

"I'm glad it's all over between you two."

"Not as glad as I am, Gaye."

"Look. Tell you what. He's spoilt the chat we were having but I think it would be great to work together during our last year. Let's have another drink now and be bitchy about Rob. Monday we'll meet for an evening meal?"

"Can you make it lunch? I'm going home to Kett in the afternoon for a few days."

"Right, lunch it is. 12:30, here."

"Fine, now let me get you a drink and tell you how bloody awful Rob's been."

18

He checked the day's date. It was September 1, 1979. He'd waited patiently. The voice on the tape had said "September or October, even sooner if I get the chance."

As he left the house to check that he had all he needed in his car he wondered if tonight he might just get that chance.

The Manville was packed when he slid unnoticed into the bar. On the juke box the theme from *The Deerhunter* was playing. He looked casually around the pub. Punks, students, locals. For a moment he thought he was going to be unlucky. Then he saw her with a group of her friends playing darts. He relaxed and walked to the bar.

"Pint of Tetley's, please."

Working his way through the crowd with his drink, he moved for a moment near the dart board. As he sipped the beer his eyes never left her. Beige long-sleeved blouse. Those same blue jeans and he noted with excitement those same high-heeled red boots. She threw a dart that clattered to the floor. Laughing, she moved forward within touching distance of him as she bent to pick it up. He could clearly read the small brass badge on her backside now. It said "Best Rump."

And that, he thought, *is exactly how I'll treat you.*

He moved away now. To the other end of the room. Frowning, he realized that some of the group she was playing darts with roomed in her building. He recognized them from previous visits to the area. If they'd come with her, then they'd go home with her. *Still, never know. She might leave alone.* From his observations on previous visits he also knew that this woman was in the habit of staying behind with her friends after closing time. Clearly they were special friends of the proprietor. Perhaps they might not all leave together. *Have to wait, just wait.*

At closing time, the group were still going hammer and tongs at the dart board. He dared not linger and draw attention to himself.

He walked up Great Horton Road to where he had parked his car. Getting in, he drove slowly down the road until he was near the pub. The road was a wide one. No problem on a Saturday night to park and just sit there, waiting, watching.

"What's the time, Roy?"

"God, nearly one in the morning. I've got to get to bed."

"Right, I'll just wash these glasses and we'll be off."

"O.K., Paul."

"You know, Alison, I think I'm beginning to crack up."

"What's the matter, Babs?"

"Well, it's my dad's birthday today and I didn't remember until this morning. Too late to send him a card. I'm going mad."

"You should have phoned home."

"I did, sang Happy Birthday to him and booked a hair appointment for Monday. Booked a perm at the same time. Last one's grown right out."

"Oh no, it looks fine."

Paul came round from behind the bar where he had been serving. "Right then, who fancies going for a curry?"

Alison went to the door and peered through a window.

"Not for me. It's raining."

In the darkened car he peered across the road as the door of the pub opened. He cursed as he saw not one but four of them walk out into the street. He watched idly as they walked up the road. Well, there was always another night. There always had been before. He watched as they paused on the corner of Grove Terrace.

The debate about the curry had ended in a majority vote against. As the others turned towards their home, Barbara paused.

"Think I'll just take a walk around the block. Clear the cobwebs away. You coming, Paul?"

"No, it's raining."

"Fair enough, but could you wait up for me? I've lost my key. Only be a few minutes."

"Right, we'll get the kettle on."

As the others started to walk down Grove Terrace, Barbara adjusted the shoulder strap on her khaki haversack, swung it onto her shoulder and began to stroll up Great Horton Road.

He saw the group leave her. Saw her begin to walk up Great Horton Road. He paused for a moment until the others had vanished down Grove Terrace, then, starting the engine quickly, made a U-turn. She walked past Claremont, then turned down Ash Grove.

Quickly he pulled up alongside Back Ash Grove. He picked up his hammer and a knife. The same knife he had used on the body of Josephine Whitaker in Halifax.

Because of his previous visits to the area he knew that this little cobblestoned passage ran parallel to the road she was walking down.

Quickly he ran down the passage. Here and there student parties were in progress. Music and laughter on the wet summer evening air. And the sound of his feet moving ever faster over the cobblestones. Halfway down he judged that he was in front of her, moved quickly through the side entrance of a house and stood in the shadows of Ash Grove. Yes, she was several hundred yards away, walking towards him, casually, without a care in the world.

He tensed himself, hammer in hand, waiting to spring out of the dark. It was always out of the dark with him. He heard her footsteps as she approached. Her boots echoed eerily as she strolled on the wet pavement, already laced with early falling leaves. Her boots. Those red high-heeled boots.

Like a vulture diving at helpless prey, he sprang. Arm coiled back. Then he smashed the hammer onto that young head.

One blow was enough. She slumped to the pavement. Dead.

Quickly, like a fevered animal, he dragged her body back. Back into the shadows of the side entrance toward Back Ash Grove. In the yard behind No. 13 he dropped the lifeless body. Panting, he stared down at her. A moment later he was pulling at her blouse, lifting her brassiere, pulling down her jeans and panties. Putting the hammer in his pocket, he began to stab and rip at her abdomen. At the life-force area. At that part of all women that he could not tolerate. Hated. The knife went into the soft flesh again and again. Eight times he stabbed her, then he was satiated. He pulled down her blouse, the white material rapidly turning red. He looked around for something, anything to cover her. It was over now. Time to pretend it had never happened. He dragged her body toward some garbage cans and there, finding a piece of old carpet, covered her. He dumped Barbara with the rubbish.

He listened. The music and laughter and life from the student parties could still be heard. Nothing had changed, except for Barbara.

He walked quietly along the cobblestones. Past houses full of light and warmth. At one flat a student was sitting half out of a window. Glass in hand. He walked on to his car and realized for the first time that the bloodstained knife was still in his hand. A hand covered with the warm blood of a twenty-year-old girl. Thrusting the knife into a pocket, he took out his car keys and unlocked the door.

Moments later he was driving home. Home to his wife.

Paul, Alison, Rob, and the others at the house waited up for about an hour. It wasn't like Babs to stay out all night; she'd never done it before. They rationalized that perhaps she had dropped in to see friends at one of the parties.

The following morning they found her bed unslept in. Doubts began to set in. They started to check with other students, including Gaye. At lunchtime they went to the Manville Arms, fully expecting that she would stroll through the door and tell of some adventure that had detained her.

When the pub closed at lunchtime on that Sunday without her appearance, they contacted the police.

At eight-thirty that evening David and Beryl Leach were deeply involved in an episode of "The Onedin Line" on television when the phone rang. David smiled at his wife.

"That'll be Barbara."

Beryl walked to the phone. The caller was a man.

"Is Barbara there?"

"No. She's coming home tomorrow. Can I take a message?"

"It's the Bradford police here. Barbara's been reported missing since Saturday night. We wondered if she'd gone home."

"No, she hasn't and that's most unusual for her to stay out like that. Most unusual."

"Right, we'll keep checking. Let you know as soon as we have any news."

David had been listening to half the conversation. What he had not heard he could read on his wife's face. She moved to her husband.

"That was the Bradford police. Barbara's been missing since Saturday night."

They both knew their daughter well enough to know that something serious must have happened to her. They felt then that first spasm of panic.

"That's just not like her, David."

Her husband felt the anxiety growing inside.

"Perhaps it's a hoax call. Somebody having a joke."

"Pretty sick joke."

After an eternity he obtained the number from information.

After a few moments on the phone he was in no doubt that the call was genuine. He offered to drive directly to Bradford and was told the journey would be pointless. That they would be advised as soon as news came to hand.

After a sleepless night, they debated what to do.

Eventually David went off to his job in a local bank. Beryl was not due to recommence teaching until the following day. A fellow teacher came to keep her company.

Throughout the day the phone rang, not the police with news but Barbara's companions in Grove Terrace to say that the police were still looking.

At seven-thirty on Monday evening David phoned the Bradford police again.

"Hello, yes, David Leach here. Can you tell me what's happening? Is there any news?"

He was told there was no news. By now a deep fear had taken

hold of this shy couple. Five minutes later the phone rang. David snatched at it. This time it was a different policeman.

"Hello, Mr. Leach?"

"Yes, who's that?"

"I'm Detective Chief Inspector Smith. Thought I'd ring and have a chat with you about Barbara. We've no news yet."

They talked quietly about the young woman, her father remarking that she was a silly girl to cause all this fuss. The chief inspector was understanding.

"Well I've got daughters too. Know what it's like."

Eventually with a promise from the chief inspector to let them know the moment the police found out anything, they said goodbye.

The void was deepening now. They phoned Graham and told him his sister was missing. They phoned other relations and warned them that there just might be something in the papers about Barbara being missing.

At 9:15 that evening the front doorbell rang. It was a local police sergeant and a policewoman. Before they spoke David thought, *Barbara's gone.* The police merely confirmed that fact.

Beryl's brother had come over during the afternoon. His kindness and reassurance had helped them through the last few hours of the hell. David and Beryl attempted to conceive the inconceivable, to grasp a nightmare and look closely at it. Barbara's father turned to the sergeant.

"I suppose you'd like me to come up and identify her tomorrow?"

"As a matter of fact, Mr. Leach, we'd like you to both go up tonight. We'll send a car around for you."

They sped north within the hour. A journey that her father knew well. Many times he had gone up to collect Barbara for vacations. Many times he or his daughter had driven back to Bradford.

They had been told at 9:15 P.M. that their daughter was dead, that she had been murdered. The police in Bradford had discovered her body five hours earlier, at five minutes past four in the afternoon. Within minutes of the discovery by a constable on routine search for Barbara they knew beyond all doubt that this was the earthly remains of Barbara Leach. Five extra hours of a living hell. Within that time Professor Gee's initial examination had already established that this was yet another in the series of murders. Still Barbara's parents in Kettering continued to suffer torment. Nothing that the police did during that five hours, and in truth they did very little, justifies such cruel insensitivity.

Shortly after midnight they were in Bradford. They met Smith and a short while later they saw what was left of their daughter.

After what passed for a night's sleep in a nearby hotel they were back at the police station again to make statements. They wanted all the details of her life, of Graham's life, of friends, relations, acquaintances. An instant biography of a twenty-year-old's life.

Later David and Beryl went to the house in Grove Terrace to see her companions. The house was full of policemen. When he walked into her attic room, her father saw that they were checking her desk for fingerprints, the desk he had made for her the previous year. Later that day, after they had refused to meet the press, they were driven back home by a constable, a young Yorkshire lad who had already had to cope with one appalling situation. It was he who had found Barbara's body under the old carpet.

As they drove back down the M.1 their minds were full of fragmented memories of a girl who was no more. Of the family car that she scraped more than once. Of her joy at horseback riding, in fact her great love for all animals. During the year that was to follow they would get many a reminder of that aspect of their daughter's life when annual subscription requests from Greenpeace, the R.S.P.C.A., the Canine Defense League and several others dropped onto their mat. They recalled earlier holidays with their children, climbing Snowdon, Cornwall, the South Coast. It was impossible to grasp. Because she had been away in a different city for so much of the previous two years, there would be many times when they half expected her to return for a weekend, moments when the horror slipped slightly out of focus and they wondered when she would next write or phone.

Graham, her brother who had always been Crow to her, caught a train from Havant to join his parents.

He sat in the restaurant car huddled in a corner, ordering drink after drink. He thought of the arguments he had had with his sister during their childhood, of how in the last few years they had begun to work at and establish a deeper relationship. His mind whirled with the alcohol and the memories and he began to cry. Eventually he shook his head and, thinking that he must pull himself together, he began to wander down the train.

He got to the guards' car. On the floor were a pile of *Daily Mirrors*. Barbara's face stared up at him from the front page. He just stood there swaying, staring back at the image of his sister. The guard wandered in.

"What are you doing?"

Graham did not respond, just continued to stare at the photograph.

The guard looked at him for a moment, then said, "Fuck off."

When Lauris was told, she collapsed. She remained heavily sedated for several days.

A few weeks later the family went back to Bradford, to Grove Terrace, to the last haven she had known. As they began to pack up her belongings, everything seemed to have a poignancy.

On the desk was her application for the new year's scholarship, half completed. They found the present she had bought for her father on that Saturday afternoon. A mug with the friendly inscription "Life is too short not to live it up a little."

Beryl wound back the tape cassette a little way. Wondering what her daughter had been listening to. The voice of Melanie filled the attic room:

"The hardest thing under the sun above is to say goodbye to the one you love."

Put all this in a film, a play, a novel and it would be said that life is not really like that.

In the corner of the room, unused, waiting for the new term, were the riding boots they had given Barbara a lifetime ago.

"Why won't they call in Scotland Yard?"

19

It was a question that had been asked with increasing frequency and growing urgency over the four-year period that a mass murderer had freely ranged. There were two reasons why, despite massive pressure from the news media and the general public, that Gregory and his senior officers continued to angrily brush aside any suggestions that Scotland Yard might have some useful contribution to make to the investigation.

Before the Second World War the various provincial police forces numbered over 130. Few, if any, had forensic laboratories to equal that in London. Fewer had such a wide cross-section of detectives as Scotland Yard. Criminal records held at the Yard were available in only very limited form to the provinces.

Today the provincial police forces have been reduced to just 43. Each has its own forensic lab. Each has immediate access via computer to all the criminal records stored in London.

The other reason that Chief Constable Gregory and his senior officers resisted calls for the Yard to be brought in was a simple one. Arrogant pride. Asked at the press conference that launched a hoax tape on the British Public why he had not called in the Yard, Oldfield was for a moment nonplussed. Not so Dick Holland; he stared at the questioner, then said, "Why should we? They haven't caught theirs yet."

Extremely witty.

Lancashire Police Chief Albert Laugharne observed at about the same time as that press conference, "Aid sought by a small force from a larger may still be done somewhat reluctantly.

"It is done less often than perhaps it ought ideally to be, if the requesting chief constable feels that he thereby throws doubt on his self-sufficiency."

In the first week of the investigation into Barbara's death, Chief Constable Gregory gave a public demonstration that even if the men he controlled were capable of crass insensitivity with regard to bereaved parents, he was extremely sensitive. On September 5, 1979, the *Daily Express*, known in Fleet Street as the *Police Gazette*, headlined a story that Home Secretary Whitelaw had ordered a top member of Scotland Yard to head a squad of very senior officers. The squad, the paper stated were going to head the hunt for "the Yorkshire Ripper."

That brought the chief constable from his bed, fast. Previous press conferences that week had been headed by Detective Superintendent Peter Gilrain. With Oldfield in a sickbed, Holland rushing back from a vacation in Scotland, Detective Chief Superintendent Jim Hobson nursing a wife with a fractured skull, the top ranks were thinning fast. Gregory came to the rescue of his beleaguered officers. He told the reporters that the article in the *Express* was "false," that he knew "nothing of this move; the Home Office knows nothing of it and I am amazed that this newspaper, who is normally helpful to murder investigations, should embark on this form of speculative journalism." He called the paper irresponsible and declared that the story could seriously undermine the morale of the investigating officers. He then stated:

"No other officers from any force other than those already involved will be coming into the enquiry."

In answer to reporters' questions about the letters and the tape that the police had received he said, "It is not one hundred percent certain that the handwriting and voice is from the man but we feel so. There are certain features about it; we feel it is connected.

"We do not want to publish the whole of the letters, otherwise we would have nothing to talk about with a suspect, but it is possible that more of the handwriting may be released in the near future. It would be wrong to publish the whole of the letters."

It is because there is powerful evidence that indicates the letters are not from the mass murderer that they are published verbatim in this book.

The subsequent events with regard to the investigation into the murder of Barbara Leach clearly illustrate that Gregory and his West Yorkshire police force certainly needed help from somebody.

Police stated that prior to the murder of Barbara they had made "certain preparations which will at last enable us to identify and arrest the man responsible." Whatever those "certain preparations" were, they were clearly inadequate. No arrest was made. The seven-minute gap from when Barbara left her companions until the moment she was murdered was not closed.

Some of the lines of inquiry followed after Barbara's murder defy explanation. They interviewed in depth all first-year students who arrived on the university campus for the first time, one month after the murder. In view of the fact that they were seeking a mass murderer who began those murders in 1975, the first-year students interviewed in October 1979 would have been about fourteen years of age when the series of attacks and murders started.

While the Chief Constable and some very senior officers stated that legal action would be taken against the *Express*, while the Home Secretary came to Gregory's aid with the statement, "There is no truth in the report that the Home Secretary has intervened in the murder enquiry in West Yorkshire or has asked Scotland Yard to do so."

While the police of West Yorkshire fumed and grew incensed, the man they were hunting grew steadily more elusive.

While the top brains from eight police forces in the north gathered in Bradford to discuss the situation and exchange ideas at a summit conference on the mass murderer, the man they hunted was going about his daily work in the same city. Not the evil work of the night but his respectable work at the wheel of a truck.

On November 16, Home Secretary Whitelaw paid a "surprise" visit to the "Ripper murder incident room" at Millgarth, Leeds. He made a particular point of talking to every man and woman on duty. Oldfield, who had defied doctor's orders, joined Gregory and the Home Secretary as reporters scribbled Mr. Whitelaw's comments.

He said: "I hope by now it is evident that everyone in the police forces of this country has the utmost confidence in the Chief Constable of West Yorkshire. There is a great admiration for what he is doing."

He dismissed as "misleading" reports that he had ordered Scotland Yard to join the case and added, "As Home Secretary I recognize the chief constable's responsibility and I have the utmost confidence in him."

Four days later, on November 20, Chief Constable Gregory announced that he had asked Scotland Yard for help.

One cannot help but conclude that either our Home Secretary does not know his right hand from his left or the chief constable of West Yorkshire was told to ask for help. Not for the Yard to take over the investigation, just to send up a couple of men as a public-relations exercise to quiet the press and public.

The unfortunate man selected for the task was Commander Jim Nevill, former head of the terrorist squad. In fact, Nevill was second choice. The first senior Yard man asked to catch a train to Wakefield was Commander Peter Duffy, but he, knowing a bad idea when he saw one, declined.

Commander Nevill and Detective Chief Superintendent Joe Bolton stayed four weeks to bring "the fresh eyes and minds" that Gregory now thought useful. It served its purpose. The editors in Fleet Street who had previously urged Scotland Yard involvement were well pleased with their efforts. Curiously, when the Yard left one month later, having made "certain recommendations," the national press gave the departure less prominence. Those in the West Yorkshire police force who bitterly opposed Yard intervention felt vindicated. They'd been and gone and while there, the feeling in certain police quarters had been "they're not going to catch our Ripper, we are."

The fallibility of the mystic Scotland Yard and the men of London's police forces had already been clearly demonstrated earlier in the year.

During April 1979 in Southall, London, in broad daylight a man was killed by a crushing blow to the head. Despite the fact that at that precise moment he was surrounded by many policemen no one has ever been arrested and charged with the murder. No one ever will be. The dead man's name was Blair Peach.

The "certain recommendations" that Commander Nevill of the

Yard made were contained in a report that has never been made public. None of it has ever been revealed. Part of it makes ominous reading:

"And it is unfortunately apparent that despite the numerous arduous lines of enquiry that have been undertaken, very little actual evidence has come to light to connect any particular person with these crimes."

On the day that the Yard men caught their train back to London it was revealed that Detective Chief Superintendent Gilrain had taken overall charge of the Ripper investigation. Gilrain was described by colleagues as an Alf Ramsey-style leader who shunned the limelight. He would have needed the expertise of Ramsey's entire World Cup winning team to have avoided the glare of publicity mechanics then in full momentum: a one-million-pound publicity drive, with one aim, to catch the mass murderer. The campaign's conception was brilliant, the organization highly professional. It was skillful, original, and imaginative. It had flair. It had everything, including one fatal flaw. The basic premise around which the entire campaign was mounted was a false one. The object of the entire exercise was to insure that millions and millions of people heard the tape recording and saw samples of the handwriting, the assumption being that voice and letters had come from the mass murderer. It is clear that they did not. It was clear before the campaign was mounted that they were a hoax.

The decision by the police to revert to a policy of massive publicity that had been made in June 1979 led to a crescendo in the autumn of that year.

It began within police circles with the idea that a free newspaper that gave what was considered "vital information" about the killer should be circulated. The initial concept was to aim for half a million copies. The Wakefield *Express* offered to print the paper free of any charge except the cost of the virgin paper.

The circulation figure quickly rose to one million copies. Meetings were held with large distributors such as Menzies and W. H. Smith. They too offered their facilities free of charge.

It was at this stage of the planning that the idea evolved to bring in the professionals. Superintendent Peter Silvester, deputy head of community affairs, was advised that the best company to handle this extraordinary project was Graham Poulter Associates of Leeds, an advertising agency with branches in Manchester, London, and Newcastle and an annual turnover of more than twenty million pounds. Keith McPhail, the company's account director, received a telephone call from Silvester in mid-September. The superintendent's opening remark was one of the great understatements of all time.

"We've got a small problem."

"Oh, yes."

"Yes. It's these twelve unsolved murders."

"Yes."

"Well, we've been hunting the killer for four years and we feel we need to do a little bit more. You know, in terms of getting public involvement, public awareness of what's going on."

Keith McPhail, Graham Poulter, and several senior colleagues met with the police. Within days Project R was rolling.

Superintendent Silvester made it clear at the outset that he had very little money to play with, ten thousand pounds. In a society where millions are spent yearly on advertising soap or dog food, ten thousand pounds would not get you to the drawing board, let alone off it. Poulter Associates offered their services for nothing and set to work. They opened the lid on a well of Ruth.

There is much that ails this country. Now and again there are impressive demonstrations that the nation is capable of showing impressive goodwill to match the evil.

The police had wanted a "few ads and the odd poster around Leeds so that we will be seen to be doing things." What they were given was a national million-pound campaign that cost the police about twenty thousand pounds. The rest was donated by the printing firms that ran off the posters and the literature, the newspapers that made space freely available to carry full-page advertisements, the companies who freely gave poster sites, the radio stations that gave free air time; the goodwill appeared to be endless. From the top of Scotland to Cornwall, posters and newspapers carried the four posters shown in this book. Two million homes from Stoke-on-Trent to Scotland found a copy of the police newspaper on their mat. Headlined HELP US CATCH THE RIPPER, it asked, HAVE YOU SEEN THE HANDWRITING? HAVE YOU HEARD THE TAPE? A chilling commercial made by the advertising company was played on nearly twenty radio stations—in part it recounted the murders, in part it played the voice of "the Ripper."

An extra fifty policemen were drafted onto the project to assist the 250 already working full time on the investigation. Some of them manned traveling caravans which, while they lacked the professional expertise of Poulter's with their displays, still showed examples of the handwriting, as they constantly played the "I'm Jack" tape. Other police officers enlarged the initial efforts that had followed the June press conference; they took the tape to every conceivable place. Two million people phoned in on the free phone lines and listened to the boasting Wearside voice.

The tape and samples of his handwriting went quite literally around the world. Every country outside the Iron Curtain and a number within, heard the tape. It had become the world's biggest manhunt.

In early February 1980 the unprecedented campaign was officially stopped. The West Yorkshire police force then promptly and very rapidly reverted to a policy of a total press blackout. They had swung full circle again. But as they moved from a positive position to a highly dangerous negative one, the publicity campaign had left one major question unanswered: why had it failed to uncover the killer?

The answer was there before the question begged answer.

When the tape recording had first arrived on Oldfield's desk, among others he consulted were Stanley Ellis, a dialect expert and senior English language lecturer at Leeds University, and Jack Windsor Lewis, a lecturer in the department of linguistics and phonetics at the same university.

Both men rapidly confirmed that the accent was "Geordie," and further that it was genuine. Ellis shortly afterward narrowed the source of the accent to the Sunderland town of Castletown or an area very near. By early September 1979, both experts felt sure the exposure the tape had already been given would have insured that someone would have recognized the highly distinctive accent. On September 23, nearly two weeks before the one-million-pound campaign was launched, Mr. Windsor Lewis wrote to the police:

The accent and voice quality of the Ripper tape-speaker are so highly distinctive that:

1. It is hardly conceivable that he was not recognized at once from the broadcasts by various people to whom he is

known, some of whom must have said so immediately to the police.

2. Presented with a suitable recording of a suspect, it is virtually certain that someone with the training of Mr. Ellis or myself could readily identify or eliminate the speaker with confidence.

3. If further evidence were needed to corroborate such a conclusion it seemed to me that it might be provided by a sample of the speaker's written English if it could be confidently decided that the three letters were truly, as they purport to be, written by the speaker.

With this last question in mind I requested permission to examine the letters. A preliminary hour on Saturday, 15th of September, the whole of Thursday, 20th September morning and afternoon examining photographs of them, and subsequent further scrutiny of the notes taken on those occasions have convinced me on the internal linguistic evidence that speaker and writer are one and the same person.

In my opinion this indicates a retracing of steps by the investigators in the direction of making speaker/writer identifications from samples of suspects' speech and writing with no prejudice whatsoever as to whether the speaker/writer in question could or could not have committed any of the murders. Mr. Stanley Ellis informs me that he is in complete agreement with this view.

In the opinion of the experts, therefore, the man who recorded that tape had already been interviewed by the police. Their considered opinion, which is based on unassailable logic, was ignored. The series of murders, the tape, and the letters had all been irretrievably knitted together by the police.

Just as there is no doubt whatsoever that the police had already interviewed and mistakenly eliminated the mass murderer from their investigation, so equally there is no doubt that they have also eliminated the man who wrote the letters and recorded the tape.

With regard to the mass murderer, doubtless the police rationale is, "Well, one of the reasons we eliminated him is because he does not have a Geordie accent." With regard to the actual hoaxer, the rationale will undoubtedly be, "Well, it could not have been him because he has a cast-iron alibi on the vital dates that the murders were committed."

In October 1979 Mr. Windsor Lewis followed up with a report of some 1500 words on the three letters. The report analyzes the highly individual characteristics of spelling, punctuation, phraseology, and handwriting style. The West Yorkshire police have paid no more attention to this report than they did to the letter.

When speech therapists told police in late 1979 that the speaker on the tape was almost certainly masking a stutter they ignored that too. They certainly suppressed that considered opinion from the public.

If they ignored their own experts they did so at peril—not to themselves, but to the women of the north of England.

By the beginning of 1980 it was clear that despite the publicity campaign, despite the huge police investigation, despite rewards totaling 30,000 pounds, the man they hunted was continuing to get away with murder. In terms of what it had actually achieved toward catching the mass murderer, the end result of the publicity campaign was so negligible that the one million pounds so generously donated might have been more effectively used if it had been given to the various women's movements throughout the killer's hunting grounds. At the end of the night it was always a woman who lay horribly mutilated and dead on northern ground. Violence toward women, which is such an acceptable part of our society, reached newsworthy peaks with these murders, yet the breeding ground for these particular crimes had been there for many years.

The johns, the flashers, the men who fondle the salesgirl or their secretary. The whistles and shouts when a woman walks down the street. The wife-battering, which is somehow a comfortable euphemism for woman-battering. The myths that surround the act of rape: all women secretly desire it, they ask for it, etc. The condescension, the patronization. The "some were prostitutes but others were innocent women" philosophy. The "next one might be your wife, girlfriend, or mother" police view. The *droit du seigneur* tradition. The "weaker sex" concept. All of these are spawned from the same source as the so-called "Yorkshire Ripper." Even with him caught, all women will still be at risk. It will still not be safe for women to walk in certain parts of certain cities. The man hunted by the police is merely the tip of the iceberg.

This problem is not unique to Great Britain. In the Third World where there is the most hideous suppression of women, in many countries this "weaker sex" grows at least 50 percent of all food produced. In a number of those countries less than one girl in ten ever goes to school. In the northern cities and towns of Brazil over 50,000 women and girls earn a living as prostitutes.

Women are 50 percent of the world's population. They work two-thirds of the hours worked on this planet. They receive 10 percent of the world's income and own less than 1 percent of the world's property.

If that all seems a far remove from the murders in the north of England it should be realized that without that global oppression this killer would indeed be unique, but those facts clearly illustrate that this killer is but the logical conclusion of "the system."

"You're the fellow that's writing the book on Yorkshire Ripper, aren't you?"

"Yes."

"Tell me, how many did that Victorian Ripper kill?"

"Five."

"What, five? I thought it was more than that."

"No. Many of the newspapers misquote the number. In fact it was five."

There was a pause, then the questioner beamed.

"Eee, our Jack's beaten him, hasn't he?"

The above was a conversation in a Leeds pub in 1980.

This man who has rapidly become part of our folklore has spread ripples of evil far, far beyond his comprehension. There are women who find it a terrifying thought that everything they have worked for, everything they have fought for, and everything they have made themselves into could be annihilated by a hammer on the back of the head from a man who hates "women."

They are women who are angry, furious that one man can determine where they walk, live, play. Inevitably they have begun to fight back.

One aspect of this fight back is a movement called "Women Against Violence Against Women." Another is the "Reclaim the Night" demonstrations. The origins of these demonstrations came directly from the murder of Jayne MacDonald in 1977. Later the same year women marched from Chapeltown, from that adventure playground where one of their number had died most horribly for no other reason than that she was a woman. Marches took place simultaneously in eleven cities scattered throughout the country. It was not merely a protest, it was also a celebration that the "weaker sex" could walk in no-go areas. It was not intended within itself to create dramatic change except perhaps in the minds of these women who marched.

You are in trouble when you live in an area where you cannot go to a pub after dark. Attend a bingo session. Go to an evening class. Open the door to a stranger. Where your newspaper tells you, "You May Be Next—if you're young, female, and out alone at night." Where the police will prosecute (and have done so) if you carry a weapon for protection. Where if you do not have a car you are vulnerable to sudden attack. Deep trouble.

It must have done wonders for the morale of northern women when Detective Chief Superintendent Jim Hobson stated one month after Barbara's murder, "The Yorkshire Ripper has now made his point after murdering twelve women in four years and should give himself up."

If any good whatsoever emerged from the murder of Barbara Leach, it was the dramatic consciousness-raising of a significant number of women in the North but particularly in Bradford itself.

It certainly needed raising. There had been no protest marches after the attacks on Anna Rogulskyj and Olive Smelt. . . .

No public marches through the streets after the murders of Wilma McCann, Emily Jackson, and Irene Richardson, all in Leeds. . . .

There was no female outcry after Tina Atkinson had been brutally murdered in Bradford, or Maureen Long attacked in the same city. Or Yvonne Pearson, murdered also in the same city. . . .

No feminists took to the streets of Manchester after the murder of Jean Jordan. They were equally mute after Vera Millward had been hacked to death. . . .

No feminist public protested in Huddersfield after what was left of Helen Rytka had been discovered.

It is abundantly clear that it took the deaths of nonprostitutes, of Jayne MacDonald in Leeds, Josephine Whitaker in Halifax, and Barbara Leach in Bradford, to produce public action from women.

Feminists have very rightly condemned the police message of

"even innocent women are now at risk." But surely, by their muteness at the time of the other murders and attacks, those same feminists display that same bigoted attitude. Is it only when *they* feel personally threatened that *they* can respond? They certainly reacted after Barbara's murder.

Over four hundred women marched through the city protesting the increasing violence against their sex. Previously, after the murder of Josephine Whitaker, a Women's Right to Self-Defense Campaign had originated in Bradford. The march in the week after the murder of Barbara carried such slogans as "Women Demand Curfew on Men" and "Cut off Male Power"—but replacing one form of sexist behavior with another is surely not the solution.

The comments are nevertheless understandable against the background of oppression. For the vice chancellor of Leeds University to issue the following extraordinary statement a week after Barbara's death is the clearest illustration that there was something very rotten in the north of England.

"I have been advised by the West Yorkshire metropolitan police to warn all women students that, until the person responsible for recent murders is brought to justice, they should under no circumstances be out alone after dark.

"I most urgently request the cooperation of all students at the present time."

The reasons for the warning are obvious. Equally clear is the absurdity of the injunction. Were they supposed to confine studying to daylight? No research at night? Never mind the mundane things of life like going out to enjoy oneself. How on earth could that directive cover the realities of university life?

When Anna Rogulskyj was attacked by the mass murderer, not one national newspaper carried a photograph.

Four years later, at the time of the murder of Barbara Leach, the killer was the best-known unknown man in the entire world.

On the beaches of Australia, in the hotels of New Zealand, in the brothels of Germany, they talked of him.

The French call him *"L'Éventreur,"* the Italians *"Lo Squartatore."*

The tape that purported to be from him was heard on the junks in Hong Kong, in the porno clubs of Sweden and the nightclubs of France.

He was now known of throughout the world. His notoriety penetrated even the Iron Curtain. *Pravda* accused Britain's "bourgeois mass media" of making a hero of this man.

In Tokyo, New York, and Sidney he was the subject of conversation. Reporters, film crews, writers poured into Leeds from all over the world with the exception of Russia.

Some film crews even filmed each other. Many of the items filmed or filed on the murders were grossly inaccurate, yet the police obliged if it was during one of their "let's talk to the press" cycles. But always the press was told precisely only what the West Yorkshire police wanted them to know. Never in the history of this country's police force has there been media exposure of this quantity. Never has such potential ever been so abused by the police, who determined what would and would not be released. This particularly, indeed almost exclusively, applied to the British press—the very group that could potentially help the police manhunt more than the rest of the world's press put together.

Sadly, Dennis Hoban, who could have taught the others a thing or two about press relations, was dead. He died suddenly in 1978. After leading the investigation into the murders of Wilma McCann and Emily Jackson, this highly talented policeman was never again in a position of control with regard to the series of murders. Careful analysis of the entire police investigation leads one irresistibly to the conclusion that, if Hoban had lived and had been placed in charge of the overall investigation, women now dead would be alive.

The police-controlled exposure this killer received both in England and abroad had many side effects. One was to make in certain sections of our society a folk hero out of a mass murderer.

When the chairman of the West Yorkshire police committee, Kenneth Davison, said in 1978 that he wanted the killer caught "dead or alive" and urged a large reward for the deed, the myths were given further impetus. After all, it was just like Jesse James, wasn't it? From the moment after the murder of Emily Jackson when the press dubbed her killer "The Ripper," the seeds of folk myth were born and flowering.

In May 1980 a Hall of Fame opened in London. The fiberglass figures moved. Just past the figures of John Wayne, James Stewart, and Clint Eastwood was an aisle; in it, a model of the Victorian Jack the Ripper stood crouched over a lifeless victim.

In a year when this nation showed far greater concern over who shot J.R. in the TV show "Dallas" than they did over the identity of that J.R. in Yorkshire, the Hall of Fame was an apt comment on current values.

In 1978 it was reported that prisoners in Armley jail, Leeds, were running a sweepstake. The prize of a pile of chocolate bars was for the prisoner who correctly guessed the date when the mass murderer would be caught. Prison Governor Dennis Ward called it "Harmless fun."

Hoaxers bedeviled police investigations for five years. Letters, tapes, phone calls came, all claiming to be from the killer; other hoaxers reported bodies in Leeds, Bradford, Huddersfield, Manchester, and many other towns.

Starved of the true details concerning the murders, many people insisted that they knew for a fact that he removed the entire skin from their faces. Others, that they knew for a fact he pushed bottles inside all of his victims. The number of these "facts" appears to be endless. One of the most common—and one that has appeared in virtually every newspaper throughout the country—is: "It is known that he always leaves a horrific trademark on the bodies; that is how police know he is responsible." As this book clearly illustrates, that "fact" is in the same category as the two previously mentioned.

There were reports in 1979 that children at parties were playing "Cops and Ripper."

Dr. Stephen Shaw, a Wakefield-based psychiatrist, has already admitted one man to a closed ward because of irrational but persistent fears that his next-door neighbor was the mass murderer.

A woman driver became frightened when she noticed that an elderly woman she had picked up hitch-hiking had a deep voice, huge hands, and hairy wrists. She stopped the car and asked her passenger if she would kindly check the rear lights, as they appeared to be faulty. When the "woman" had got out, the driver roared off into the night. Getting home, she discovered that her passenger had left her shopping basket behind. In it was a blood-stained meat cleaver.

The story is total myth, complete fantasy. By the end of 1979 West Yorkshire police had over fifty reports of this "fact." It first emerged as a "fact" in the middle of the nineteenth century.

Then the "car" was a pony and trap.

It is a fact than an American executive wrote to the Yorkshire *Post* in April 1980 offering the "Yorkshire Ripper a job tending Shetland ponies on a two-hundred-acre ranch, with free accommodation for him and his next of kin for a salary of seven dollars an hour for an eight-hour day, five-day week."

Many have profited out of the fear that abounds in the north. Taxi fares in Leeds and Bradford have invariably risen after a murder. The publicity campaign prompted one American company to send a sample of their product to Poulter Associates, who conducted the publicity campaign. It is called "Rapel"—a small can the size of a pen which women are advised to keep with them. If threatened, the woman breaks the phial, which releases an appalling odor. The same company also offered whistles in gold and silver.

A variety of "Ripper alarms" have had massive sales in northern cities: necklaces with built-in whistles, pocket-size alarms, screechers, all have found a market.

One of the most nauseating attempts to cash in came from self-styled rock star and show-business impresario Jonathan King. He announced plans to market a record of "The Ripper's Speech." When there were protests, he offered to give royalties to the mass murderer. When there were further protests, he slid back under his rock.

A punk band called The Diks have made a habit of dedicating songs to the killer "if he happens to be in the audience." Another group called The Gonads brought out a number entitled "Ripper's Delight."

A few weeks before Barbara was murdered, the BBC's Soccer Match of the Day was Sunderland v. Fulham. Clearly, throughout the commentary, could be heard the persistent chant of "There's only one Jack the Ripper" being sung to the tune of "Guantanamera."

In October, a few weeks after Barbara died, the police as part of the big publicity campaign played the tape at Elland Road during a Leeds home soccer match. The tape was drowned by the chanting fans: "You'll never catch the Ripper" and "Twelve nil. Twelve nil."

Outside the stadium badges were on sale: *Leeds United Whites. More feared than the Yorkshire Ripper.*

Outside Sunderland stadium a month later were badges that referred to the team's center forward, John Hawley. The badges said *John Hawley strikes faster than the Ripper.*

In July 1978 a twenty-five-year-old mother sleeping with her two children was terrorized for three hours by a man who broke into her home and raped her three times. He told the petrified woman, "I am the Yorkshire Ripper." He was sentenced to four years' imprisonment.

In the same month another mother of three was raped on her way to her Leeds home. She feared he was the Ripper and, after being half strangled, ceased to struggle. Her attacker was sentenced to four years' imprisonment.

In October 1978 Stuart Siddall was sentenced to life imprisonment. Freed from jail only five months previously after serving a sentence for raping and killing a woman, Siddall indicated to his latest victim that he was "the Yorkshire Ripper," punched her in the face, tried to rape her in the street, then forced her to take him home, where he "submitted her to humiliating and degrading practices."

Later in 1978 a 35-year-old man threatened a woman with a knife very close to where the body of Helen Rytka had been discovered at the beginning of that year. He told her he was "the Yorkshire Ripper" and threatened to murder her. When a police car appeared, he ran away. He was later arrested and given a 12-month suspended sentence for assault and theft.

In May 1978 two vice-squad police officers arrested a woman for soliciting in Moss Side. Taking her to a local police station, they initially said they wished to photograph her in the nude. She refused. She was then driven to waste land and the officers demanded sexual intercourse. At first she refused. One of the police officers said, "Unless you let us do it, you'll end up dead and we'll make it look like a 'Yorkshire Ripper' job." She allowed them both to have sex. The two men were dismissed from the force, the director of public prosecutions having decided to take no action.

"Ripper" jokes abound in the north. One example should suffice:

Jack's mother to her son: "I'm getting worried about you, Jack. Why is it I never see you with the same woman more than once?"

In the streets of Chapeltown the little children have a modern nursery rhyme:

> "Ripper, Ripper,
> Hunt. Hunt.
> Ripper, Ripper.
> Cunt. Cunt."

His evil spread far and wide. He poisoned the well.

Chapeltown, Lumb Lane, Great Northern Street. They are still much the same five years later. Some of the Victorian terraces have been knocked down in Chapeltown. Reginald Terrace is at present a waste land. There is currently talk of grand schemes designed to radically alter the area. The people there have heard it all before. Perhaps this time it will happen. Perhaps not. If it does not happen soon in some of these areas, there will be conflagration on a par with the Watts riots in the United States.

The police spread their net far and wide in the hunt for the mass murderer.

Men with prison records in the north going back ten years who were free at the times of the murders were checked.

A widely held theory that the killer was a policeman was checked.

The theory that the man they hunted was a member of Her Majesty's Forces and that the long gaps between some of the killings might be explained by overseas periods of service was checked.

Every conceivable occupation from lighthouse keepers to miners was checked.

On the theory that the letters and the tape bore a marked resemblance to phrases used in letters allegedly written by the Victorian Jack the Ripper, libraries throughout the north were checked in an attempt to obtain information on readers who had borrowed books written on the nineteenth-century murderer.

Checks were made of confidential records, including medical and social security records. The Inland Revenue refused to make tax records available.

In view of the fact that many of these checks were based on the premise that the letters and tape were genuine, the investigations made in this area were a total waste of time, money, and manpower.

We live at a time when men have been placed on the moon. We can pick up a telephone in Great Britain and a few seconds later talk to someone in New Zealand. Heart transplants are now an everyday event. This computer age that we live in has made astonishing breakthroughs on many fronts. And yet.

And yet one evil man with a ball peen hammer, a screwdriver, and a collection of knives and chisels murdered again and again and again with impunity. Forensic science, sophisticated communication techniques, the national police computer, were powerless against his ball peen hammer. A modern-day Luddite causing havoc.

In February 1980 the total inconsistency of the police with regard to publicity was demonstrated yet again. From unique exposure on an international scale, from a period in which the world could obtain interviews with Oldfield and other senior officers, shoot film in the murder incident room at Millgarth, Leeds, follow the police around during the inquiries and indulge in whatever angle took the media fancy, from this situation a total press blackout again descended on the investigation. No interviews, no filming, no access, no go.

In early 1980 the West Yorkshire police entered into another bizarre conspiracy with the murderer. A conspiracy solely designed to achieve one purpose, to make the killer react. It was reasoned that he enjoyed publicity. This reasoning was based on the letters and the tape. It was felt, therefore, that to starve the killer of publicity would be to force his hand. Initially it was hoped that the press blackout would provoke him to write "another" letter. The previous letters had all been received in the month of March. March 1980 passed; no letter came. It was then hoped that he might send another tape in June. June 1980 passed; no tape was received. There was only one thing left to expect. Privately many police officers expressed the view "We won't catch him unless he murders again."

The policy to legalize prostitution in a small corner of Bradford was changed in June 1980. For eighteen months the women had been free to sell their bodies at certain hours in a certain area. Live bait, dangled on a line. It had been a highly dangerous policy, not to the police who sat in their cars in Church Street and the surrounding area, but to the women on the streets looking for business. Just how dangerous was demonstrated in January 1980. A prostitute was violently attacked by a man; other prostitutes went to her aid. Police were sitting watching in a car but made no effort to intervene. When one of the women ran screaming to a police car for help, they told her that they had been instructed not to move, that they were there to collect license numbers. The attacker got away.

The women who walked Church Street during the "amnesty" were placed in appalling danger. Just how appalling can be seen from the method used by those police who sat there night after night "just taking license numbers." Whenever a motorist is stopped by the police they can communicate back to the station to check his license plates. The station will switch into the national police computer and usually within minutes the details have been fed back to the policeman on the street. This system was not used during the observations carried out during the "amnesty." At that time the watching officers in Bradford logged the license numbers on a tape cassette. The following day the cassettes went to Leeds; then and only then was the information checked on the national police computer. By this time the murderer would have been home, cleaned up all traces, unscrewed the false license plates, spent a night in bed with his wife, worked through the following day and again got away with murder.

The months of 1980 began to slip by. Leeds, Bradford, and the other towns where this man had left his mark began to relax.

Shortly after Barbara's death in September 1979, a siege mentality prevailed. Women canceled all but the most essential engagements. One man had set back the liberation of half the population by a hundred years. Clubs, pubs, cinemas, night classes, bingo halls. If women went at all they rarely made the journey home unescorted. Feminists might be boiling inside but many would not go shopping alone after dark. Women telephoned back home as soon as they had arrived at a destination, to reassure the family that they had in fact arrived.

Church services in the evening were either canceled or held earlier. Fathers drove daughters sometimes hundreds of miles back to colleges and universities rather than put them in jeopardy after dark. Autumn 1979 in the north was dark in many ways.

By the spring of 1980 the tension was visibly slackening. The approaching summer reassured people and by the middle of the year it was evident that most had totally relaxed. There was a general feeling as the death of Barbara Leach receded further and further in memory that he had gone away or that he had committed suicide. People cannot live in constant fear. Cannot go through life minute by minute fearing sudden violent attack. At times when the bombs ceased to drop on British cities during the Second World War that same easing of tension was clearly discernible.

In Bradford, young girls and women went to the dance halls, cinemas, public houses, and could be seen often walking home at night, unescorted. In Bowling Back Lane, young girls tripped about in their high-heel shoes on the cobblestones; with plunging necklines and skirts split to the thigh they displayed not a care in the world.

In Huddersfield as the summer reached its height the women there reverted to normality and lived lives uninfluenced by him. At Halifax, Manchester, the same return to a normal pattern was in evidence. In Leeds the contrast between the siege mentality of September 1979 and the relaxed manner of August 1980 was particularly marked. Young women walked apparently without fear through the streets of the city at two and three in the morning. It seemed that the majority had reached a conclusion: he has gone away; he will not murder again.

He knew differently.

Machine oil, ball peen hammers and that fiver had brought the police back to his works in January 1980. They took him down to the station. Again he fooled them. The man that Oldfield and other senior Yorkshire police officers have stated they would know instantly was still free to kill again.

He had read in his local Bradford newspaper in April the murder squad hunting him had been cut from three hundred men to one hundred and even further reductions had been made since then. It seemed to him that they were almost inviting him to kill again. Further confirmation that the time was ripe for another murder occurred during that summer.

One warm evening he had gone out alone for a few drinks. Old habits die hard.

On the way back home, he couldn't resist driving through Manningham. That night he had not been so cautious, had not taken care. He'd had a drop too much and was driving his Rover in an erratic manner. He was stopped by the police.

The man about whom Oldfield, Holland, and many many other senior police officers had asserted "will give himself away if questioned, we'll know him when we see him," this man who had already outwitted them during at least three police interviews, perhaps more, yet again fooled them.

He was breathalised and would eventually have to go to court. He might lose his license. As a lorry driver without a license, he'd have to change his job. He'd warned his boss that he might have to leave. The car was stopped in a red light area with a driver under the influence, a car with a number that had already been noted a number of times in red light areas, a fact that had resulted in yet another interrogation.

There were no cross-references, no routine checks, no assessments of previous interrogations, not even an awareness that he had been previously questioned *at least three times*. It all added up to another murder.

On the evening of August the twentieth the lights in a section of the Department of Education and Science at Farnsley, mid-way between Leeds and Bradford, burned unusually late. At her desk, executive officer Marguerite Walls was clearing a backlog of work.

The forty-seven-year-old spinster was in theory already on holiday. Conscientious Margo Walls was determined to clear her desk before leaving. She was that sort of person. Quiet and unassuming, with few close friends, her main interest was her work. At ten-thirty, her work completed, she left the building and began to walk towards her home. Always a careful woman she deliberately avoided a short cut that would have taken ten minutes off her journey. She preferred the brightly lit main roads. Work finished, only a holiday to think about, she stepped briskly through the respectable suburb. The clatter of her high-heeled shoes was the only sound to be heard as she walked along New Street. As she approached the entrance of a local magistrate's house, the man who had quietly waited in the shadows leapt out of the driveway and aimed a blow at her head. She staggered on the pavement. As blood gushed from the wound she screamed. Again she was struck on the head. Still she did not fall. He moved closer to her. He had to stop those screams. In a moment the hammer was back in his pocket and his hands were around her neck. As he strangled her he began to drag her into the driveway of the house. She had been but four hundred yards from her own home. A home she would never see again.

With his hands still gripping her throat, he dragged her through the over-grown grounds of the house called Claremont. Eventually he reached the side of the garage, deep in the garden. By now Margo was dead. He began to rip at her clothes feverishly. Her black gaberdine coat was torn from her body and thrown into the bushes. Her cardigan and blouse tossed into a flower bed. The purple skirt was thrown high in the air. Brassiere, panties, shoes, tights, handbag were scattered over the garden. He cursed the fact that his knives were still in the car. Pulling the hammer from his pocket he began to rain blows on the body but it wasn't the same. It failed to give any of the satisfaction that came from the knife. Calmly he re-pocketed the hammer and stared down at the lifeless body. Yet again he felt the need to cover it, to mask the deed. It was foolish to have thrown her coat away, as foolish as forgetting the knife. Nearby he saw a large pile of dead leaves. In a moment the naked body was covered. It made him feel better, wiped the deed from his mind. Cautiously he stared towards the large house. It was in darkness. Moving quickly across the garden he reached the spot where just a few minutes previously he had listened to the footsteps of Margo Walls. He paused, aware that in the next door house lived a policeman. It wouldn't do to bump into him on his way out. Choosing his moment he emerged into an empty street. In less than fifteen minutes he was home; home to his loving wife.

The following day he carefully read all the newspapers. The body of Margo Walls had been found and journalists were speculating "New Yorkshire Ripper Victim?" The headlines on the next day gave him particular cause for satisfaction. Detective Chief Superintendent Jim Hobson had ruled out the possibility that the dead woman was the thirteenth victim of "The Ripper."

Well he was right. Marguerite Walls was his twelfth victim.

He smiled as he read that Hobson was concentrating his inquiries in Doncaster, seeking links from Margo's past. He shook his head in disbelief as he tinkered with his Rover V8 in the garage. They held him responsible for a murder in Preston that he hadn't committed. They cleared him of a murder in Farnsley that he had perpetrated. He had always considered that he was invincible. The mounting errors in the police investigation merely served to confirm that self opinion. What gave him particular cause for satisfaction was the knowledge that the cities that he preyed upon would still be relaxed. Women would still be off guard. While the police hunted for a non-existent murderer among Margo Wall's small circle of friends and acquaintances and maintained a press blanket on information about a Sunderland Yorkshire Ripper with a Geordie accent, who was equally non-existent, this Yorkshireman with a Bradford accent was being given a risk-free invitation to kill again. He was not a man likely to decline such an invitation.

During the first week of September there were several newspaper references to the fact that it was one year since the murder of Barbara Leach in Bradford which, as far as the police and the press were concerned, was the last time he had struck. Recalling that murder he grew thoughtful. The students would be returning soon from their summer vacations. He checked out the areas around both Bradford and Leeds universities and chose Headingley. Many of the students attending Leeds lived in this quiet respectable suburb.

In the days that followed he spent several evenings in Headingley. He went to the pubs that were popular with the students. Explored the roads and alleyways that lead off the main Leeds Otley road.

On the evening of the twenty-fourth of September 1980 he crouched in the darkness, waiting. Shortly after eleven P.M. a slim, dark-haired woman approached. Seconds later she was lying in a pool of her own blood that poured from head wounds. Only the fact that other people were also returning to their homes saved her life. Hearing footsteps he had melted away into the darkness and returned to his car.

The following day he read that his latest victim was thirty-four-year-old Dr. Upaehya Banbara, a native of Singapore. She had just finished a twelve month study at the Nuffield center after winning a scholarship with the World Health Organization. Ironically she had, like Margo Walls, been about to commence a holiday when the man who was an ideal husband and a highly regarded employee had smashed her upon the head.

Yet again he noted that the police had failed to link the

attempted murder with him, though they thought it was linked with the murder of Margo Walls. Yet again that failure ensured that he was free to roam the northern cities. The inhabitants of those towns unconcernedly went about their everyday lives. The women in those cities remained oblivious to the fact that he had returned and in truth had never gone away.

He shrugged off the fact that this latest victim had survived and began to plan the next attack. It was nearly three years since Helen Rytka's murder in Huddersfield. He knew from recent visits to the city that he had little to fear from police patrols. Recalling the bonfire-night of 1975 when he had been thwarted of his second victim he decided to "celebrate" that anniversary.

He sat quietly sipping a pint in the Minstrel pub in the centre of Huddersfield. Watching. This place had certainly changed. At the time he had killed Helen it had been full of likely victims but now there was not one obvious prostitute to be seen. An attractive young woman sitting by the bar caught his attention. His interest quickened. She was young, too young to be in a pub on her own. Obviously she was on good terms with the landlord, who from time to time came over to share a laugh and a joke with the pretty girl. Recalling that evening in the Manville Arms when he had sat and watched another attractive young woman, the excitement grew within him. When he saw her give the landlord an affectionate kiss before leaving, he knew who the next one was going to be. A moment later he quickly finished his drink and followed her into the street.

The affectionate kiss, the sixteen-year-old's presence in the pub alone, were without significance. It was her father's pub but the true facts would have made no difference to this man. He stalked Teresa Sykes through the Huddersfield streets as she returned home to her three-month-old son. She was close to home when he struck, always from behind. The ball peen hammer smashed down on her head. Three times. One blow was of such severity that the hammer went through her skull. She screamed in agony. Forty yards away waiting in her home was boyfriend Jimmy Fury. For a moment he watched horror struck from a window as the murderer smashed at Teresa's head. Moments later he was out in the street rushing towards the attacker. The killer saw him coming and turning away, ran down the street. Fast as her boyfriend was, the attacker was faster. He vanished into the darkness leaving yet another victim alive. Alive with a nightmare for the rest of her life.

Yet again the police ruled out any connection with the mass murderer. Teresa's father felt differently. He remained convinced that his daughter had been attacked by the Yorkshire Ripper. Others in Huddersfield felt the same. It was a feeling that clearly irritated the police. Weeks later after another murder was definitely linked with the killer, the head of West Yorkshire Police Southern Area, CID Detective Superintendent Tony Hickey, declared:

"I said at the time that this was a local incident and that I was convinced that a local man was involved."

"Nothing has happened to change my mind. All this talk that Teresa may have been attacked by the Ripper is only making it more difficult for me to catch her assailant."

What was making it more difficult for Hickey was his own stubbornness. By the time he made those remarks, certain events in Headingley clearly demonstrated that Hickey did not have a monopoly on obtuseness.

20

Barbara Leach, a third-year student, highly regarded by her tutors, with a great love of animals, described by her friends at the time of her death as "a girl who cared for people."

Jacqueline Hill, same age, same stage of education, same love of animals, same caring quality for people. Indeed, she was planning to become a probation officer when she left Leeds University, and was already a trainee.

She was engaged to a young man in the R.A.F. She had every single thing to live for.

After the murder of Barbara, Jaqui's parents were fearful for their daughter. She was in lodgings, as Barbara had been. But the realization that the mass murderer was now hunting women in such areas worried Mr. and Mrs. Hill. To allay their fears she moved back into a hall of residence, Lupton flats in Headingley. The area was well lit and the parents relaxed.

This evil that has been glorified with the name of a nineteenth-century murderer, stalked the Headingley area for many nights. His cunning demanded that he continue to measure twice.

On the evening of November 17, 1980, Jacqueline attended a probation seminar in Cookridge Street, Leeds. When it finished shortly after 9:00 P.M. she caught a No. 1 bus back to her apartment. She got off the bus just after 9:20 P.M. She was in sight of her home. She crossed the main road near the Arndale Center, a large shopping mall. She began to walk down Alma Road toward the block of apartments.

At that moment he struck. From out of the blackness he leaped into the road. Again the ball peen hammer was used to kill.

He again dragged a lifeless body into nearby bushes to mutilate. To stab in the eye. To tear at her clothes. To stab this young woman, already dead.

This man they call "the Yorkshire Ripper" murdered Jacqueline Hill.

On December 19, 1980, Jacqueline Hill was buried in the village that had been her home, Ormesby, near Middlesborough.

With parents, fiancé and two hundred other mourners, her coffin was carried to the grave. While those she had loved stood in the rain at her grave her favorite record was played in the church where she had been baptized, confirmed and had planned to marry. It is a poignant song. A beautiful song. Never has it sounded more poignant as Art Garfunkel and Paul Simon sang "Bridge Over Troubled Water."

As the cold rain fell, and the words about darkness and pain filled the air, Jacqueline's fiancé threw a silver coin into the grave, a final tribute to his own "silver bird."

To commit murder is easy. To get away with murder is more difficult. He smiled at the thought. He could afford to indulge the smug feeling creeping up from the pit of his stomach. He stopped pacing, poured another cup of tea, added milk and two carefully measured spoonfuls of sugar.

He checked his watch. Nearly five o'clock on the evening of Friday, January 2, 1981. A new year, full of promise for many, had just begun. If his expectations for the year were realized, all the new year would hold for a number of women was brutal death.

He began to pace again and found himself staring at his reflection in a mirror. He smiled at himself. *What was it that the blonde who had survived had said? "He was good looking with come-to-bed eyes."* Who was he to argue with that opinion?

He continued to stare at his reflection. That same blonde had given a very accurate description of him. It hadn't made any difference. He'd committed murder many times before that particular attack. He'd committed murder many times since. Even the police did not know exactly how many. They were still insisting that he had murdered that woman in Preston in 1975. What was her name? Harrison. Joan Harrison. Well, they were wrong about that one. That other man could take the credit for her. That other man who also claimed the victims that were *his* and *his* alone.

It had made murdering that much easier. Had probably helped him enormously on the number of occasions he had been interviewed by the police. They had questioned him quite a number of times. He'd walked away from every interrogation.

He checked his watch again. Plenty of time. He'd told the wife he intended to go out tonight. She was happy watching TV. Just as well, he could hardly take her along with what he had in mind.

He sipped his tea and recalled some of the moments of the past five and a half years. The recollection that he had not always achieved total success, that there had been some women who had survived, brought a frown to his face. But he would never forget other moments. Successes scattered over half a decade. Successes that had made him the best known unknown man alive in the world today.

His wife. His family. His workmates all knew him by his real name. None, not a single person suspected that this quiet married man living in Bradford was the Yorkshire Ripper.

Images of dead women swirled into his mind. As an automatic reflex his right hand closed, the grip tightened, the knuckles whitened. For once the action was harmless. The hand held no hammer. Still the hand clenched ever tighter as in his mind's eye their faces came into focus.

Later he kissed his wife goodbye, climbed into his Rover car and headed for Sheffield.

Epilogue

On the evening of Friday the 2nd of January, 1981, two police officers on routine patrol of a Sheffield red-light district questioned the occupants of a Rover car.

Inside the car were Peter Sutcliffe and a prostitute. The car was bearing false license plates.

Sutcliffe, a native of Bradford and resident in that city, occupation truck driver, was taken to a Sheffield police station for questioning.

Sutcliffe, a married man living with his wife, was held in custody.

On Monday, January 5, 1981, Peter Sutcliffe was brought to Dewsbury Magistrate's Court in West Yorkshire. He was charged on two counts. One that "between the 13th of November, 1980 and the 2nd of January, 1981, you did steal two motor vehicle number plates."

The second charge was:

"That between the 16th and 19th of November, 1980, you did murder Jacqueline Hill."

The deliverance from this evil had begun.

Conclusions

Random murder. The most difficult to solve. When the victim has no link with the attacker, one of this society's vulnerabilities is exposed. It has always been so. It will always be so.

And yet. And yet.

I began my research into this series of murders in early 1979, with marked reluctance. The study of murder, any murder, is not pleasant. I had been offered the opportunity to accept a commission for this book but declined; I did, however, begin to research quietly.

In June 1979 the infamous tape exploded upon us all. Soon after followed samples of the handwriting and extracts from the letters.

Further research established to my satisfaction that the accent on the tape was genuine. As a drama writer I am very aware that the Wearside accent, or to give it its popular though erroneous description, the "Geordie" accent, is one of the hardest to impersonate. I have many times written a colloquial part in a play for a Yorkshire, a London accent, anything but Geordie, for the simple reason that it is so hard to imitate accurately and with total belief in its authenticity. It's possible but very difficult. Expert opinion rapidly confirmed my own view that the accent was genuine on the tape recording. Fully aware of the massive national and international exposure the tape had received, I began to experience a nagging doubt. Police asserted that the murderer lived in West Yorkshire. If he did and the tape was genuine then I was convinced that he would have been exposed very rapidly. Certainly by September 1979.

In the first week of September he gave an appalling demonstration that he was still at large. He murdered Barbara Leach. It was the death of this young woman that caused this book to be written. Many of the earlier murders received scant coverage in London, largely, I believe, because so many of those earlier victims were prostitutes. I take the view that all these women were innocent victims. That none deserved their ultimate fate. All were equally entitled to live. Barbara's death was for me the moment of truth. No excuses now about lack of coverage to blame for the fact that my own consciousness on this series of killings was pitifully low. With an eldest daughter the same age as Barbara the fact was driven home to me of the disgusting, obscene waste that had occurred. That a life with all yet to offer had been snuffed out sickened me. I determined to research, investigate, then write.

In early 1980, leaving a family that it seems I am constantly leaving, professionally, I moved to Leeds. The fear in the northern cities at that time was very evident.

Alone in a strange city, I began to research. In view of recent emphasis on the fact that observation by the police in all red-light districts that were potential targets for this killer was maintained, the reader may find it of interest that I visited every red-light district many times. I visited every murder site many times. Not once was I challenged, not once stopped. I refer here to the visits made to those places before, as well as after the West Yorkshire police press office was notified by me as to what I was researching.

A BBC "Man Alive" film crew, plus researcher and producer, were compiling a profile on how I set about writing a book such as this one.

It was when the researcher and then the producer attempted to obtain a small measure of police cooperation that we all discovered just how heavy the police blackout of information had become. The chief press officer of the West Yorkshire police, one Bob Baxter, acting clearly on instructions from much higher up the line, declined to give the BBC any cooperation whatsoever. This extended to even basic factual information such as the current statistics on the investigation: The cost. Man-hours. Cars checked. Statements taken. Information that had been handed out to all a few months previously was now being treated as top secret and highly classified.

Much of the information contained within the body of this book would doubtless be classified as top secret or highly classified. None of it came out of the West Yorkshire police force. Thus my growing anger had nothing to do with lack of cooperation but rather with the realization that a conspiracy existed. Members of the police force in general and Assistant Chief Constable Oldfield in particular were very frank about this. The premise was to starve the "Ripper" of publicity and force a reaction from him. They hoped initially for a letter. The other three had been written in the month of March and the reasoning was that a press blackout might force another in March 1980. It did not.

I became frightened. Extremely frightened. It seemed to me that the killer was more likely to react with another murder.

By early April 1980 it was freely stated to me by senior police officers that "our only hope of catching him is if he kills again." Thus a conspiracy between a police force and a force for evil had been made. An initial meeting with George Oldfield in early April merely confirmed that conclusion.

On April 20 the BBC team again came to Leeds. The plan was to film throughout the coming week. The following day after interviewing the mother of Jayne MacDonald, I found myself in the intensive-care unit at St. James Infirmary, Leeds, the initial diagnosis being that I was suffering from pulmonary embolisms. There was the possibility of massive clotting. I mention this for one reason only. Speaking to my wife from that hospital, I told her not to visit me, not to travel from London to Leeds. I had no wish to die and even less wish to die alone, but I was frightened. But my overriding concern, my deeper fear, was for my wife's safety in Leeds. Not only was there a killer on the loose but I knew, as did the BBC team, that those who controlled the hunt for him were attempting to provoke him into action.

March had gone, no letters. What was left to hope for? Surely not another bizarre tape in June?

After I was five days in the hospital, the doctors decided that my illness was merely pleurisy and I was allowed to leave. Two weeks later I recommenced the research for this book.

As my interviews with a large range of people progressed, I became increasingly disturbed; the awareness that this man could strike again at any time and the fear that created within me was in marked contrast with the growing relaxation in the north. The press blackout was clearly lulling not only the public in general but the police in particular into a false sense of security. The announcement that the investigation was being scaled down, that two hundred men had been taken off it, seemed a particularly dangerous gambit. Clearly a police force cannot keep hundreds of men tied up indefinitely on a specific investigation—crime goes on—but to announce it in the press was, in my view, to play with life.

Also very disturbing was the clear evidence that was coming to my hand that the police had bungled the investigation, that lives lost forever could have been saved.

It has always been one of my cardinal principles when investigating murder that first lines of inquiry, in many cases subsequently abandoned by the police, often hold the answers. Working on that principle, I saw the following facts beginning to emerge:

• Anna Rogulskyj is considered by the police to have been the first woman attacked by the mass murderer. Anna, who miraculously survived, was attacked in an alleyway in Keighley, a small town miles from Bradford. There is no red-light district in the town, no night life. Why would a man with murder in his heart come to such a place? I felt the explanation could be that Keighley was close to the man's home. That perhaps he lived on the Keighley side of Bradford and that instead of turning in toward his own town he had chosen to drive out, on the Keighley road that runs directly from Bradford. I felt one fact highly significant. *He never returned to Keighley. Without exception the murderer returned to every other town.* Immediately after he had smashed Anna to the ground, a nearby resident, disturbed by the noise, engaged the killer in conversation. The resident was reassured and went back to his bed. My research clearly indicates that the man that resident spoke with, the man crouched over the unconscious body of Anna, *spoke with a Yorkshire accent.*

• When Olive Smelt survived a murderous attack in Halifax on August 15, 1975, she recounted to the police her conversation with a stranger at the entrance to the ginnel, or alleyway, near her home. Not a long conversation, to be sure, but an exchange about the weather. I questioned Olive about this and other aspects for many hours. Olive is a bright, intelligent woman. There was no doubt whatsoever in her mind about that man's accent. *He spoke with a Yorkshire accent.* She elaborated on aspects of this man. *He was good-looking.* She estimated that *the man was in his early thirties and that he was under six feet tall, about five feet ten inches. She was adamant that the voice on the tape was not that of her attacker.*

• When Wilma McCann was murdered on October 30, 1975, Hoban, the man in control of that investigation, believed *that a long-distance driver was responsible.*

His reasoning was sound. The area where Wilma had last been seen attempting to either hitch a lift or pick up a john is a route that is extensively used by trucks bound for Hull, Manchester, and Liverpool. Indeed, Wilma was seen to enter a truck, only to be put back down a few hundred yards further on. Hoban and his officers interviewed over 6000 long-distance truck drivers during that particular murder investigation. They quickly eliminated the man who had picked her up and then dropped her. *They never eliminated a stationary half-track parked opposite Rakusen's factory*, a place close to the scene where Wilma was last observed alive.

That particular truck vanished into the October mists. This line of inquiry was never again pursued with the same diligence.

• When Joan Harrison was murdered in Preston in November 1975, the killer had sexual intercourse with her very shortly before her death. If this particular murder was to be included in the series it would mean that *for the first and only time the murderer had indulged in sex.* Further, with the exception of the murder of Yvonne Pearson, he had also *killed without using knives* or other sharp instruments. Further, it was highly likely, again with the exception of Yvonne's death, that he had *killed without using a ball peen hammer.* The evidence, therefore, *strongly indicated that Joan Harrison was not killed by the mass murderer but by someone else.*

• When Emily Jackson was murdered in Leeds in January 1976,

police were convinced that the man they sought was the john in the Land Rover, the Irishman so accurately described in this book. He danced in and out of subsequent investigations. He was seen picking up Emily Jackson at 7:00 P.M. *Virtually every other attack and murder took place late in the evening or in the early hours after midnight.*

The Irishman certainly fitted into my principle of following up the first major lines of inquiry, but it seemed inconceivable when studying the entire sequence of attacks and murders, up to and including the death of Barbara, that the killer had calmly sat in a Land Rover while Emily and her friend chatted, *knowing he was being observed by the friend, and then murdered. None of the tracks found at subsequent murder scenes were made by a Land Rover.*

• It was the murder of Jean Jordan, usually called Jean Royle, that the murderer clearly made his biggest mistake to that date. I do not believe that in the normal way of commerce a new five-pound note can cross the Pennines from near Bradford to Manchester in at the most forty-eight hours, and probably twenty-four hours, and find its way into Jean Jordan's handbag other than from the hand of her murderer. Are we to believe that two men set out from near Bradford, one looking for a good time with a prostitute in Manchester, the other man with murder in his heart, that the first has his "good time," and that the second then chooses precisely the same prostitute? It is a nonsense. George Oldfield considered I was mistaken. He talked to me about men getting cash in their pay packets these days to the tune of eighty pounds, of men then buying gasoline and having to use a fiver. I was convinced that the five-pound note held the key to the identity of this so called Yorkshire Ripper, so called not by himself but by a murderous hoaxer and the media. *The five-pound note leads directly to the killer.* Jack Ridgeway remarked after his officers had given up that particular quest, "I am convinced we have interviewed the man responsible." In my view he had never been more accurate in his entire life. Hence the scene in this book between murderer and police.

If my deductions to date were correct, it pointed unquestioningly to the Baildon/Bingley/Shipley areas near Bradford as the killer's place of work and almost certainly his residence. *All are areas on the Keighley side of Bradford.* His astonishingly intimate knowledge of so many cities also strengthened my view that he was a long-distance truck driver. Trucks are so commonplace, so everyday. At the end of any day, if the average person were asked how many trucks he had seen in one of these cities he would be hard put to give an accurate number. A description of all such vehicles would be an impossibility.

Clearly, from the evidence of the tire tracks found at the various murder sites, the killer did not use this mode of transport for the actual night of the murder, with perhaps the exception of the very first one. But while on his many working trips he would be able to reconnoiter, again and again. Further, the tire tracks indicated a variety of vehicles. The contradictory sightings of a variety of cars had to my mind several possibilities. Witnesses were wrong or confused, or the murderer had access to a variety of cars. *To have a heavy-goods-vehicle license it is necessary to have a certain degree of mechanical knowledge. Further, it seemed inconceivable that a man as clever and as cunning as this killer is would allow anyone other than himself to work on his car. Further, he might well repair other people's cars, either to earn money or as a favor. The favor would have been amply repaid if while he had a friend's car he used it on a murderous mission.*

• The attack on Marilyn Moore on December 12, 1977, yielded a number of very important clues. There were the descriptions that Marilyn was able to give, *of her attacker, of his car.* Her observation *"He was good-looking and knew it. He had 'come-to-bed' eyes"* fits closely Olive Smelt's answers to my questions. The car she described was, to use a phrase from a confidential police report, "almost certainly either an Austin Cambridge A55 or a Morris Oxford Mk 5." There is little difference between the two. There are other makes that fit the general description: Wolseley 15/60, MG Magnette Mk 111, Riley 4/68.

In view of the fact that a car answering the description of either an Austin Cambridge or a Morris Oxford was seen in the vicinity of a number of the murder sites at crucial times, it seemed incomprehensible that all such cars still existing had not been checked on the national police computer. I then discovered that this much-vaunted piece of information-giving equipment is less than perfect. Many older types of cars such as the two in question are not recorded on the computer. Many manual records relating

to them have been either lost or destroyed. The police were aware
of this with regard to the investigation in December 1977. If they
had really wanted our help in catching this murderer one might ask
why they did not come clean with the general public on many
aspects. This inability to eliminate cars is just one of the many
examples. Doubtless they will respond that to have done so would
have given the murderer an opportunity to get rid of his car. It
would. But if the police had cared to publicize this as heavily as
they have other worthless information, if they had asked that we
all contact them and advise them if we owned such a car, knew
anyone who did, anyone who had just bought or sold one, *anyone
who used to have one but now apparently did not,* they may have found
the information they needed. The general public has a great deal
more intelligence than the police of this country credit them with.
This killer did not live in a cave in the Orkneys; he bought
groceries, house paint, newspapers, drinks, from someone.
However, when the search for these vehicles was begun after the
attack on Marilyn Moore, the instruction went out from the West
Yorkshire police to all officers:

"This information is the main lead that we have in tracing the
Ripper and no information must be disclosed to the press or any
unauthorized person."

If the police had done their work efficiently when that five-
pound note was traced to the Shipley, Bingley, and Baildon areas
near Bradford, if they had done their work efficiently when
attempting to trace the car that carried Marilyn Moore to near
death, *seven women later destined to die would still be alive.*

Marilyn Moore told the police that her attacker refused to hand
over his five pounds when the car had stopped. There was an
argument. Still he refused to part with his fiver. When they got out
of the car and he attacked her he still had not parted with his
money. *What greater confirmation the police needed that their colleagues,
who were at that very time attempting to trace the source of the five-pound
note found in Jean Jordan's handbag, were very close to the killer, is hard
to imagine.*

One aspect of the attack upon Marilyn Moore continues to
puzzle. She described the man, who called himself "Dave," as
having a Liverpool accent. How sure she was of this aspect I do
not know.

The West Yorkshire police declined to help me trace Marilyn Moore or pass on my request for an interview with her. In view of the fact that Marilyn had already been interviewed by several newspapers, the police refusal to assist in any way was puzzling. But at least their lack of cooperation was consistent.

• The murder of Josephine Whitaker in Halifax in April 1979 gave the police several invaluable clues. Her killer left a footprint, again size seven, he also left minute traces of machine oil, probably from his fingernails. It was this clue plus the hoax letters with their Sunderland postmark that convinced the police that their killer worked for an engineering company, but ignoring the location that the five-pound note pointed to, the Bradford area, they concentrated their efforts in the region of Sunderland. They sought a skilled or semiskilled engineer. *Long-distance truck drivers are also men who will carry traces of machine oil on their hands, particularly if they work for an engineering firm.*

Equally important was the sighting of a particular man in Halifax. At 9:00 P.M. on the night Josephine was murdered a man of about thirty attempted to pick up a woman in Halifax town center. He was driving what was described as a Ford Escort. Later at a time very close to the murder a similar car was seen in Saville Park.

The description given of this man tallies very closely with that given previously by Marilyn Moore, yet when newspapers printed that composite, George Oldfield furiously attacked them. Oldfield was wrong, the newspapers correct.

• The three letters and the tape cassette held for so long to be highly significant will, I am quite sure, be totally discredited later this year. The fact that in two of the three letters the murder of Joan Harrison is referred to is seen by the police as very important. It is. They consider that it ties the letter writer to all of the murders. It does not. It ties the letter writer to one murder—that of Joan Harrison. He is preoccupied with it for one reason alone. He committed it.

Here is a man who in two of his letters and his tape is clearly concerned with the number of women he has murdered.

It is my belief that certain sections of that tape have been deleted by the police and that those edited sections refer specifically to the murder of Joan Harrison. If that is so it is yet a further indication of how preoccupied "Jack" is with one particular murder.

Careful analysis of the *entire* letters reveals that all the information contained is either generalized self-opinion or *information readily obtainable from newspapers prior to the sending of the letters.* The one exception to this is the threat contained within the second letter: "next time try older one I hope." This, directly after the murder of eighteen-year-old Helen Rytka. In view of the fact that the vast majority of prostitutes on the streets of this country are indeed older than eighteen years, the writer could have claimed credit for accuracy if the next victim had been twenty years of age.

In the first two letters he chides the police for not including Joan's murder in the body count. *Yet he totally ignores the then dead but undiscovered Yvonne Pearson. He ignores her murder in his gruesome sum total of death for only one reason. He had no knowledge of it.*

What those letters and tape do tell us is that the sender almost certainly murdered Joan Harrison. Forensic has established that the letter writer has blood type B. Very rare. Only 6 percent of the male population are B secretors. B secretion was discovered also in the semen deposited in Joan Harrison very shortly before she was murdered. The bite above her breast clearly reveals a gap in the upper front teeth. There is a sibilant quality of voice on the tape entirely consistent with such a gap. A door-to-door saliva test in certain selected areas would have rewarding results.

It is my understanding that Peter Sutcliffe has a gap in his upper front teeth and also that his blood type is B. If that is so it would appear that an overwhelming case against Sutcliffe with regard to the murder of Joan Harrison exists. Men have been hanged on less. One fact and one fact alone totally exonerates Sutcliffe from any connection with this particular murder. *He is not a secretor. He has that very, very rare type of blood B that does not secrete blood cells into body fluids such as saliva or semen. The man who killed Joan Harrison is a secretor.*

If I am correct with regard to my conclusions concerning the letters and the tape, and correct about Sutcliffe, then a truly extraordinary state of affairs exists. A situation that one would associate only with fictional crime.

Two men, both murderers, sharing the same rare blood type, acting entirely independently of each other murdered, in the north of England.

These two men also have fetishes that are identical. Both have a fetish concerning the repositioning of brassieres. Both have a fetish concerning footwear. While the mass murderer remained silent, the other boasted of murders committed by the first.

If those conclusions are indeed correct they demonstrate just how wrong the police theory concerning a press blackout was. If there was any credibility whatsoever in the theory that the mass murderer adored publicity, responded to the limelight, if any single factor was designed to provoke such a man, it would be another claiming the "credit" for the mass murders. Yet the real mass murderer remained silent throughout all the publicity. There was only one way, I believed, that he would react; that was with murder. That was why I grew not only fearful but angry during those many months in the north of England. The people were being lulled.

At an initial meeting with Assistant Chief Constable George Oldfield I had advised him that I wanted no more at that time than a general discussion of the entire case. That I wished to complete a great deal of intensive research before coming back to him. He agreed to that.

Several months later I attempted to obtain that second interview. The West Yorkshire police chief press officer at this stage denied I had ever seen Oldfield. It was not logged, he stated. No one knew of it, he declared. The obdurate Baxter continued in this vein over many telephone conversations. It became a point of honor with me that I was going to get that second conversation with Oldfield.

George Oldfield finally agreed to see me again and we met at his Wakefield office at 10:30 A.M. on Wednesday, June 25. All of this might seem of little consequence. I refer to it for one reason. After publication of this book I fully expect the West Yorkshire police force to deny that this second meeting ever took place and that if it did it was for only a few minutes. I'm sure that they will produce a press log to prove this.

I have a tape recording of that second interview with Oldfield— an interview that lasted one hour.

I reached a point in the interview at which I wished to discuss that five-pound note found in Jane Jordan's handbag. Up to that stage of the interview I had not been encouraged by his responses to my questions. The man, clearly dedicated, clearly working himself into the ground, was also clearly obsessed with the case. From where he sat behind his desk there was on the wall opposite and to the left a large white board. On it the names of the victims of the mass murderer. From where Oldfield sat, his eyes would have constantly played upon that board. It was clearly for George Oldfield still very much "my case." That above all else is what discouraged me. I put it to George Oldfield that in my opinion that five-pound note had come from the killer. That he most certainly worked in the Baildon/Bingley/Shipley area and equally certainly lived there.

Oldfield answered: "Again you're falling into the trap. We're dealing with a prostitute. That fiver that was in her possession was more than likely from a previous client, because Jack isn't going to kill them and leave a bloody fiver."

I went at it a number of ways. I failed with every attempt to convince him that he should reopen that aspect of the investigation. That failure hangs heavily upon me. Jacqueline Hill is dead.

Later in the interview George Oldfield remarked: "If we had a roomful of suspects, twenty or thirty men in one room, we would know very quickly which was the Ripper."

Peter Sutcliffe, the man now charged with the murder of Jacqueline Hill, has been interrogated at least four times by the police in the past three years.

It was clear from my interviews with the Assistant Chief Constable that he still clung to the theory he has held throughout the past five years: the theory that the murderer was a man with a hatred of prostitutes, that the murder of Jayne MacDonald had been a case of mistaken identity, a young woman in a red-light district in the small hours, etc.; that the killer had turned his attacks to nonprostitutes *deliberately* only with the killing of Josephine Whitaker.

It is a view clearly and heavily influenced by the three hoax letters and the tape. Putting those aside, what do we have?

We have a man whose first two murderous attacks on women who have fortunately survived were perpetrated on nonprostitutes. We have a man who, far from expressing regret for the murder of Jayne, goes out two weeks after that murder and attempts to kill yet another nonprostitute, Maureen Long.

What nature of man is this?

He is a man who by his actions shows a massive hatred of and anger at all women.

Why is there within him such anger and hatred? I believe the nature of the injuries sustained holds the key. In attack after attack, in murder after murder, there is clearly shown a pattern of behavior. The women are smashed on the back of the head with blows that would have produced instantly a very deep unconsciousness and almost certainly a very quick death. If the purpose were to kill, it had been achieved at that moment. The killer can then make a rapid departure. Time and time again this man stayed with the dead body, moved it, sometimes a few yards, sometimes a greater distance. It was then, in my opinion, that the real acts that this man was hell-bent upon took place. The lifting of brassieres, the lowering of panties, the undoing of outer clothing and the appalling attacks on the stomach and abdomen, the life-force area. The life-force area that at one time has held us all. This murderer never stabs through clothing. He is very careful to insure that nothing will come between the naked skin of the life-force area and his weapons. The victims are already dead. This is not additional violence designed to kill. This is *the* act for the murderer, to attack and mutilate the life-force area. Virtually every single victim suffered the killer's need to give vent to this specific fixation.

Consider Jean Jordan in Manchester. *The attack on her abdominal area took place over one week after her death.* Why this particular obsession? Was it self-hatred, an attempt to pluck himself from the womb? Doubtless Freudians would embrace that view.

Or is it something far less complex, is it a raging evil jealousy because so many of his victims have something he does not have? Children. Excluding Joan Harrison's murder, twenty-three children have been deprived of their mothers by this man.

If Maureen Long, Olive Smelt, and Marilyn Moore had not all miraculously survived, eight more children would have been rendered motherless. All the victims were of child-bearing age. My theory was to a degree based on the assumption that the killer is married but childless. That he desperately wanted children and for some reason could not have them. That the frustration and sadness that are normal healthy reactions to such monthly disappointments in this man grew to a violent evil hatred of all other potential child-bearing women.

Research indicated that with regard to the killer's overwhelming hatred of women there would probably be at least two exceptions. His mother, with whom he probably had a very close relationship, and his wife. It would be entirely consistent that with his hatred for women in general went an extraordinary degree of devotion to his wife. She would be on a pedestal, far above what he would consider the common herd.

There has been much expert speculation on the nature of this killer over the years, on what kind of man he is. Virtually every psychiatric label has been fastened to him.

He has been termed an overcontrolled aggressive psychopath. He has been called psychotic, impotent, a religious maniac, sexually motivated, a highly aggressive lesbian, and again and again "mad."

It has been asserted that the murderer has an inability to provide or experience love and affection, that he is essentially cold, callous, and unfeeling. That he failed to learn from past mistakes because, in the view of many experts, he could not conceive that he ever made any.

Experts have declared that the killer is a schizophrenic, that he had what is commonly called a Jekyll and Hyde personality.

Others observed that he might be suffering from an insanity brought on by long-term syphilis. Others felt that he was heavily influenced by the Victorian Jack the Ripper and pointed to similar phraseology in letters allegedly written by the Victorian murderer and letters allegedly written by "the Yorkshire Ripper."

The vast majority of experts who commented on his domestic life were insistent that the killer was not married, that if he had been, his wife must be aware of what he was doing. The experts thought it more likely that either he lived alone or with aged parents.

The infamous tape recording was seen by at least one expert, who heavily influenced police thinking, as the ultimate example of egotism. These are just a few of the considered opinions expressed over the past five years.

In my view, this murderer can be described in one word. A word no longer fashionable in the latter part of the twentieth century. I do not believe that this man is insane or that he can get off the hook by accepting any one of the vast number of psychiatric labels that have been fastened upon him. The word to describe this man, to sum up his mind, his personality, is "evil."

In a society in which a majority are no longer practicing Christians the concept of evil has lost vogue. Yet it still remains valid as a description.

Raymond Morris, the Cannock Chase murderer, the man who took a little girl in his car, suffocated her, sexually interfered with her, murdered her, threw her body on the naked earth, then calmly drove home to lunch with his wife, went shopping with her and bought cakes for his mother-in-law for an afternoon tea, enjoyed while the body of that little girl was still warm—this man was not insane. No attempt was ever made at any time by Morris or his defense counsel to argue insanity. He serves his life sentence not in a hospital for the criminally insane but in the maximum-security wing of Durham prison. Morris is not insane. He is evil.

Consider the creatures known as the "moors murderers," Ian Brady and Myra Hindley. These two who tape-recorded the pitiful last pleas for mercy from terror-stricken children, then murdered them, and buried their bodies on the Yorkshire moors. No hospital for the criminally insane holds them. Hindley is in Holloway Prison in London. Brady is in the same maximum-security wing at Durham as Raymond Morris. Brady and Hindley are not insane. They are evil.

Many may find that description inadequate for the man who has terrorized the north of England for over five years. Clearly this killer has necrophilic tendencies. Clearly he has a variety of obsessions, not least his fetishes concerning women's shoes, panties, and brassieres. Often with murder one can argue extenuating circumstances. Indeed, in a number of my own studies I have done precisely that. Sometimes there are no such extenuating circumstances, no mental illness that can be attributed and thereby give comfort not only to the killer but to society in general. There is darkness within us all. The majority have that darkness under control to varying degrees. A small minority are totally immersed in their darkness. They do not fight it. They enjoy it. Such a man is that mass murderer. A man that football crowds have hailed with "There's only one Yorkshire Ripper."

They are wrong. This minority are like buses. When one has gone, another comes to take its place.

There has been much speculation about the gaps between the murders. Theories have abounded, including the view that the killer was prevented from striking during the long gaps because he was in prison. I firmly believe that once all is known of the murderer and his life, an inner rhythm concerning the murders will clearly emerge. An inner rhythm affected perhaps by periods of time when he believed that his wife was pregnant—and indeed, perhaps she was, only to miscarry. An inner rhythm affected by the mundane—moving his home, vacations, or *working trips abroad.*

It has been said by many, many experts over the past five years that this man could not have close friends, family, relatives, or a wife. Perhaps not close friends, but I firmly believe he has the rest. How then could he mask his awful acts from these people? Were they part of the murderous conspiracy? Surely they would know?

I referred earlier to the BBC "Man Alive" team filming a program about the creation of this book. In one of the sequences filmed on March 25, 1980, when speaking of this mass murderer I spoke of an earlier notorious case that occurred in England in 1968. It was known nationally as "the Cannock Chase murders." Three little girls were murdered in an area near Stafford between 1965 and 1967. They had been sexually assaulted, suffocated, then their small bodies dumped. The anger and hatred at their killer was immense, not merely in the Midlands but throughout the entire country.

It was not until November 1968 that a man was arrested and charged with one of the murders. I have already referred to him, Raymond Morris. Despite the fact that a very accurate police composite had been circulating over those years, despite the fact that Morris had been interviewed by the police between 1967 and 1968 on three different occasions, he had fooled them and slipped through the net. There was one reason and one alone why this had occurred. On each occasion his wife, Carol, had supported his alibi and confirmed to the police that they had been together during the crucial hours when the third murder had occurred. It was only after

he had been arrested that Carol reconsidered the statements she
had made to the police not once but three times. Arrest of one's
spouse can concentrate the mind wonderfully. Discussing those
earlier interviews *after* her husband's arrest she said:

"I said at the time my husband had got home at his usual time,
about two o'clock in the afternoon on Saturday, August nineteenth, and that we were shopping together in Walsall all
afternoon before visiting my mother at half-past four.

"I realize now that this could not have been so, but I was not
telling lies. I thought what I was saying was accurate, but now I
think again I realize that I cannot possibly be sure of anything
except that my mother had asked me to get some cakes which she
had forgotten to get when we were out shopping together in
Walsall that morning."

She had seen the roadblocks in Walsall on the afternoon of the
murder, had read all the appalling details in subsequent weeks,
knew that the police were looking for a gray Austin A55
Cambridge car, like the one her husband owned, and yet . . .

"I never dreamed that my husband could be the man they were
after. I trusted my husband implicitly and if I was mistaken, it was
an honest mistake and with no intention to cover up for my
husband."

The alibi had been blown away. Then, and only then, was
Morris charged with the murder of Christine Darby.

His workmates were shocked. They all spoke highly of him, of
what a good worker he was but that he was not very sociable,
would never mix. His neighbors shared their sense of disbelief.

During his trial his wife gave evidence, for the prosecution. She
was their key witness. Her husband's lawyer mounted an attack on
her honesty. With regard to the three statements she had made
that confirmed her husband's version, the defense counsel forced
from her the admission that she had been lying on those occasions.
Technically of course this was accurate, but Carol's other remarks
in the witness box demonstrate a picture with shades of gray as
well as the legalistic "Then you were lying?"

"I did not think it could be him. . . . Well, if a person comes
home acting normally and eats his meals and shows no sign of
emotion you could not believe . . . I agreed with him because I
couldn't believe he was responsible."

I believe that the very human and natural response of Carol Morris will be repeated by the wife of the man who has murdered at least twelve women.

After Jacqueline Hill's murder in November 1980 a team for Granada Television's "World In Action" created a program on the manhunt for the killer. "Ripper" task force officers were shown in one sequence conducting house-to-house inquiries. One of them discussing this task with the interviewer observed:

"When you knock on a door and the husband says, 'Never went out—stayed in and watched telly with the wife and went to bed,' that's a nice one. No further checking needed."

By November 1980 this book had been written. In view of that fact, my British publishers invited me to attend their annual sales conference and talk to their representatives.

On Monday, November 17, I spoke to them for over an hour. At one point one of their northern reps underlined the view that I had found so predominant during the later stages of my research. He expressed the opinion that "the Ripper" had either killed himself or decided to stop killing. I told him and the other fifty people present of the fears that had been ever-increasing within me during 1980: that this man was not dead.

I continued, "It is only a matter of time before he murders again. He may have murdered last night. He may murder tonight."

Six hours later, Jacqueline Hill was murdered, in Headingley, a few hundred yards from where I had been staying.

It had not required any extraordinary powers to make that prediction. I do not claim any psychic, clairvoyant, mystic or any paranormal ability. It did not require great intelligence to state with total sureness what was going to happen, before it happened. Any ordinary member of the public who had been aware of the press blackout, of the deliberate and evil suppression of information, would have come to precisely the same conclusion.

Another young life had been needlessly lost. Who are these men who gamble with women's lives? How dare they? Honest mistakes are one thing. A policy such as that implemented from February 1980 until Jacqueline died cannot, must not, be tolerated.

It is my deeply held belief that the police of Britain are accountable. Accountable to all of us with regard to the hunt for this mass murderer. It is time for that accounting. Doubtless when the public-relations department of the West Yorkshire police gets under way after the arrest and trial and verdict, any demand for these men to answer to us all will be swept away in the general euphoria, and within twelve months the chief constable of West Yorkshire, Ronald Gregory, will have been granted a knighthood. George Oldfield should be good for at least an Order of the British Empire.

After the murder of Jacqueline Hill in November 1980 the police press blackout was torn to shreds. What followed was a national outburst of anger. Of demands for action. Of expressions of fear and hatred. All fired by this further awful death and by the realization that the public had been conned. Conned into thinking the nightmare was over. Conned into relaxing. Conned into forgetting that this man still walked among us.

On November 19, 1980, when it was confirmed that Jacqueline had been murdered by the mass murderer, George Oldfield stated, "I have always held the view that this man will continue to kill until he is caught. No woman is safe while he's at large. I appeal to all members of the public, especially to all women, to think carefully about all males with whom they come into regular contact, including those to whom they may be married or related, and ask themselves, 'Could that be the man we are seeking?'"

I can find no record of such public utterances from February 1980 until after Jacqueline's murder.

Female students at Leeds and Bradford Universities were urged, "Do not go out after dark. Take no risks. Keep to well-lit areas. Keep all doors and windows locked."

The siege had returned to northern England. Spontaneous living had ceased. At that time of the year in the north it is dark by four-thirty in the afternoon. It was "no go" the launderette. No go the pub. No go the telephone booth. No go life.

Jacqueline had been murdered in a respectable suburb. Well lit, busy at nine-thirty in the evening. If a young woman was not safe there, then where lay sanctuary?

When Oldfield expressed his opinion that the killer was in "all probability living in Leeds," the tension in that city mounted to near panic. "I hate Leeds," said one petrified young woman student. Others promptly left the university, for the safety of homes far away.

An "old square-shaped car" was reported speeding the wrong way down the one-way Alma Road, where Jacqueline had been murdered.

Another witness came forward and described a man she had seen in the area at the crucial time. His description fitted that given by Marilyn Moore. It fitted that of the man seen in the town center at Halifax and also Saville Park, shortly before the murder of Josephine Whitaker.

Moments after her killer launched himself at the young woman and having killed her, dragged her body some fifteen yards across waste ground, another young woman student walked down Alma Road. Nineteen-year-old Andrée Proctor saw movement in the bushes. If she had been a few minutes earlier it would have been her dead body in those bushes.

It was only after the discovery of her friend's body that Andrée realized that what had seemed odd was highly significant. Recalling that moment, Andrée said, "I had this horrible sense of evil."

It was clearly a retrospective awareness. Why should a nineteen-year-old student be particularly on her guard after nearly a year of consciousness-lowering? If members of a supposedly ever alert police force could fail to attach any significance to a bloodstained handbag, Jacqueline Hill's bloodstained handbag, handed in within hours of her death, found at the precise spot on the pavement where a ball peen hammer had ended her life, why should Andrée have attached any particular significance to wildly moving bushes?

The police had blundered, fatally, with regard to Jean Jordan's handbag in Manchester. Fatally, that is, for the seven women who followed Jean to the grave. Now, immediately after the murder of Jacqueline, there had been criminal blunder.

The handbag had been found within ten minutes of the attack. A male student discovered it on the pavement. He took it back to his rooms and, putting it to one side, made a cup of tea.

Later he took the bag to a student who was acting as key-holder for the block of apartments. The key-holder's roommate, as well as being a mature student, was also an ex-policeman, a former

Hong Kong inspector. He saw the bloodstains on the bag, noted from its contents that it belonged to student Jacqueline Hill, and immediately dialed 999. The time now was approximately 11:30 P.M. Chief Constable Ronald Gregory, when subsequently attempting to put the best possible light on what then happened, commented that "a crucial two hours had been lost before police received that emergency call." Indeed two hours had been lost. Very largely because of a lack of awareness by the foreign student who had initially found the handbag. His awareness might have been greater if during the previous ten months there had been continued publicity about "the Yorkshire Ripper," with reminders that his apparent last victim had been a student at Bradford University.

Gregory still has to offer anything approaching a satisfactory explanation for what followed. He never will. There is no "satisfactory" explanation.

A black-and-white police car responded to the 999 call. The students gave the two police officers the bloodstained handbag and urged them to find Jacqueline Hill's apartment and make sure she was unharmed. It would appear that the two officers had other ideas. After a three-minute search of the area where the handbag had been discovered, they returned to their police station and logged the bag as "lost property." They did not discover on the pavement the items that had fallen from the handbag. They did not discover the body of Jacqueline Hill some fifty yards from the spot.

If "two crucial" hours had been lost by an unaware student, ten more "crucial hours" were lost by unaware police officers. Their superior at the station obviously considered bloodstained handbags an everyday occurrence in Headingley. It was later to be said in defense of these three police officers, "They were only small bloodstains." He duly entered it in the lost-property book. It stayed there until after Jaqui's body had been discovered, until after the students asked the police about the handbag again. Then and only then, some two hours after the discovery of the body, was the bag linked with its owner, nearly twelve hours after the police had been notified.

Doubtless even if they had performed their duties efficiently after responding to the 999 call, the killer would have already been at home. But a few roadblocks set up, flooding the area immediately with policemen, immediate visits to the homes of suspects, a whole series of standard police procedures, could and should have been operating at full capacity before midnight.

Gregory was later to talk of "hindsight" and imply that if the three officers concerned had had their fair share of that virtue, the body would have been rapidly discovered.

Others seemed equally unimpressed with the chief constable's explanation. The calls to bring in Scotland Yard could be heard up and down the land. Various M.P.s demanded it. Various women's organizations demanded it. Editorials in a number of national newspapers called for it.

West Yorkshire police were reported as being "hurt" by criticism of their lack of success; they considered that most of the comments made about the investigation were "ill timed and misinformed." Senior officers were also concerned about the morale of their men. Their views on the morale of the families that had been devastated by this killer remained unexpressed.

Again West Yorkshire's chief constable asserted that he was not going to call in Scotland Yard. Against a foreground of anger that had now taken to the streets in many forms, he clearly was not going to satisfy public opinion with yet another "I have every confidence that everything possible is being done" type of statement.

George Oldfield found that it was no longer "his" case. It became the overall responsibility of Detective Chief Superintendent James Hobson, who was given the acting rank of Assistant Chief Constable to go with the task. Hobson, known to criminals and fellow officers as Lucky Jim, was of course no stranger to the investigation. His first involvement reached back to the murder of Irene Richardson in February 1977. More important, perhaps, this was a man who had worked under and been heavily influenced by the late Detective Chief Superintendent Hoban.

This appointment, made in late November 1980, should have been implemented much sooner. Hobson's first significant act was to promptly demonstrate his own view about calling in help from outside West Yorkshire. From Lincolnshire he brought in Assistant Chief Constable Andy Sloan. From the Midlands he brought in Assistant Chief Constable David Gerty. From Thames Valley came Deputy Chief Constable Leslie Emment. He added the director of the Home Office research establishment at Aldermaston, Stuart Kind. The last member of this super "think tank" was Commander Ronald Harvey, adviser to the Chief Inspector of Constabulary on crime.

The impetus for this new move had come from Home Secretary Whitelaw, but the men were hand-picked by Hobson. He changed the man in charge of the murder incident room. He changed the communications officer. Most significantly, he stated his determination that all five thousand officers of the West Yorkshire police force should play a greater part. He told them:

"What we want is to create luck for ourselves by concentrating a great deal of effort down with the officer on the beat, by making sure that the five thousand officers do something constructive every day toward the investigation."

It was a public acknowledgment of something that Hobson and many of his colleagues had believed for a long time. It echoed a view that I and many others had also held for a while. If this man was ever going to be caught, it would be by a copper on the beat, a police car making a routine check. This was the unique weapon that had always been at the disposal of the man in charge of this murder investigation. Not "it's between him and me." On November 15, 1980, that weapon was finally brought to bear on the mass murderer.

The "think tank" was there to assess overall strategy, but it was never likely that this or any other group of vastly experienced senior men would feel the collar of the killer. The odds were always on just a plain copper.

The same week that these changes were announced the Yorkshire *Evening Post* accurately caught the mood of millions of people. It ran a boxed headline that was designed to be cut out and used as a car sticker or placed in windows or on garden fences: LET'S CATCH THE BLOODY RIPPER.

The News of the World announced on November 23, 1980, that it was offering twenty thousand pounds for the capture of "the Yorkshire Ripper." This brought the total reward to fifty thousand pounds.

In the cities most vulnerable to the killer there had been in the

days that immediately followed Jacqueline's murder a fear that
spread like the wind. It is difficult for any man to comprehend the
depth of that fear, of how totally it affected every thought and
deed of the women in those cities. From London I talked to a
number of them, people in direct danger from a mass murderer. In
danger for one reason alone, because they are women. One of
them is Ann, a social worker who lives in Chapeltown. This was
the same week that Jacqueline Hill had been murdered. When I
telephoned, she was in the middle of recording her information
and feelings on a tape for me. A few days later it arrived.

Some extracts are given here. They are extracts from a woman
who is not only extremely intelligent and articulate but, because of
her feminist views, had always before this murder taken an angry,
defiant view about curfews for women. Indeed, after previous
murders in Leeds, Ann had continued to walk home, late at night,
unescorted, through Chapeltown. Previously she had taken the
view that this one man was not going to impinge on her freedom.
Her voice contains none of her normal cheerful confidence.
Instead there is a nervousness, an anxious fear, in her words:

"I was at a meeting yesterday evening with probation
officers; of course young Jaqui was a probation volunteer.
You can imagine the feelings there, around the table. We
went home in a numbed silence and there wasn't a soul in
sight in the city center. That was half past six, seven
o'clock at night.

"I really don't know what to say. You told me he would
come back. You told all of us. I didn't want to believe it. As
summer went by, it seemed you must be wrong, that he'd
gone away for good. Oh, I wish you'd been wrong.

"As the days go by, instead of feeling less shocked about
the events here, it begins to get worse. Worse when you talk
to people. Worse when you think about the situation and all
of its implications and take a look around the city here.

"You know how I take things pretty much for granted
and I suppose I was pretty complacent about the whole
thing. It's the 'can never happen to me' syndrome. I feel

absolutely stunned. The whole thing is so motiveless and pointless, except to our friend Jack.

"This is quite a different situation; it's really gone home for the first time. The murders in Chapeltown were almost exotic in a way, compared with this. Perhaps there was the comforting feeling for all us so called 'good girls' that it was 'the other people' that these things were going to happen to. You can't say that about our little Jaqui, can you? We all identify with her very much. What a very ordinary activity, going home from an evening's teaching session as a probation volunteer at the respectable hour of nine-fifteen on a perfectly ordinary number-one bus. In one of our respectable suburbs.

"The atmosphere is grim, not helped by the depressing November weather. It's so damn' dark at half past four. Everyone seems to rush behind their doors like scared rabbits. That's the womenfolk anyway.

"University Union meetings have been banned in the evenings. Women students are being escorted everywhere. The hall of residence behind where you stayed used to have an ever-open door. Now it's bolted and barred. We've had a Welfare Rights course on there this week. I spent twenty minutes trying to get into the damn' place. Eventually had to shin up the fire escape and virtually break in before we could commence the course. It's things like that that show you the tenor of anxiety that is about, in the city, amid all age groups of previously nonfrightened people. I foresee some very unhappy weeks ahead of us.

"I hear my feet clanging down empty pavements in the early evening. I suppose not having a car makes one feel more vulnerable, though my friends with cars tell me that they are terrified to cross parking lots or any open spaces at all.

"You know my feelings about curtailment of movement. Now when I go down the road about 250 yards to where my mother lives, where before I used to trot up and down the road without a thought, now even in the main road as I pass the Sikh temple I find myself glancing nervously at *every gap in the wall and walking practically in the gutter or in the face of the traffic to avoid any gate entrances. It's damn ridiculous but that's the state we're in.*

"You've probably heard about the telephone threat to the Daily Mirror that there will be another murder in Leeds next Friday. I foresee the most silent night of the year in the city. Shops were already shutting early before that. They might as well all close up for the next few months. . . .

"Stopped then for a telephone call. It was my dear mother. 'Had I got home yet? Have I come home by myself? Be careful coming down the drive. Never go anywhere alone, etc., etc.' A friend of mine was here earlier this evening for a meal. She demanded that I go out into the drive in case anyone should leap out of the trees. I reminded her that I then have to get back into the house after she drives off. Do we watch each other until we are both out of sight?

"It is the only topic of conversation. At work today we had a conversation trying to work out the best forms of protection. The suggestions ranged from crash helmets, glasses with which you can see behind you, like a periscope, a mechanical canine that could be dragged along uttering mechanical 'woof woofs,' switchblades on the back of our heels and elbows, like James Bond. Conjures up a strange composite picture.

"The modern woman of today with everything! I think our slightly hysterical laughter was rather forced. Doubtless some entrepreneur will make a fortune.

"From what you've told me of how he kills there seems to be no adequate protection.

"I think all evening work and late training sessions are going to be banned in the department.

"I think it will take us a long time to recover from this."

That widespread fear rapidly turned to massive anger. When the lunatics and the mentally disturbed yet again crawled out of the woodwork and, posing as the mass murderer, telephoned and wrote threatening to murder again, it created not only fear but even more, anger.

Leeds General Infirmary received three calls within days of the latest murder. Each time the caller declared that the next victim would be a nurse. Massive security arrangements were made at the hospital. District nurses began traveling to mothers in pairs. If a midwife was called to an unexpected birth in the middle of the night she was advised to take her husband or a male friend. What comfort they derived from taking a member of the sex that includes in its ranks the mass murderer is not known.

Another hoaxer phoned the police direct and told them he was the Ripper. This call was traced. It had been made nine days after Jacqueline's death by twenty-two-year-old Raymond Smith of Rotherham. He later told police officers he had "been a bit bored that day, so I decided to pose as the Ripper for a bit of fun. We've only had the telephone since August and it's still a bit of a novelty." He was fined £50.

Some of West Yorkshire's five thousand police officers demonstrated that they had taken to heart Hobson's call for all of them to be involved in the hunt.

A police officer in Morley approached a friend of mine and asked, "Excuse me, sir, do you have any idea who the Yorkshire Ripper is?"

Many women had also taken to the streets. The questions and demands they made were of a different order.

In Manchester, over four hundred women marched through the city demanding a right to walk the streets free of abuse and assault. Halting outside a police station, they protested at what they considered police hypocrisy. "Lock yourselves up at night, do not move, do not stir. By the way, if you should venture out and take with you anything we deem to be an offensive weapon, we will arrest and charge you."

In Margate, protesting women forced a cinema to abandon screenings of a film entitled *Dressed To Kill*.

In Coventry another protest march by women culminated in a foot-high message being painted on the plinth of Lady Godiva's statue. It stated: "Women are angry—they will fight back."

In London's Underground, many posters that advertised films

that a group of women considered objectionable were scrawled over with: "Women Against Violence Against Women."

As mentioned earlier, this was the title of a group formed in Leeds, shortly after Jacqueline's murder. The concept quickly spread throughout the country. One of their principal targets was any film that was considered to exploit sex and violence.

The founding branch in Leeds also wanted all men who were out on the streets after dark to be issued with licenses to show that they were engaged on legitimate business. The group wanted the right to challenge any man they saw.

At Bradford University, the students' union pledged itself to help in the defense of any woman arrested for carrying a weapon.

In the same city, eleven women were arrested after picketing a cinema showing *Violation of the Bitch*. As they were put into police vans they chanted, "It's taken five years and you've not caught the Ripper yet. You can arrest us but not the Ripper."

In Leeds there were more arrests after two hundred chanting women descended on the Plaza cinema, which was showing *The Beast* and *Climax*. They were led away chanting "Police support porno," and "Get men off the streets." Male reporters and men passing by were attacked, some kicked and punched, others spat upon.

Yet another Leeds cinema that bore the brunt of feminine anger was the Odeon. There was a screening of *Dressed to Kill* ended abruptly. A special "hit squad" of over fifty women forced their way past a line of policemen, walked into the cinema and threw paint bombs at the screen. The bombs were a mixture of bad eggs and red paint.

On the same night in Leeds other groups of women attempted to batter down the doors of the BBC. They then attempted to storm a nearby public house.

Cinema screens in a variety of places throughout the country had rotten eggs sliding down them.

A "sex shop" in, of all places, Chapeltown, had its windows smashed. The slogans "Women are angry" and "No men after dark" began to appear on walls in many cities. Poems dedicated to Jacqueline began to be circulated. One written by a Leeds woman contains the line "We know only that each man, or group of men on these streets, is an enemy."

All of these demonstrations and acts of protest had many police officers in attendance. In the northern cities, police who were scheduled to work on the murder investigation had to be switched to cover these demonstrations.

Mrs. Mary Whitehouse, observing so many of her sex violently advocating what she had been peacefully advocating for seventeen years, stringent censorship, welcomed all her new supporters though she considered that "if they achieve the objective through violent means it is a sad example for society."

In an article in the *Guardian*, Jean Stead urged that "the time has come for primary schools to get some supervised mixed infant fighting courses going in the playgrounds."

She hoped to engender in the male population generally "a healthy physical fear of women instead of an irrational fear of their tongues."

She advocated that women should become like their sisters of yesteryear, during the Roman occupation, and carry around large stones "to attack any strange man who came near them."

Jacqueline Hill's mother made a television appeal to the public in general to help find her daughter's killer. She also suggested a poster campaign throughout the north to declare "The Ripper Is a Coward."

The police later expressed grave doubts about this suggestion, but a Morley businessman had eight thousand posters printed. Soon they were on walls and windows.

On November 27 came the most extraordinary aspect. An item on BBC 2, a hymn of hate to the killer. A number of the living victims of the killer's acts spoke directly to the man responsible via the screen.

Mrs. Irene MacDonald: "You are a beast with no feelings—a coward, not a man. All people hate you. I think you are the Devil himself."

Mrs. Avril Hiley, the mother of Josephine Whitaker: "You are a very inadequate person, certainly physically and mentally. You can't make a relationship with a live woman. Possibly your only relationships are with dead women."

Mrs. Olive Smelt: "Doesn't it bother you to think people hate you for doing this? It is nothing to be proud of, the things you do."

Mr. Haydn Hiley, Josephine's stepfather: "You are the worst coward the world has ever known, and that should go down in the Guiness Book of Records."

Mr. David Leach: "You are an obscenity on the face of the earth. When they catch you and put you away they will throw away the key."

Mrs. Beryl Leach: "Look over your shoulder, Ripper. Many people are looking for you. They hate you."

The hunt ended as many had felt it would end—but it oh, so nearly did not. After the arrest there was an extraordinary sequence of events. A euphoric Chief Constable Gregory held press conferences during which he clearly indicated that the police had caught the mass murderer. The arresting officers were seen on television reading out a telegram of congratulations from their colleagues in West Yorkshire. The final irony had been that it was not Gregory's men who had brought the hunt to an end but police from a neighboring area, South Yorkshire. What has not been revealed is how very close Peter Sutcliffe came to yet again fooling the police, yet again slipping through the net.

Two uniformed policemen on vice patrol in one of Sheffield's red-light districts on the evening of Friday, January 2, 1981, saw a Rover V8 parked. The license plates appeared to be false. Casually the two officers approached the Rover.

Inside the car they discovered prostitute Olivia Reivers and a young man. He was questioned about the plates. The officers checked with the national computer and ascertained that they were indeed false. They asked the couple to accompany them to a police station. Peter Sutcliffe, the young man in the car, asked if he could urinate in some nearby bushes before going to the station.

Subsequently, after being questioned at the station, it was established that the number plates were allegedly stolen from near Dewsbury. Stolen number plates, a Bradford man who closely resembled Marilyn Moore's "Dave" picked up in the red light area with a prostitute, all these factors ensured a phone call from the Sheffield police to their colleagues on the Ripper Squad. Sutcliffe, who had initially given his name as Peter Williams, had by now admitted his real name and address. The response from the Ripper Squad? "Oh he's all right. We've already questioned him."

On Saturday morning Sutcliffe was taken to Dewsbury police station for processing on the minor charge of the stolen number plates. The paper work having been duly completed the Dewsbury police had no objection to granting Sutcliffe immediate bail. Only the nagging doubts of a woman police officer about Sutcliffe prevented him from walking out of the station. Because of her insistence the Ripper Squad were sent for. Sutcliffe remained calm and unruffled during the day-long questioning.

Back at Sheffield, Sergeant Bob Ring, one of the arresting officers, came back on duty on Saturday night and was told that Sutcliffe was still being questioned. Acting on a hunch, he returned to the scene of the arrest. In a pile of leaves near the spot where Sutcliffe had apparently urinated, Bob Ring found a ball peen hammer and a knife.

Confronted with this evidence on Sunday morning, Peter Sutcliffe began to tell a different story. An horrific, unbelievable story.

Since 1975, this murder hunt has become the biggest in the history of this country, if not in the entire world. Over thirty thousand statements have been taken. Over two hundred and sixty thousand people have been interviewed. Nearly two hundred thousand cars have been checked. The police have worked over seven hundred thousand man hours. The cost is in excess of six million pounds.

At the time of writing Peter Sutcliffe stands accused of one murder, that of Jacqueline Hill. If Sutcliffe is indeed guilty of that murder then certain conclusions can irrefutably be drawn.

Peter Sutcliffe is, in my opinion, the so-called and mis-called "Yorkshire Ripper." I believe that of the thirteen victims that have been attributed to this mass murderer, Peter Sutcliffe murdered twelve of those women.

I am convinced on the evidence I have accumulated over the past two years that Peter Sutcliffe is responsible for the following:

The murder of Wilma McCann, Leeds, October 1975.

The murder of Emily Jackson, Leeds, January 1976.

The murder of Irene Richardson, Leeds, February 1976.

The murder of Patricia Atkinson, Bradford, April 1977.

The murder of Jayne MacDonald, Leeds, June 1977.

The murder of Jean Jordan, Manchester, October 1977.

The murder of Helen Rytka, Huddersfield, January 1978.

The murder of Yvonne Pearson, Bradford, January 1978.

The murder of Vera Millward, Manchester, May 1978.

The murder of Josephine Whitaker, Halifax, April 1979.

The murder of Barbara Leach, Bradford, September 1979.

The murder of Margo Walls, Farnsley, August 1980.

The murder of Jacqueline Hill, Leeds, November 1980.

I am equally convinced on the evidence I have accumulated that the murderer of Joan Harrison in Preston in November 1975 is still at large. That *this* murderer is the man responsible for the three letters and the tape-recording that have sent the police of this nation and many other countries around the world on the greatest wild goose chase in the history of crime.

If this second murderer is ever apprehended, he should also be closely questioned concerning the unsolved murder of Patricia Elizabeth Maguire in Bradford in April 1979.

With regard to Peter Sutcliffe I believe he is also responsible for the following:

The attempted murder of Anna Rogulskyj in Keighley in July 1975.

The attempted murder of Olive Smelt in Halifax in August 1975.

The attempted murder of Marcella Claxton in Leeds in May 1976.

The attempted murder of Maureen Long in Bradford in July 1977.

The attempted murder of Marilyn Moore in Leeds in December 1977.

The attempted murder of Dr. Upaehya Banbara in Leeds in September 1980.

The attempted murder of Teresa Sykes in Huddersfield in November 1980.

He should also be closely questioned concerning the murder of

Carole Wilkinson in Bradford in October 1977. This murder causes particular anxiety. Carole was smashed on the head with two heavy stones. Three months later, in January 1978, Yvonne Pearson was murdered in an identical manner, *three miles from the scene of the attack on Carole Wilkinson*. At the time of Yvonne's death, investigating police officers declared that it was not a "Ripper" murder, not one of the series. Police officers further stated their belief that the death of Yvonne was "a copy cat murder," someone attempting to emulate "The Yorkshire Ripper." Eighteen months after the death of Carole Wilkinson, Bradford police arrested and charged twenty-two-year-old Anthony Steel with the crime. At his trial in December 1979, the case against Steel depended very largely upon a confession he was alleged to have made to the police after being arrested. The defense stated that the confession was false and had only been made after "intense pressure" had been brought to bear upon the accused. Anthony Steel was found guilty and sentenced to life imprisonment.

By the time of Steel's trial, the murder of Yvonne Pearson was no longer thought to be "copy cat" by the police. It had, from June 1978, been included in this list of murders attributed to "The Yorkshire Ripper."

Peter Sutcliffe should also be closely questioned on the following:

Attempted murder of Barbara Miller in Bradford in March 1975.

Attempted murder of Caroline Tracy Browne in Silsden in August 1975.

Attempted murder of Barbara Brearly in Doncaster in October 1976.

Murder of Barbara Ann Young in Doncaster on the 23rd March, 1977.

Murder of Carol Reeves in Hyeres in the South of France on the 16th June, 1978.

Attempted murder of Ann Rooney in Horsforth on the 2nd March, 1979.

Attempted murder of a twenty-one-year-old woman in Derby on the 3rd August, 1979.

Attempted murder of Yvonne Jane Mysliniec in Ilkley on the 11th October, 1979.

Murder of Gertie Jensen in Gothenberg, Sweden, in August 1980.

Murder of Theresa Thurlong in Malmo, Sweden, in August 1980.

Attempted murder of Maureen Lea in Leeds on the 25th October, 1980.

All of the above attacks and murders are at present unsolved. I am convinced that some, if not all, are the work of this man who is the embodiment of evil. The man *they* call "The Yorkshire Ripper."

David A. Yallop   London
                                                  20th January 1981

Deliverance

Peter Sutcliffe, the eldest of six children was born on June 2, 1946. His father, textile worker John, and his mother, Kathleen—a native of Connemara—were both devout Christians. John was a member of the choir at nearby Church of England St. Wilfred's. Kathleen attended the Catholic church of St. Joseph's. As is usual in what Catholics would term a mixed marriage, the children were brought up in the Catholic faith. Sutcliffe's first school was St. Joseph's R.C. primary at Bingley. Subsequently he went to Cottingley Manor Secondary School, where he is remembered as an intelligent boy, always near the top of his class, with a particular aptitude for English, history and art.

Neighbors on the Gilstead estate in Bingley, where Sutcliffe spent most of his formative years, speak of the happy childhood that Peter and his brothers and sisters had. They recall the children's parties and a mother who was clearly devoted to her family. Peter in particular was close to his mother. This is a view shared by his own family.

Examination of Sutcliffe's early life shows no abnormal features, no traumatic events, nothing to trigger him into mass murder.

Neighbor and childhood friend Wendy Turner:

"I do not recall him being in any kind of trouble. He was always the first to respond if a neighbor needed help. I never saw him show violence in any form. His brothers used to get into fights. Not Peter. He would walk away."

Neighbor Marjorie Varley:

"Peter was just a normal healthy child. A really nice boy. I don't know what has happened but clearly something has gone seriously wrong."

Brother Michael Sutcliffe:

"I could not believe it. My brother was not a man who was violent. I was the violent one in the family and he was the quiet one."

When he left school at the age of sixteen, Peter Sutcliffe's life continued on an uneventful course. He was initially employed as an apprentice by a local engineering firm, then at Fibre Products, then at a local garage where he could utilize an earlier interest in repairing cars and motorbikes. In 1964 his work took a more unusual turn. He became a gravedigger at Bingley Cemetery. Work for which he showed an unusual relish as fellow gravedigger Laurie Ashton recalled:

"Sutcliffe volunteered to work overtime at the local mortuary. He really used to like his job—especially in the mortuary at nights. On one occasion when we were out having a drink, he told us he had the mortuary keys and that 'there are two right ones in there. Do you want to go and have a look?'" His colleagues declined the offer.

Laurie Ashton recalled another far more macabre moment.

"On one occasion Peter was re-opening a grave so that a second coffin could be buried in a family plot. His spade struck the rotten wood of the coffin. The next moment he was chasing a couple of schoolgirls along a nearby path with the skull held out in front of him. He came back laughing and joking."

Fellow gravedigger Eric Robinson recalled another incident that took place shortly after a funeral service. The coffin had been lowered into the grave during the ceremony but before the earth was shoveled over it, "Peter jumped into the grave and took the lid off the coffin."

He gave his colleague the impression that he was looking for rings as still standing in the grave he remarked, "Oh, there's nowt there."

Eric Robinson continued, "Later we were in the Royal Standard pub in Bradford and Peter put his hand into his pocket and pulled out five or six rings. He told us that he had offered one of them to his sister Maureen for her wedding and that when he had told her they came from bodies at the cemetery she had jumped back in horror. Peter thought it was a big laugh."

During this period he was courting Carol Jones, a Keighley girl. She recalls a shy young man with a soft voice who throughout their four-year courtship never attempted to advance sexually past passionate kissing.

"He was very well mannered. Motorbikes, cars and me were the main topics of conversation. Now that I am older I can see that he was shy of going further than kissing and cuddling."

Shy with the living. Desecrator of the dead.

In 1965, normality returned to the cemetery when Sutcliffe was sacked because of bad timekeeping. His inability to arrive at work on time is a recurring theme. After two years' employment with a local water board, he was fired again for the same reason. He is also remembered at T. Lund & Son Ltd. in Bingley for the same reason. In 1968 he joined an engineering company, Anderton International, and elected to work on the night shift.

It was at this time that he met the woman who was destined to become his wife, Sonia Szurma. The eighteen-year-old student teacher had her first date with Sutcliffe in the same pub where a few years before he had produced gold rings from his pocket and boasted of removing them from the dead, The Royal Standard, Bradford. The attractive Sonia clearly captivated Sutcliffe. Intelligent, articulate, the young woman of Czechoslovakian parents was different from the run of the mill town girls in his eyes.

In 1974, they married. Not at the local Catholic church—Sutcliffe had long abandoned his faith—but at Clayton Baptist Chapel. At the time Sutcliffe was unemployed, having recently been made redundant. The wedding reception at a nearby public house was paid for by Sonia as was their honeymoon in Paris.

Subsequently they lived with Sonia's parents in Clayton, a quiet suburb of Bradford.

Within one year Sutcliffe had obtained a Heavy Goods License and work as a long distance truck driver. One month after obtaining that license in June 1975 he attempted to murder Anna Rogulskyj.

While Peter Sutcliffe and his wife saved every penny, with Sonia rigidly controlling the purse strings as she dreamed of the day when they would have their own home, her husband was creating a nightmare existence for all women living in the north of England.

The reserved arts teacher and her hardworking truck driver wanted children as badly as they wanted a home of their own. Within that first year of marriage and prior to the murderous attacks Sonia suffered two miscarriages.

In 1977 the couple achieved at least half of their ambition when they moved into their own home, 6 Garden Lane, Heaton, Bradford, a detached, pebble-dashed house next to a playing field called Salem. The purchase price was £16,500. It was quite a leap for the boy from the mill town of Bingley.

They maintained the house well. The gardens were kept neat, the woodwork painted. During that first year, while they tended their home with care, Sutcliffe went out and murdered three women and attempted to murder a further two.

This man who would wax indignant about other men who were unfaithful to their wives, who would hold forth to other members of his family about morality, not only went out and murdered women, he also frequently paid prostitutes for sex. Psychologists might see this behavior as an indication of multiple personality. I see it as simple hypocrisy.

While Peter Sutcliffe played the dutiful husband and impressed his in-laws, he was also smashing, gouging, knifing and killing. The hands that passed the tea cakes or stroked his wife's hair were the same hands that deprived so many children of their mothers, that stole daughters from parents, for ever. His wife shed tears when her husband was sent for trial.

Diminished responsibility?

This man boasted to his friend Ron Barker of the women he had. Told his mate of two he had picked up and made love to, one in the car, the other on the hood. He bragged about "never having to pay for it." Yet frequently he did just that.

He would wander into the Mecca ballroom at Bradford, the

same ballroom where Barbara Leach danced a few days before her death.

Barker recalls, "He would walk around in the ballroom sort of inspecting the merchandise. He liked the girls with tight dresses and long legs. Thought he was God's gift to women."

What a gift.

Ron Barker's recollections also have a more ominous aspect.

"One night when we were out drinking, Peter drove through Chapeltown. I had had quite a lot to drink and when he pulled up he told me to stay in the car and have a sleep. He was gone quite a long time, and when he came back he told me he had followed a girl to her flat. He never said a name but I know shortly afterwards the Ripper struck in Chapeltown."

Ron Barker also recalls a similar experience with Sutcliffe in Manchester and speaking of these events observed, "I suppose I should have thought about it at the time but you never imagine your friend is the Ripper. I thought he was just looking for girls.

"Now looking back I can see he was using me as a decoy while he went out and chose his next victim."

Another friend, Trevor Birdsall, has similar recollections of his drinking friend Sutcliffe. Indeed, Birdsall became convinced that Sutcliffe was the mass murderer. In 1980 he walked into Bradford Central Police Station and told listening officers, "Peter Sutcliffe is the Yorkshire Ripper." Some time later he left the police station in disgust. Presumably they brushed aside his accusations on the grounds that Sutcliffe did not have a Geordie accent.

The man who was considered an excellent employee by T. & W. Clark haulage where he has worked since 1975, excellent, that is, apart from bad timekeeping—the man whose photograph was taken sitting in his truck and hung in the reception area and utilized in the company's brochures, this man will shortly have his photograph flashed around the globe. This man with the dark good looks of a Greek has stared at the dead remains of at least thirteen women whom he has murdered. This man evaded the biggest manhunt in the history of Britain for over five and a half years. And while he evaded the police he would from time to time discuss the activities that he was responsible for.

To his friend John Johnstone he always referred to the killer not as "The Yorkshire Ripper," but as the "headbanger." Johnstone recalls, "Once in a pub he became quite emotional over the murder of Jayne MacDonald. He said she was an innocent victim and whoever did it virtually killed two people because her father never got over the death and died of a broken heart. He said, 'It's terrible, whoever is doing all these murders has a lot to answer for.'

"After the Barbara Leach murder we were talking about whether the police were any nearer catching the Ripper and Peter said, 'They are no nearer catching him now than they were at the beginning.'

"Following the murder of Jacqueline Hill last November someone said that the Ripper had bloody struck again. Sutcliffe responded, 'It's about time that sod was caught.'"

As well as being a mass murderer, having dalliances with prostitutes, being the ideal husband and a man who expressed apprehension for the safety of his sisters because of the killer, Sutcliffe had yet another role, that of lover. Since 1979 he has had a love affair with a woman living in Motherwell, Scotland. He told the woman his name was Peter Logan, that his wife had been killed in a car crash ten years previously. He played with the five children of the divorced woman and told her how badly he had wanted children of his own. Whenever his work took him to the far north, he would invariably appear at this woman's home. They corresponded frequently. Her letters, addressed to Peter Logan, went to his father's address. He told his father that the letters were for a friend serving a prison sentence. That the friend's wife did not know her husband was in prison. When his girlfriend in Scotland asked him for a memento while he was away, he gave her a photograph of himself and Sonia and told her that Sonia was a family friend. This was no secret other "personality." Sutcliffe would boast to his workmates at Clark's of his girlfriend in Scotland.

Shortly before his arrest Sutcliffe confided in his brother Michael that he and Sonia intended to adopt two children, probably Vietnamese boat children. Thank God he was arrested before that.

January 4, 1981. In the middle of the day I receive a telephone call. *He* had been arrested in Sheffield two days earlier. It is *him* my caller assures me. "He's coughed [confessed]. There will be a press conference later today."

January 5. The press conference held by the police yesterday was by any standards extraordinary. A grinning Chief Constable Gregory sat flanked by the equally delighted George Oldfield and James Hobson. The media were told that a man had been arrested in Sheffield on Friday in connection with a matter which was identified as theft of number plates from motor cars. Gregory continued: "This man is now detained in West Yorkshire, and he is being questioned in relation to the Yorkshire Ripper murders. He will appear in court before Dewsbury magistrates later today."

If at that point the Chief Constable had closed his mouth and kept it closed there could be no complaint. Regrettably he opened it again.

"We are all absolutely delighted, totally delighted with the developments at this stage.

"The officers who detained the man in Sheffield were outstanding police officers, who have my heartfelt thanks."

One reporter asked if the Ripper hunt was being scaled down. Gregory replied: "You are right."

In a few stunning minutes Chief Constable Ronald Gregory had eliminated two of the cardinal points of the British judicial system. That a person is innocent until proven guilty. That guilt must be established beyond reasonable doubt.

Today, before Sutcliffe has been officially named and before he has appeared in court, *Yorkshire Post* readers are advised of his name and address and for good measure given a photograph of his home taken the previous night.

The *Sun* quotes Gregory as saying, "The hunt for the Ripper is being scaled down." It also quotes an elated police officer at Sheffield.

"These lads (the arresting officers) are real heroes. This is a great day for us. They did a wonderful job. We know the girl the man was with when he was arrested. She's very lucky indeed. She could easily have been his next victim."

The vast majority of this country's newspapers are carrying similar stories with additional information about what they called "the five-year reign of terror."

This afternoon the *London New Standard* publishes a photograph of Sutcliffe. Press and television are by now committing gross criminal contempt.

Sutcliffe is rushed into Dewsbury Court handcuffed to a detective and carrying a blanket over his head. Court proceedings are delayed because of the noise emitting from over two thousand sightseers who apart from booing and screaming are calling out "Hang the bastard" and other similar sentiments.

January 6. A letter is sent to all editors of newspapers, television and radio programs, from the Solicitor General acting on behalf of the Attorney General. It informs editors "of his concern about the publicity which has been given to the 'Yorkshire Ripper' case since the arrest of Mr. Sutcliffe."

February 6. One wonders what Attorney General Sir Michael Havers makes of the checkbook journalism now flourishing in the north of England. For a month now reporters have been hurtling over the Pennines and up the M1 motorway like salmon returning to spawn. The Sutcliffe family have been predictable targets. Members of the family have been moved by the *Daily Mail* to the Stirk House Hotel, near Gisburn. John Sutcliffe, the father, has been signed by the *Mail*, price £5,000. The same paper is also in hot pursuit of Sonia. Despite the vast amounts being dangled before her, to her great credit she has to date refused to be bought up. The *Sunday People* has paid £500 down, plus £65 per week "expenses" to Sutcliffe's close friend Trevor Birdsall who will almost certainly be a witness at the trial.

Olivia Reivers, in my view one of the luckiest women in England, has been signed by the *Daily Star* for £4,000 so that after the trial readers can learn exactly what Sutcliffe did during his last thirty minutes of freedom. Clearly Olivia Reivers is also a potential witness. Sutcliffe's friend Ronald Barker has been paid £700 for a photograph of Peter and Sonia by the *Sun;* Barker is also clearly a potential witness.

Even more disturbing is the clearly criminal activity of certain reporters. Posing as police detectives, reporters have called on Anna Rogulskyj and obtained a "statement." Other reporters have shown a photograph of potential witness Birdsall to potential witness Olive Smelt. Yorkshire police are having to contact some of the above-named newspapers who have hidden their purchases in order to obtain official statements.

February 20. Peter Sutcliffe was today sent for trial. Charged with murdering thirteen women and attempting to murder a

further seven. Their names appear on earlier pages of my book. I
am correct on all twenty counts. It gives little cause for satisfaction
when one knows that many of those lives lost should have been
saved.

March 27. A telephone call advises me that Sutcliffe and his
lawyers are plea bargaining and that this man is prepared to plead
guilty on all counts but only guilty to manslaughter on the murder
charges on the grounds of "diminished responsibility." We have a
Prime Minister who is constantly asserting with regard to men in
the H block of The Maze that "we will not do deals with
criminals." Is it possible, that with regard to Sutcliffe another
member of her Cabinet takes a different position?

April 3. Another telephone call. A deal has indeed been done. It
will be asserted on Sutcliffe's behalf that he is suffering from
paranoiac schizophrenia. This assertion has been accepted by the
Attorney General. Only the trial judge stands between Sutcliffe
and a hospital door that some time in the future may be opened to
let him walk among us once again. If the judge accepts this
argument, there will be no jury and the hearing will last less than
two days. Clearly such a limited hearing will prevent the many
appalling errors of certain investigating police officers from becoming public knowledge.

April 28. When collecting my Press ticket from the Old Bailey, I
am calmly advised by a number of court officials that the trial will
finish this week in less than three days. My own personal hopes
that justice will be done now rest entirely on one man, Mr. Justice
Boreham.

April 29. The circus has come to town. The queue for the small
public gallery of Number One Court began forming yesterday
evening. By 9:30 A.M. the number waiting for the thirty seats had
risen to several hundred. At 9:34 A.M. the one man who has no
need for such measures sweeps past the queue in an armored
police van, escorted by two police cars with sirens blaring and
lights flashing. Peter Sutcliffe has arrived at the Old Bailey. As I
am about to enter Number One Court, an American journalist
offers me £1,000 for my Press ticket.

At the back of the court are the parents and brother of Barbara
Leach. Anna Rogulskyj. Olive Smelt. The mother of Jacqueline
Hill. The mother of Jayne MacDonald. I had over the past two

years spent many hours with all of these people, with the
exception of Mrs. Hill. When Jacqueline had been murdered in
November 1980 I could not face even attempting to intrude on
such recent grief.

In the well of the court the array of barristers and QCs begin to
take their places. For the Crown, Sir Michael Havers, QC, and
Harry Ognall, QC. For the Defense James Chadwin, QC, and
Sidney Levine. Directly opposite these men sit James Hobson,
Jack Ridgeway. In the court foyer I saw the ever-immaculate
figure of Chief Constable Ronald Gregory. At the table where his
colleagues sit are an assortment of exhibits. Plebeian objects that
had been put to an obscene use: seven ball peen hammers, a claw
hammer, a hacksaw, three carving knives, eight screwdrivers, a
long thin-bladed kitchen knife, a cobbler's knife, a length of rope.

Shortly before 10:30 A.M. Sonia Sutcliffe and her mother come
and sit directly in front of me. Reporters begin to leave their seats
and come to stare at Sonia, their faces inches from hers.

Sonia, her shoulders slumped in abject defeat, sits quietly. She
looks dreadful, like a woman who has slept the night in a hay field.
Like hundreds of other people she has been caught up in a
nightmare of one man's making. Shortly before 11:00 A.M. that
man, the sole reason drawing all of us to this courtroom, walks up
the steps from his cell below the court.

Since early 1979 this man had ever increasingly occupied my
thoughts. Day after day, night after night, I had attempted to
catch the physical and mental reality of him. For a brief moment
our eyes meet as he enters the dock. The face of a Greek waiter.
As Olive Smelt had said to me, "He wouldn't frighten anybody."
But he had. He'd frightened us all. He had reduced a large part of
this country to a siege mentality. It takes over seven minutes to
read out the twenty charges he faces. He stumbles over his
responses as he pleads guilty to seven attempted murders and not
guilty to thirteen murders but guilty to manslaughter on the
grounds of diminished responsibility. Attorney General Sir
Michael Havers tells the Judge that the Crown accepts Sutcliffe's
pleas.

The Attorney General advises the Judge that he has before him
the reports of four psychiatrists, that each man has interviewed
Sutcliffe on a number of occasions and that "I have met with them

to discuss their reports with the greatest care and anxiety and at great length. The general consensus of the doctors is that this is a case of diminished responsibility, the illness being paranoiac schizophrenia."

For a moment it hangs in the balance. If Mr. Justice Boreham accepts the argument presented to him by the Attorney General then this so-called "Trial of the Century" will not run for two days, there will be no jury and whatever evidence is adduced will be a masterpiece of brevity. But late comes the hero.

Mr. Justice Boreham: "I have very grave anxieties about Sutcliffe and his pleas. I would like you to explain in far greater detail than usual any decision that you are going to make about the acceptance of these pleas."

There follows a truly extraordinary and remarkable situation. For the entire morning the Attorney General of this country, the leader of the Crown Prosecution in the case of *Regina v Sutcliffe*, assumes the mantle of defense counsel and argues on *behalf* of Sutcliffe.

When a defendant pleads state of mind as a defense as Sutcliffe has done, the onus, the burden of proof, is always upon that defendant and his counsel. Now on the morning of the 29th of April, 1981, that tenet of law has been reversed. While Sutcliffe's leading counsel, James Chadwin, QC, says hardly a word, his adversary the Attorney General struggles for two hours to convince the Judge that he should accept pleas of manslaughter because of diminished responsibility. Of Sonia, "She has a history of mental illness which needed hospital treatment in 1972."

He tells the court that the death of Sutcliffe's mother "greatly distressed him."

A few moments later comes the kernel of Sutcliffe's defense.

"He is saying that he is under the direction of God and that he has a mission. In fact he desires to be God."

His mission it transpires is "to kill all prostitutes." It further transpires that Sutcliffe is advised by God's voice exactly who is a prostitute and exactly whom he should kill.

In view of the fact that out of at least twenty women attacked, ten are not and never have been prostitutes, it would appear that God is not infallible.

Sutcliffe, the Attorney General advises the court, first heard the voice of God when he was working as a gravedigger at Bingley.

I have previously contended that this mass murderer can be described in one word, hence the title of this book. He is evil. Just how evil is being demonstrated in this courtroom at this very minute. Sutcliffe is, in effect, attempting to rid himself of the guilt or burden of his crimes, is attempting to climb out of the dock and leave God on trial.

This dark-headed man, mid-thirties, slim, apparently lacking completely in muscle tone, looking taller than his five feet ten inches because of his built-up shoes—this man, with his girlishly high voice, claims to be guided by the voice of God.

The tale that Sir Michael is quietly unfolding, so quietly that most of those in the courtroom cannot hear him, grows more bizarre by the moment. In 1968, while courting Sonia, Sutcliffe became convinced that she was having an affair with another man. She denied this but it continued to prey on his mind. In 1969 to "set the balance right" he decided to pick up a prostitute in Manningham. He gave her ten pounds for a five-pound session, became so disgusted with the girl on the way back to her flat that when she told him she had no change he attempted to cancel the agreement. The girl insisted that they go to a local garage to get change. In the event Sutcliffe lost his ten pounds and never had any "business."

Some weeks later he saw the same prostitute in a public house. He attempted doggedly to collect at least five pounds change and was laughed out of the pub. The event filled him with hatred for prostitutes.

In September 1969 while out driving with close friend Trevor Birdsall, Sutcliffe stopped his car in the Manningham area. Clutching a sock that contained a stone he approached a woman and smashed her on the head with the weapon. Returning to the car the two men drove away. *Police interviewed both Sutcliffe and Birdsall at the time but no charges were pressed by the injured woman. Nevertheless, as both men were interviewed over a potentially serious charge, records of those interviews should have been kept on file.*

Within weeks, on the 29th of September, 1969, Sutcliffe again went out with murder in mind. This time he took a hammer for company. He pursued a prostitute but she ran away. He was found on waste ground in the Manningham area, clutching a hammer. In October 1969 he was fined

£25 at Bradford Magistrates Court for "going equipped for theft" with a hammer.

I listen to this stunned. Surely to God when Ridgeway and his men came over the hills from Manchester in October 1977 they applied basic police procedure? Surely when in pursuit of the owner of that five-pound note, they looked up the previous criminal form of all whom they questioned. A man with a hammer in a red light area in 1969. Six years later women are lying dead all over the north of England, smashed to the ground by a hammer.

Who needs God's protection?

His conversations with the psychiatrists were sprinkled with references to his mission. "I know it's wrong to kill but prostitutes are still out there on the streets, even more now. The mission is not finished."

The Judge says very little during all of this until shortly before one o'clock. "The matter that troubles me is not the medical opinions because there is a consensus. It seems to me that all of these opinions—and I say this without criticism—all these opinions are based simply on what this defendant has told the doctors, nothing more."

Then devastatingly.

"Moreover what he has told the doctors conflicts substantially with what he told the police on the morning of arrest. I use the word 'conflict' advisedly. In statements to the police he expressed a desire to kill all women. If that is right—and here I really need your help—is that not a matter which ought to be tested? Where lies the evidence which gives these doctors the factual basis for these pleas? It is a matter for the defendant to establish. It is a matter for a jury."

I have never before felt the almost overpowering urge to get up in a courtroom and cheer a judge.

He then makes perhaps his most astonishing remark of the morning.

"We have in a sense conducted a trial which has satisfied us."

Mr. Justice Boreham says, "It seems to me it would be more appropriate if this case were dealt with by a jury."

The look of consternation spreads over a sea of faces like the wind. I see it on the Attorney General's face, on Defense

Counsel's, on the faces of Hobson and Ridgeway and, outside the court, on the face of Chief Constable Ronald Gregory. Clearly not one of them has bargained for Mr. Justice Boreham.

After some discussion the judge finally agrees to the defense request for an adjournment until Tuesday the 5th of May.

May 5. For a man allegedly suffering from a very serious mental illness, Sutcliffe gives a remarkable display of mental alertness. As the jury is being sworn in he moves rapidly to the bar of the dock twice to challenge prospective jurors through his counsel.

The Attorney General opens on behalf of the Crown and rapidly gets to the very heart of the issue that the jury must decide.

"You have to consider whether this man sought to pull the wool over the doctors' eyes. You have to decide whether, as a clever, callous murderer, he deliberately set out to create a cock and bull story to avoid conviction for murder."

Sutcliffe sits impassively in the dock staring directly ahead. He does not fidget, does not stir, does not scratch himself. Hour after hour he sits there, immobile. Whatever control he has had or not had over his mind during the past five and a half years, his control right now of his body is extraordinary.

Sir Michael quotes at length from the doctors' reports. We hear much of Sutcliffe's "mission," his "messages from God that instructed him to go out and kill prostitutes." These are the utterances that have convinced four of the top psychiatrists in this country that Sutcliffe is suffering from paranoiac schizophrenia. For over half a decade this man fooled the best police brains; has he now, this truck driver from Bradford, fooled four psychiatrists?

The Attorney General talks of the discrepancies between what Sutcliffe had told the police and what he subsequently said many weeks later to the doctors. Some of these discrepancies he states are "very significant."

As he turns to details of the twenty attacks, the Attorney General demonstrates that the sliding scale of value put on human life that was such a feature of the entire murder inquiry is not confined to the north of England.

"Some were prostitutes, some were women of easy virtue, but the last six attacks from 1979 to 1980 involved victims whose reputations were unblemished."

On the previous Wednesday both Mr. Justice Boreham and Sir Michael Havers had both shown concern for the number of "perfectly respectable victims."

Is there then a license to kill those whom society decrees are blemished or disreputable? If six victims are "innocent" are then fourteen "guilty"?

The three letters and the tape that by the middle of 1980 I was convinced were hoaxes are now in May 1981, for the first time, publicly and officially accepted as just that.

"The harsh truth is that the author of the letters and tape has nothing to do with this case. . . . Most regrettably it became widely accepted by a number of senior police officers that this man [the hoaxer] was in fact the Ripper and that he spoke with a Wearside accent. One of the things which affected the investigating officers was that if people interviewed did not speak with a Sunderland accent or if their writing did not compare with that on the letters, they tended to be eliminated."

Reading extracts from Sutcliffe's confession to the police, Sir Michael's words pull me back to early 1980. To places visited, to people interviewed.

Anna Rogulskyj: "I asked her if she fancied it. She said 'not on your life' and went to try and get into a house. When she came back, I tapped her up again and she elbowed me. I followed her and hit her with the hammer. I intended to kill her but I was disturbed."

Olive Smelt: "I saw her in the Royal Oak. She annoyed me, probably in some minor way. I took her to be a prostitute . . . I hit her on the head and scratched her buttocks with a piece of hacksaw blade or maybe a knife. My intention was to kill her but I was disturbed by a car coming down the road."

Wilma McCann: "She said, 'Come on get it over with,' I said, 'Don't worry I will,' and I hit her with the hammer. She made a lot of noise and kept on making noise so I hit her again. I took a knife out of my pocket and stabbed her about four times." In fact it was fifteen times.

Explaining to the police why he had stabbed a number of women in the heart Sutcliffe observed: "You can kill them quicker that way."

Emily Jackson: "I pushed a piece of wood against her vagina to show how disgusting she was."

He also stabbed Emily Jackson over fifty times with a screwdriver.

Marcella Claxton: "She went behind some trees to urinate and suggested that we 'start the ball rolling on the grass.' I hit her once on the head with the hammer, but just couldn't bring myself to hit her again. For some reason or another, I just let her walk away and I went back to the car."

He actually hit Marcella on the head nine times. He also returned to where he had left the seriously injured woman but she had fortunately managed to get away.

Irene Richardson: "I used the hammer and a Stanley knife on her. As she was crouching down urinating on the grass I hit her on the head at least two or three times. I lifted up her clothes and slashed her abdomen and throat."

Tina Atkinson: "I heard her using foul language. It was obvious why I picked her up. No decent woman would have been using language like that at the top of her voice. When I had killed her I picked her up under the arms and hoisted her up onto the bed."

Sutcliffe then utilized the claw end of this particular murder weapon to tear at her lifeless body.

The list of horrific details seemed endless. He'd wiped his knife clean on the back of Jayne MacDonald. After the hammer blows to the head, after being dragged across open ground at which point a jagged bottle top entered her chest, and after several stab wounds, Jayne was still alive. At some point in the remainder of the twenty stab wounds the sixteen-year-old girl died.

When he had returned to the dead body of Jean Jordan, six days after he had murdered her, he attempted to saw off her head to make this particular murder "more mysterious."

He smashed Yvonne Pearson's head in with a walling hammer. Smashed it into seventeen fragments. At one point during this attack he had been interrupted by passers-by. He had stuffed filling from the nearby settee into her mouth, and pinched her nose, yet still she continued to moan. Alone again, he continued to smash at her head.

Helen Rytka: "She undid my trousers and seemed prepared to

start sexual intercourse right away in the front of the car. It was very awkward for me to find a way to get her out of the car. For about five minutes I was trying to decide which method to use to kill her. She was beginning to arouse me sexually. I got out of the car with the excuse that I needed to urinate and managed to persuade her to get out of the car so that we could have sex in the back. As she was getting in I realized that this was my chance but the hammer caught on the edge of the car door frame and only gave her a light tap. She said, 'There is no need for that, you don't even have to pay.' I expected her to immediately shout for help. She was obviously scared and said, 'What was that?' I said, 'Just a small sample of one of these,' and hit her on the head hard. She just crumbled making a loud moaning noise. I realized that what I had done was in full view of two taxi drivers who had appeared and were talking nearby. I dragged her by the hair to the end of the woodyard. She stopped moaning but was not dead. Her eyes were open and she held up her hands to ward off blows. I jumped on top of her and covered her mouth with my hand. It seemed like an eternity and she was still struggling."

The two taxi drivers, Helen Rytka's only lifeline, continued to chat obliviously. Sutcliffe lay on the ground, panting, waiting for them to leave before he resumed his attack on Helen Rytka.

"I told her that if she kept quiet, she would be all right.

"As she had got me aroused a moment previous, I had no alternative but to go ahead with the act of sex as the only means of keeping her quiet. It didn't take long. She kept staring at me. *She didn't put much into it.*"

The taxis eventually left the woodyard. Sutcliffe, who had dropped his hammer after the initial attack, scrabbled in the dirt for it as Helen staggered to her feet and ran towards the car.

"This was when I hit her heavy blows to the back of the head. I dragged her to the front of the car and threw her belongings over the wall."

But the virtually naked body of Helen Rytka still clung to life.

"She was obviously still alive. I took a knife from the car and stabbed her several times through the heart and lungs. I think it was a kitchen knife which I believe the police later retrieved from my home."

They did, they found it with the other cutlery in a kitchen drawer. In such a manner died eighteen-year-old Helen Rytka.

Arriving at the murder of Josephine Whitaker, Sir Michael observes, "Now we come to another sad one."

No tears for Helen Rytka, Sir Michael?

Earlier in this book one of the many questions raised is "Did Josephine meet and walk through Saville Park with her killer?" The Attorney General now gives the answer.

"She left her grandparents at about 11:40 P.M. and a man walking his dog about fifteen minutes later saw a man and a young woman walking side by side towards Saville Park. This was Josephine Whitaker and Sutcliffe. Shortly afterwards another man was walking by the park and he heard an unusual noise, 'the type of noise that makes your hair stand on end.'"

Sir Michael holds up the most fearsome weapon I have ever seen in a courtroom. It began life as a giant Phillips screwdriver. It must be nearly two feet long. The end has been converted into a sharp point. As it passed round to members of the jury, the Crown Prosecutor continues.

"Sutcliffe told the police, 'I used it on Josephine Whitaker and Barbara Leach.' It was badly worn and had been converted into a bradall."

He used the hammer too.

"Josephine's skull was fractured from ear to ear. She had been stabbed twenty-one times in the trunk, six times in the right leg. Her vagina had been stabbed three times in the awful way of using the same entry each time."

I am fully aware of what is coming next. So is David Leach, sitting behind me.

"Barbara had a large laceration on the back of her head and seven stab wounds in her trunk, three of them round her umbilicus. The knife was reintroduced again and again into the chest wound. She had numerous bruises and abrasions and had been struck on the head with a hammer and stabbed with a three-sided instrument. When interviewed about Barbara's death, Sutcliffe started talking about his earlier victim Whitaker, saying: 'It was forty-six weeks after the last one. I was never urged to do it again until then. I killed Barbara Leach. I took her to the back of the house before I stabbed her.'"

I feel like being sick. More than anything, what keeps me seated in this courtroom is the knowledge that a man sitting behind me is displaying great courage.

Alan Royle, the de facto husband of the late Jean Jordan, has already left the court with his hand to his mouth. Others have visibly winced as if actually bearing the blows that the man in the dock rained on people they knew, loved and cared for. Throughout, Sutcliffe sits impassively. I swear to God he actually looks bored. Sir Michael holds up a length of cord. It had been found on Sutcliffe at the time of his arrest. He used it to strangle Margo Walls. When asked why he had changed his method of killing, Sutcliffe has said, "Because the Press and the media had attached a stigma to me. I had been known for some time as the Yorkshire Ripper. I didn't like it. It wasn't me. It didn't ring true. I had been on my way to Leeds to kill a prostitute when I saw Margo Walls. It was just unfortunate for her that she happened to be walking by. I don't like the method of strangulation. It takes them even longer to die."

Of Dr. Banbara: "She was walking slowly like a prostitute and I hit her on the head with a hammer. I didn't have any tools with me to finish her off so I used the rope. I dragged her down the road and her shoes were making a scraping noise. I apologized to her and took her shoes off and put them over a wall with her handbag."

Of Teresa Sykes: "I attacked her because she was the first person I saw. I think something clicked because she had on a straight skirt with a slit in it."

The court rises for the day. Peter Sutcliffe, like a man in a hurry for his dinner, moves quickly out of the dock to his holding cell below.

May 6. The tale of human carnage continues. Sir Michael reads yet again from Sutcliffe's confession. A confession that took nearly sixteen hours as police officers who had wives and daughters took it down.

"The last one I did was Jacqueline Hill at Headingley. I sat in the car eating some Kentucky Fried Chicken, then I saw Miss Hill. I decided she was a likely victim. I drove just past her and parked up and waited for her to pass. I got out of the car and followed about three yards behind her. As she drew level with an opening I took the hammer out of my pocket and struck her on the head. By this time I was in a world of my own, out of touch with reality. I dragged her on to some waste ground. A car appeared and I threw myself to the ground, but the car passed by. I can't imagine why I was not seen. She was moving about, so I hit her again. Then I dragged her further into the waste ground as a girl was passing by. I pulled most of her clothes off. I had a screwdriver with a yellow handle and I stabbed her in the lungs. Her eyes were open and she seemed to be looking at me with an accusing stare. This shook me up a bit so I stabbed her in the eye."

As Sir Michael tells the jury that the medical evidence suggests that Miss Hill may not have died straight away, the fiancé of Jacqueline Hill leaves the court, grim faced. Throughout the morning, the Attorney General continues to read extracts from the Bradford truck driver's confession, and it comes almost as light relief when, after the lunch adjournment, he turns to a report from psychiatrist Dr. Hugo Milne.

We hear that a few years before her death Sutcliffe's mother embarked on an affair with a policeman. His father responded with an affair of his own and the marriage was destroyed. Of greater significance perhaps is the fact that Sonia spent three weeks in a Bradford psychiatric hospital in 1972. The diagnosis was schizophrenia. Is it perhaps catching like measles? Did it give Sutcliffe, who at that time was courting Sonia, an example of the symptoms?

Milne's report is riddled with the most extraordinary rationalization, hence the fact that Sutcliffe has apparently returned to his childhood Catholic faith while in prison is seen by the doctor as "itself diagnostic with his mental illness." It gets even more absurd: "There is no suggestion that he is a sadistic sexual deviant. I am convinced that the killings were not sexual in any way and the stabbings which were a feature of the assaults had no sexual component." A piece of wood pushed up into Emily Jackson's vagina? A screwdriver three times inserted into Josephine Whitaker's vagina?

Clearly God has been joined in the dock by four psychiatrists.

Their professional reputations are obviously at stake. In my view, there are, broadly speaking, three concepts of madness: medical, legal, lay public. I study the jury who at the end of the trial will tell us all which opinion they collectively embrace, arrived at on the evidence.

A writer from *Stern* magazine sitting next to me murmurs in my ear, "When we talk to God it's called praying. When God talks to us it's called schizophrenia."

The more I hear, the more convinced I become that Sutcliffe has indeed fooled these doctors.

May 7. Yorkshire accents from the witness box. Trevor Birdsall is giving evidence. He looks like a very sick rat. Already the Judge has lectured him about the newspaper deals that he and his girl friend have made with the *Sunday People*. Now he sits in the box, constantly sipping water and glancing across the court at Sutcliffe. If Sutcliffe returns the look it is without turning his head. I do not understand why Birdsall is not himself under arrest.

This man Birdsall was in the car when Sutcliffe left him for a few moments and smashed a woman over the head with a stone in Bradford in 1969. He was out with Sutcliffe, in Halifax, the night Sutcliffe attempted to murder Olive Smelt.

"On the way home we passed through the Boothtown area of Halifax, which is not a red-light area. Peter stopped the car and got out and said he was going to speak to somebody. I didn't take any notice if he had anything with him but he seemed to put his hand down the side of the seat. There was a couple of people walking past, and I remember seeing a woman. She was walking quickly and Peter went round the back of the car and disappeared. He didn't seem to go in the same direction as the woman but was away ten to twenty minutes. When he came back he said he had been talking to a woman, but he was quiet, unusually quiet. The next evening I read in the *Telegraph & Argus* a report about a brutal attack on a woman in Boothtown. It crossed my mind that Peter might be connected with it."

Did it indeed?

It also crossed Birdsall's mind that Sutcliffe might be the mass murderer in 1977 when his friend was interviewed about the five-pound note. He justified not contacting the police until November 1980 by stating the tape recording with the Geordie voice "destroyed the link." But the tape recording was not received by the police and made public until June 1979. At that time Birdsall's companion in their tours of red-light areas had murdered at least ten women and had attempted to murder at least a further five women.

Birdsall finally sent an anonymous letter to the police on the 26th of November 1980, nine days after the murder of Jacqueline Hill. Then, "I worried more about it and very shortly after that I went to see the police myself."

The full public inquiry that will hopefully follow the end of this trial should attempt to establish why the Bradford police did not act upon Birdsall's allegations.

In the courtroom a clear picture was emerging that Sutcliffe had indeed held to the maxim of measure twice and cut once. He had reconnoitered areas, sometimes with friends, before returning to murder. Ronald and David Barker, next door neighbors to Sonia's parents, and therefore neighbors of Sutcliffe during the time he lived with his in-laws, had accompanied him on a variety of trips.

On the 28th of May 1977 the two Barkers and Sutcliffe had gone drinking in York. Sutcliffe vanished during the course of the evening and upon his return said he had followed a young woman out of the pub. Later on the return journey to Bradford, Sutcliffe made a detour to Chapeltown, Leeds. Asked why, he remarked, "This is Ripper country." He left them in the car and went for a walk for about fifteen to twenty minutes. On the night of the 25th of June he was again out with the two brothers in Bradford. He dropped them home at 1:30 A.M. and within thirty minutes he had murdered Jayne MacDonald in Chapeltown.

The reason why the majority of the attacks and murders occurred on weekends has also emerged. Sonia had a part-time job on weekends, sometimes baby sitting, sometimes working on Saturday nights as an auxiliary nurse.

The Mecca ballroom at Bradford, a dance hall used by Maureen Long and Barbara Leach, was also, it transpires, patronized by Sutcliffe and his friends. The three men had been together on the evening of the attempted murder of Maureen Long.

Olivia Reivers, appearing by courtesy of the *Daily Star*, tells the court about the last twenty minutes of freedom that Sutcliffe will ever know. Her description of Sutcliffe's sexual fumblings, of his

fifteen-minute inability to get an erection, reduce one of life's
most beautiful acts to sordidness. The only reason she is alive to
give her testimony is because she declined Sutcliffe's suggestion
to get into the back of the car.

The final witness for today, Detective Inspector John Boyle,
recounts a moment that he will remember for the rest of his life. It
occurred on January the 4th of this year. Sutcliffe had been in
custody for nearly forty-eight hours. He had already been subjected to intensive questioning about the many times his car had
been noted in red-light areas. Testimony established that when on
at least one occasion Sutcliffe had lied about being in Manchester,
the police had double-checked and had established that the car
had indeed been logged in that city's red-light district. Astonishingly there does not appear to have been a follow-up
interview with Sutcliffe.

Sutcliffe had also given the police samples of saliva and blood
and handwriting. *This was the first time he had ever been asked to give
blood and saliva samples with regard to the murder, yet it is clear that he
has been interviewed at least nine times.*

At about two o'clock on that Sunday afternoon, Boyle asked
Sutcliffe why he had wandered away from the arresting officers at
Sheffield. The truck driver, who had been up to that moment
hoping to be bailed, whereupon he planned to catch a taxi to
Sheffield and collect the hammer and knife he had dumped, knew
now he had reached the end of the road.

"I think you've been leading up to it."

"Leading up to what?"

"The Yorkshire Ripper."

"What about him?"

"Well, it's me."

May 8. Since Sutcliffe's arrest there is one question that I have
been asked more than any other. "What about Sonia—surely she
must have known?" I have explored this aspect earlier in the book.
Now Sutcliffe's comments on this aspect as reported by a police
witness give further credence to my view that Sonia had no
knowledge. "Sonia automatically gave me an alibi on the occasions
I was questioned. These occasions were weeks, sometimes
months after the event. My wife would agree that we were at
home, as we were practically all of the time."

Prison officer John Leach recalls Sutcliffe's remarks to Sonia on the 8th of January, six days after his arrest and long before any talk of a "mission from God."

"I wouldn't feel any animosity towards you if you started a life on your own. I am going to do a long time in prison, thirty years or more, unless I can convince people in here I am mad and maybe then ten years in the loony bin."

Prison officer Anthony Fitzpatrick recounted a conversation he had had with Sutcliffe on the evening of April 5th.

Sutcliffe said, "I'm not going to a long-term prison. I am going to Park Lane [a special secure hospital in Leeds]. A bed has been reserved for me there.

"An agreement has been reached between the defense and the prosecution for a plea of diminished responsibility to be accepted. Kerry Magill [his solicitor] has told me.

"I've been told by a psychiatrist that I will have to do no more than ten years, to satisfy the public."

Frederick Edwards, another prison officer, takes the oath—"He was saying to me that the doctors considered him disturbed and he was quite amazed by this and was smiling broadly and leaning back on his chair. He said to me, 'I'm as normal as anyone.'"

This is the case for the prosecution.

May 11. James Chadwin, QC, opens the case for the defense. He calls to the witness box Peter Sutcliffe. Again that incongruously high voice can be heard in Number One Court.

"I have killed these thirteen women. I intended to kill the other seven. I intended to kill Olivia Reivers."

And that was in the first minute of his testimony. This personification of evil then turns his thoughts to God.

When working as a gravedigger in Bingley cemetery he remembered, "Something that I felt was very wonderful at the time. I heard what I believed then and believe now to have been God's voice."

At this point Sutcliffe's face has about it an almost evangelical expression. He elaborates: "I was digging a grave in the Catholic section at the top of the cemetery. I heard something that sounded like a voice similar to a human voice, like an echo."

He told the court that he then climbed out of the grave and

walked towards the direction where the voice appeared to be coming from.

"There was no one there at all. I heard again the same sound. It was like a voice saying something but the words were all imposed on top of each other. I could not make them out. It was like echoes. The voices were coming directly in front of me from the top of a gravestone, which was Polish. I remember the name on the grave to this day. It was a man called Zipolski. Stanislaw Zipolski."

He is shown photographs of the cemetery and he picks the gravestone of a Bronislaw Zapolski as being the one where the voices spoke to him. He told his counsel that he looked at the inscription on the tombstone and read the words "Poko Jago" and took that to mean Jesus, which it does not. He read the words "Wehvy Ecko" and took that to mean "We be Echo," which it does not.

"I thought the message on the gravestone was a direct message telling me it was the voice of Jesus speaking to me."

His counsel points out to him that none of these words appear on the tombstone.

"I remember seeing them. It had a terrific impact on me. I went down the slope after standing there for a while. It was starting to rain. I remember going to the top of the slope overlooking the valley and I felt as though I had just experienced something fantastic."

It transpires that Sutcliffe told no one of this experience.

"I thought that if it was meant for everyone to hear they would hear. I felt I had been selected. I don't know why."

Clearly neither did he know what the "voice" was saying to him. This young man of then twenty years of age, brought up in the Catholic faith, an altar boy. A youth with a very good basic religious grounding has what would be the most traumatic experience of anyone's life. He tells no one, which is perhaps understandable. *He also makes no attempt then or at any time in the future to obtain a translation of exactly what the Polish words on that tombstone really mean.*

As his evidence unfolds there is much irrelevance. A rival for Sonia, an Italian ice cream salesman. A motorbike accident that has no bearing. Of greater relevance is the incident with the prostitute who conned him out of £10. It is curious that a man in direct communication with God, with a mission from God to kill all prostitutes, should, less than two years after hearing God's voice, pay money to have sex with one of these "scum."

Sutcliffe tells the court: "Soon after this incident my attitude towards prostitutes changed. I heard a voice which kept saying I had got to go on with the mission and it had a purpose. It was to remove the prostitutes. To get rid of them."

The theme throughout his evidence is constant.

"It was God's will. God was controlling me. I don't know who sent the letters and the tape, I thought it was an indirect act of God. I can't remember how many times the police interviewed me. So many times I've lost count. The police did not catch me before because everything was in God's hands. They had all the facts. They knew it was me. They questioned me at work and at home. One of them said he knew it was me, that he had no doubts at all, but he went away. God was in control."

May 12. Sutcliffe continues where he left off yesterday.

"I did not expect to be charged with murder even when I was caught with that prostitute in Sheffield. I had confidence in God. I gave a false name and address to the police, because the fact that I had been caught in that situation had no bearing on the mission being terminated whatsoever. Even when I was transferred from Sheffield to Dewsbury I told the police lies because the point had not been reached where I could do otherwise. I was waiting and hoping that I would get advice from God. God had given me the signal through the police when they asked about why I had left the car and gone over to the wall that it was time to tell."

The reason that not once during the days of questioning and not once during the statement that took nearly sixteen hours to write down he had not mentioned the incident at Bingley cemetery was "because I thought that would lead them to find out about the mission. I had not wanted them to find that out, as I was by no means convinced that it was finished."

His explanation about only doing ten years in a "loony bin" was that he wanted to cheer Sonia up.

"Do you think you are mad?"

"No."

"Do you think there is anything wrong with you mentally?"

"Nothing serious at all, no."

"Do you think you will spend less time in custody if people think there is something wrong with you mentally?"

"No. There would be something wrong with me mentally if I thought that."

And this is the man who not once in five and a half years would the police publicly acknowledge as clever. His voice, that oddly high pitched voice has had virtually throughout his counsel's questions a pathetic quality. His face, perhaps because of the mustache and beard, creates the illusion when he speaks that at any moment he may roar with laughter and admit that he is trying to pull the greatest card trick in criminal history. His counsel makes the mistake of asking him about the alleged conversation with a prison officer concerning the plea bargaining.

"I simply told the truth of what I believed and what I had been informed, and that was that the prosecution had agreed to accept the plea of diminished responsibility."

A few minutes later, after a further reiteration that God had advised him on all the occasions that he had murdered or attempted to murder with the exception of Yvonne Pearson, and that murder had been "arranged by God"—his counsel sits.

The Attorney General stands and faces the most notorious British murderer of the century.

As the cross-examination proceeds, the Yorkshireman in the witness box is reminiscent of Boycott in top form batting against Lillee and Thomson bowling at half pace. The batsman at the other end appears fairly useful too. The Almighty.

"On the night of your arrest you picked up Miss Reivers, intending to kill her?"

"Yes."

"Because God expected it?"

"Yes."

A few moments later the Attorney General turns to Sutcliffe's confession. A confession that was only given after the murderer had realized that the police had found his hammer and knife on the waste ground at Sheffield.

"Do you understand the phrase 'bang to rights'?"

"No."

"Do you understand when I say 'I have got you. I have all the evidence well and truly. The game is up'?"

"Yes."

"And you say 'God told me to tell,' or was it just that you realized the game was up. Did you say you were the Ripper because you knew the game was up?"

"I knew it was the time to tell them."

"When found out, you decided to tell the truth. Like any other criminal?"

"Like any criminal, not any other."

Asked to explain why he told the police nothing of God's visit to Bingley cemetery and then subsequently omitted to tell any psychiatrist until March, the answer is, "I was waiting for a direct message, saying that it was over, to fully convince me that the mission was terminated."

"What you are saying is that you had to have a 'mission finished' or a 'mission terminated signal.' Did you ever get that?"

"No, never."

"When did it first pass your mind that the God you were in touch with was very evil, quite contrary to the sort of miracles you had been told about as a Catholic boy?"

"It seemed similar to the contradiction between the Old Testament and the New."

Sutcliffe, a man with an estimated IQ of 110, at the very top end of the average rating, sips from a mug of water as the Attorney General increases pace.

"After you had been taunted by a prostitute, the first one you had met, you developed a hatred for her and her kind?"

"Yes."

"So, God jumped on the bandwagon after that and said, 'You have a divine mission, young Peter, to stalk prostitutes and avenge me by killing them'?"

"It's a very colorful speech, sir, but it does not apply."

The case of Mark Rowntree, referred to earlier in this book, becomes the subject of discussion. Rowntree, a random murderer of four people *after Sutcliffe had started to murder* had subsequently been found guilty of manslaughter on the grounds of diminished responsibility. It transpires that Sutcliffe several months before mentioning his divine mission to the doctors had discussed Rowntree's case with a prison officer.

The fact that he had never murdered inside his car, because "it would have left evidence and also would have been very difficult," that all of his actions were those of a man in total control, all of this was laid firmly at God's door. Sir Michael concludes with, "The mission was the floater and the bait on the hook was God's message, and they fell for it hook, line and sinker. Is that what happened?"

"No."

After brief re-examination from his own counsel Peter Sutcliffe returns to the dock.

May 13 to May 19.

An impressive array of psychiatrists give evidence for the defense. All contend that Sutcliffe is suffering from paranoiac schizophrenia. Three doctors with a collective experience of over sixty years in the field of psychiatry surely cannot be wrong. And yet . . .

Dr. Hugo Milne. "Yes, he could have learned 'ideas of reference' and learned some of the symptoms from Sonia's mental illness but I do not believe that anyone could learn schizophrenic thinking.

"I am not saying because someone is a multiple killer that it would point to schizophrenia or any other abnormality.

"Yes, I agree that my inquiries have shown that Sutcliffe never displayed to family, friends or workmates any external indications of mental disturbance.

"Yes, Sonia suffered from schizophrenia in 1972. She had the delusion that she was the second Christ. She heard voices talking to her.

"I could have been duped by Sutcliffe into believing he was a paranoiac schizophrenic.

"Perhaps I have been duped. It is for the jury to decide.

"I agree that as he lied to the police he could also have lied to me."

Harry Ognall, QC, for the Crown. "I put it to you that the injuries to these women betray quite clear and sexual components in the attacks. Do you agree?"

"Yes."

"This isn't a missionary from God, it is a man who gets sexual pleasure out of killing these women?"

"I don't accept that."

Dr. Malcolm MacCulloch. "I concluded within half an hour of my first meeting with him that he was suffering from schizophrenia of the paranoid type."

Under cross-examination from Harry Ognall, QC, for the Crown, "When did you first learn of the Crown's case?"

"On April 28th."

"Are we to understand that the first time you considered the Crown's case against Peter Sutcliffe was the day before he was due to stand his trial?"

"Yes."

"You say that with remarkable calm and apparent indifference. How were you going to, if called upon, justify your diagnosis on oath, without knowing the nature of the Crown's case? How on earth do you diagnose a man's psychiatric condition without knowing the nature and quality of that which he is alleged by outside evidence to have done?"

"By examining the mental state and taking history."

Mr. Justice Boreham: "Are there not truly occasions when that homely old phrase applies that a man's actions speak louder than his words?"

"Yes, I am sure there are occasions."

"Do you not think it is wise to look at a voluntary statement before you make up your mind?"

"Yes, I think it would be wise."

"And in this case you did not do that?"

"No, my lord."

"Yes, Mr. Ognall, I would agree that in reaching my diagnosis I made no enquiries of Sutcliffe's family, friends, workmates or general practitioner.

"I am sure he deceived me here and there on one point or another. I think it most likely. However, I had been asked specifically to consider deception by another psychiatrist.

"I will admit that I could not determine whether Sutcliffe was a liar."

Mr. Justice Boreham: "If what he has told you is not true, then what of your diagnosis?"

"It falls."

Dr. Terence Kay. "The prison officers, who are with him twenty-four hours a day, told me that we [the three doctors] were being fooled.

"Sonia Sutcliffe also complained about having the stigmata of the cross on her hands and she complained of wanting to be a teddy bear."

The Attorney General: "Do you know of a reported experiment in the United States where eight perfectly normal people simulated schizophrenia?"

"Yes, I do."

"I understand they stated they could hear voices and that they also described other symptoms. Apparently they were all diagnosed by psychiatrists as schizophrenic and admitted to various hospitals?"

"That is correct."

"I understand they fooled doctors at seventeen mental institutions, but the patients considered them fakes declaring, 'You are not crazy—you're just journalists checking up on hospitals'?"

"That is correct."

"Would you accept that if Sutcliffe was a cold-blooded killer who had an enormous desire to kill prostitutes or just to kill women, he could be bad rather than mad?"

"Yes, I would accept that."

Late morning on May 19. The Attorney General rises to his feet to make the final speech for the Crown. He takes the jury carefully through the evidence that had been adduced and asks them the question that has so preoccupied my mind over the past two and a half years. "The crimes are horrible and sadistic, beyond our ordinary comprehension. Does it mean he must be mad or just plain evil?"

James Chadwin, QC, makes his final speech on behalf of Peter Sutcliffe. He too examines much of the evidence that has been heard during this trial. He also finds a phrase that encapsulates the very issue.

"Either, as the doctors have expressed their belief, this series of events arises because of the schizophrenic illness, or he must be a man, who, for some reason, enjoys killing."

May 22. Mr. Justice Boreham concludes his summing up to the jury. He has spoken for nearly eight hours. Slowly and carefully he has taken the jury through the evidence. A point for the prosecution was promptly balanced with a point for the defense. It has been the most balanced direction to a jury that I have ever heard. Other observers felt it was too finely balanced, displaying perhaps their own personal view and hoping the Judge would lean one way or the other but the Judge is clearly conscious that such a device would leave open grounds for appeal and has kept his personal opinion very much to himself, but there were clues.

Referring to the evidence of Dr. Hugo Milne, he reminded the jury that the doctor had cited the fact that Sutcliffe had once worked in Bingley cemetery as partial confirmation of his claim to have heard the voice of God there.

"I do not mean to be flippant but this is very much like claiming to have swum the Channel and your friends doubting it and taking them and showing them the Channel as proof. Well it doesn't prove very much, does it?"

This morning in his final words he touched upon the very theme of this book.

"There has been some reference to the defendant being 'bad or mad.' It is perhaps a convenient shorthand way of putting it, but you stick to the words I gave you, whether he was suffering from abnormality of mind.

"In the end you may think the real question, and the one that will be decisive is, do you think it more probable than not whenever he killed he acted under a deluded belief that he had a divine mission to kill prostitutes." The jury files out to consider its verdict. The time is 10:21 A.M.

Outside the circus is in full swing again. Positions in the queue for the public gallery are being sold for up to £100. A whole battery of television cameras are mounted directly opposite the court entrance. Behind the cameras the television crews have erected a hut. All that is needed is a sports commentator.

On the third floor of the building is the restaurant. Groups gather at tables sipping endless cups of tea. Groups with a common interest.

At one table sit a dozen reporters endlessly discussing who has been bought up by whom. The burning topic appears to be Sonia Sutcliffe. Still she has resisted all offers. A bid of £100,000 is just one that she has declined.

At another table sit a group drawn together by the most awful common interest. Olive Smelt and her eldest daughter Linda. Olive, a Halifax housewife, a woman branded as a prostitute, who is not. A woman awarded less than £1000 by the Criminal Compensation Board. Over one hundred thousand for Sonia's story, less than a hundredth of that for a skull that was smashed and a life that has been shattered.

At the same table sit Irene MacDonald, David and Beryl Leach. Doreen Hill has also arrived at the Court for this bitter day.

Sutcliffe was charged with the murder of Jacqueline Hill on what would have been Barbara Leach's twenty-second birthday. Today would have been the twenty-first birthday of Jacqueline.

Outside in the street the protesting voices of representatives of the English Collective of Prostitutes float up to the restaurant. They are rightly objecting to the sliding scale of values put on human life in this country. Innocent victims *vis à vis* prostitutes.

Minutes pass into hours. At 3:20 in the afternoon the jury returns. They cannot arrive at a unanimous verdict. Mr. Justice Boreham tells them he will accept majority verdicts of no less than 10–2. The jury retires again.

At eight minutes past four the jury has returned. They have reached a majority verdict.

Peter William Sutcliffe is found guilty of murder on all thirteen counts.

No madness. No voices from God. No divine mission. He has been declared sane.

He is evil.

For the last time Sutcliffe and the Judge look directly at each other. The truck driver from Bradford is standing. Three of the prison officers with him move automatically close to him. So close they are touching the man.

"The jury have found you guilty of thirteen charges of murder, if I may say so, murder of a very cowardly nature. For each was a woman.

"It was murder by getting behind her and beating her on the head with a hammer from behind.

"It is difficult to find words that are adequate in my judgment to describe the brutality and gravity of these offenses.

"I am not going to pause to seek those words. I am prepared to let the catalogue of crimes speak for itself."

A few moments later Mr. Justice Boreham also let the sentence speak for itself.

"I sentence you to life imprisonment. I shall recommend that you should not be released from prison for at least thirty years."

Moments later Peter Sutcliffe, showing a total lack of concern is gone from the dock.

The evil damage that he created lives on. His ripples have now spread and touched many aspects of our society.

The reputation of the West Yorkshire Police force is in shreds. The reputation of psychiatry is in pieces.

The reputation of the judiciary has been mauled. We are not a country that officially indulges in plea bargaining.

But from the man the world will always know as the Yorkshire Ripper we have been delivered.

David A. Yallop
London
May 22, 1981